Vivan

THE
AMAZING
DINOSAUR
QUIZ BOOK

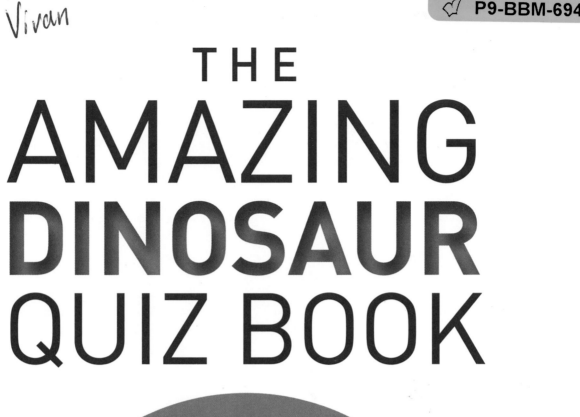

DK

Project Editor Victoria Wiggins
Senior Designer Jim Green

Managing Editor Linda Esposito
Managing Art Editor Diane Peyton Jones

Category Publisher Laura Buller

Production Controller Sophie Argyris
Production Editor Rebekah Parsons-King

Jacket Editor Manisha Majithia
Jacket Designers Silke Spingies, Nim Kook

Publishing Director Jonathan Metcalf
Associate Publishing Director Liz Wheeler
Art Director Phil Ormerod

DK INDIA

Senior Art Editor Chhaya Sajwan
Art Editors Pankaj Bhatia, Suhita Dharamjit,
Niyati Gosain, Shipra Jain, Kanika Mittal,
Namita, Payal Rosalind, Priyanka Singh,
Mahipal Singh, Shruti Soharia Singh,
Amit Varma, Vidit Vashisht
Managing Art Editors Priyabrata Roy Chowdhury,
Arunesh Talapatra
Senior Editor Monica Saigal
Editors Gaurav Joshi, Vibha Malhotra,
Suparna Sengupta
Managing Editor Pakshalika Jayaprakash
DTP Designers Rajesh Singh Adhikari, Neeraj
Bhatia, Jaypal Singh Chauhan, Anita Yadav
DTP Manager Balwant Singh
Production Manager Pankaj Sharma
Picture Research Sakshi Saluja

First published in Canada in 2014

DK is represented in Canada by
Tourmaline Editions Inc.
662 King Street West, Suite 304
Toronto, Ontario M5V 1M7

14 15 16 17 18 10 9 8 7 6 5 4 3 2 1

001—273915—Aug 2014

Published in Great Britain by Dorling Kindersley Limited.

Library and Archives Canada Cataloguing in Publication
Brusatte, Stephen, author
The amazing dinosaur quiz book / contributors, Stephen Brusatte and John Woodward.
ISBN 978-1-55363-243-6 (pbk.)
1. Dinosaurs--Miscellanea. I. Woodward, John, 1954-, author II. Title.
QE861.95.B78 2014   567.9   C2013-908683-8

DK books are available at special discounts when purchased in bulk for corporate sales, sales promotions,
premiums, fund-raising, or educational use. For details, please contact specialmarkets@tourmaline.ca.

Printed and bound by Leo Paper Products Ltd., China

Discover more at
www.dk.com

THE
AMAZING
DINOSAUR
QUIZ BOOK

Contributors: Stephen Brusatte and John Woodward

Contents

Quiz number
Each quiz is numbered, so you can look up the relevant set of answers by quiz number.

Quiz **1**

Sauropods swallowed **stones** to ... mash up f...

1 Some Triassic crocodile relatives had sharp teeth and claws, and could run fast on two legs. They looked similar to…

a Frogs | b Fish
c Dinosaurs | d Birds

2 Which dinosaur's name means "three-horned face"?

a Triceratops | b Brachiosaurus
c Tarbosaurus | d Homo sapiens

3 Which of the following theropods had large crests on its skull for display?

a Dilophosaurus | b Tyrannosaurus
c Velociraptor | d Crocodylus

4 Where did ichthyosaurs live?

a In the air | b Underground
c In the sea | d On dry land

5 Which was one of the largest of all the carnivorous dinosaurs?

a Velociraptor | b Coelophysis
c Archaeopteryx | d Tyrannosaurus

6 According to experts, how many years ago did dinosaurs appear?

a About 230 million | b About 230
c About 230,000 | d About 230 billion

7 When did pterosaurs become extinct?

a End of Cambrian | b End of Cretaceous
c Start of Jurassic | d Middle of Permian

8 Which famous sa... longer forelimbs th...

a Saturnalia
b Brachiosaurus

9 Which of these is...

a Tyrannosaurus
c Canis

10 Which feature he... dinosaurs like this A...

a Large and powerful h...
c Short neck.

6

Fast Facts

What is a dinosaur?
Dinosaurs were reptiles, but they were not like typical reptiles. Even though the word dinosaur means "terrible lizard," they did not stand or move like lizards, and some even had feathers. This probably means that their bodies worked more like those of birds or mammals.

Tyrannosaurus walked tall.

Reptiles with attitude
Imagine a reptile and you might think of a crocodile, lizard, or snake. But the dinosaurs were not like these sprawling, slithering creatures. They were clearly dynamic, agile animals, and some were fast movers too.

Walking tall
One thing that we have always known about dinosaurs is that they walked with their legs beneath their bodies, like birds or mammals—and not like lizards. We know this from the details of their hip and leg bones.

Long tail improved balance at high speeds.

Feathers retained body heat.

Warm blood
The dynamic stance of dinosaurs suggests that they were warm-blooded, like modern mammals or birds. This would explain why many small dinosaurs like this *Gallimimus* had insulating feathers. It also fits in with the fast growth rate of the bigger dinosaurs. However, scientists still disagree about this.

Strong legs were built for running.

Eggs and...
As far as we... laid eggs w... similar to b... the smaller... certainly in... in nests like... nested in bi... There is eve... food to the...

Family tr...
There were... and ornithi... eating saur... The plant-... thyreopho...

Saur... had f... pub...

130

Picture questions
Every quiz has at least two picture questions, testing your visual memory.

How to use this book

Each quiz is given a difficulty rating—easy (green), medium (blue), or hard (red)—as well as a quiz number. The questions are also numbered, with multiple-choice answers. Each question is color-coded, so you know which Fast Facts page to turn to if you want to find out more about a particular subject. The answers are laid out in a clear, easy-to-use section at the back of the book.

Learning more
You'll find fun facts on every page.

Difficulty rating
Choose between easy, medium, and hard quizzes, depending on how bright you're feeling. The level of each quiz is clearly indicated.

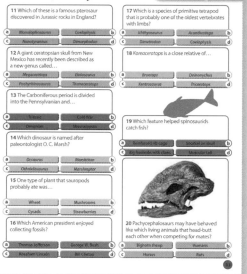

Fast Facts color
Match the color of the question to the color of the Fast Facts page tab, and find out more about the subjects that interest you.

Sauropods swallowed **stones** to

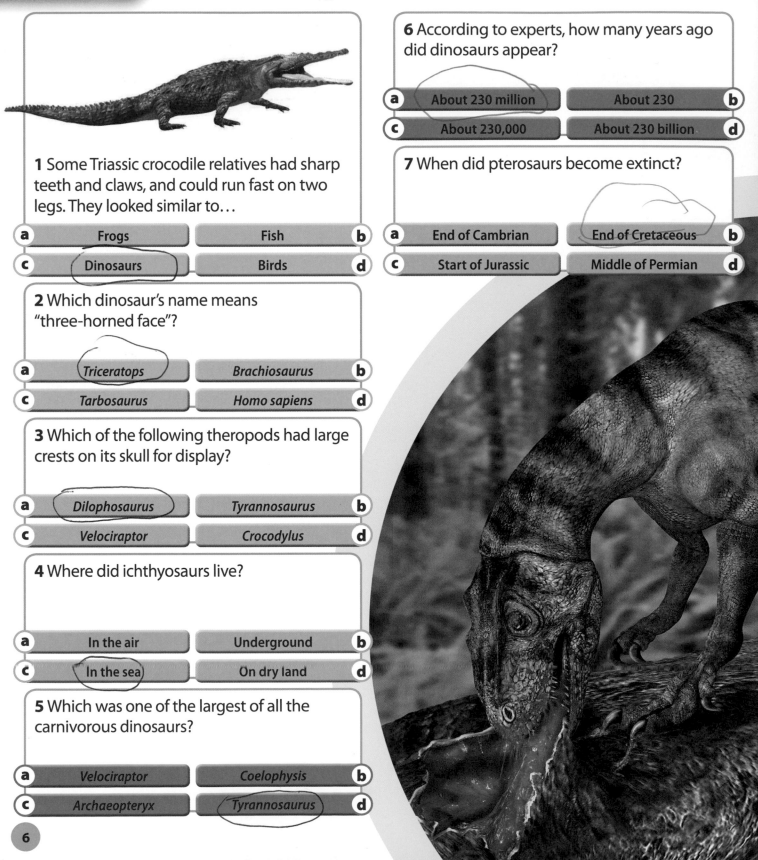

1 Some Triassic crocodile relatives had sharp teeth and claws, and could run fast on two legs. They looked similar to…

a	Frogs	Fish	**b**
c	Dinosaurs	Birds	**d**

2 Which dinosaur's name means "three-horned face"?

a	Triceratops	Brachiosaurus	**b**
c	Tarbosaurus	Homo sapiens	**d**

3 Which of the following theropods had large crests on its skull for display?

a	Dilophosaurus	Tyrannosaurus	**b**
c	Velociraptor	Crocodylus	**d**

4 Where did ichthyosaurs live?

a	In the air	Underground	**b**
c	In the sea	On dry land	**d**

5 Which was one of the largest of all the carnivorous dinosaurs?

a	Velociraptor	Coelophysis	**b**
c	Archaeopteryx	Tyrannosaurus	**d**

6 According to experts, how many years ago did dinosaurs appear?

a	About 230 million	About 230	**b**
c	About 230,000	About 230 billion	**d**

7 When did pterosaurs become extinct?

a	End of Cambrian	End of Cretaceous	**b**
c	Start of Jurassic	Middle of Permian	**d**

mash up **food** in their stomach.

8 Which famous sauropod dinosaur had longer forelimbs than hind limbs?

- **a** Saturnalia
- **b** Thecodontosaurus
- **c** Brachiosaurus
- **d** Plateosaurus

9 Which of these is a sauropod?

- **a** Tyrannosaurus
- **b** Stegosaurus
- **c** Canis
- **d** Apatosaurus

10 Which feature helped carnivorous dinosaurs like this *Allosaurus* catch prey?

- **a** Large and powerful hands
- **b** Stocky feet
- **c** Stiff necks
- **d** Skull horns

11 Which of the following were not a display structure in dinosaurs?

- **a** Crests
- **b** Claws
- **c** Horns
- **d** Frills

12 Which time interval is called the Age of Mammals?

- **a** Medieval times
- **b** Great Depression
- **c** Reign of dinosaurs
- **d** Cenozoic

13 Dinosaur fossils are often found in which modern environment?

- **a** Atmosphere
- **b** Deserts
- **c** Lakes
- **d** Ocean floor

14 Which of these did not exist when the first dinosaurs evolved?

- **a** Mountains
- **b** Rivers
- **c** Bacteria
- **d** Flowers

15 What does the word *dinosaur* mean?

- **a** Like a dragon
- **b** Creature from the sea
- **c** Terrible lizard
- **d** Giant animal

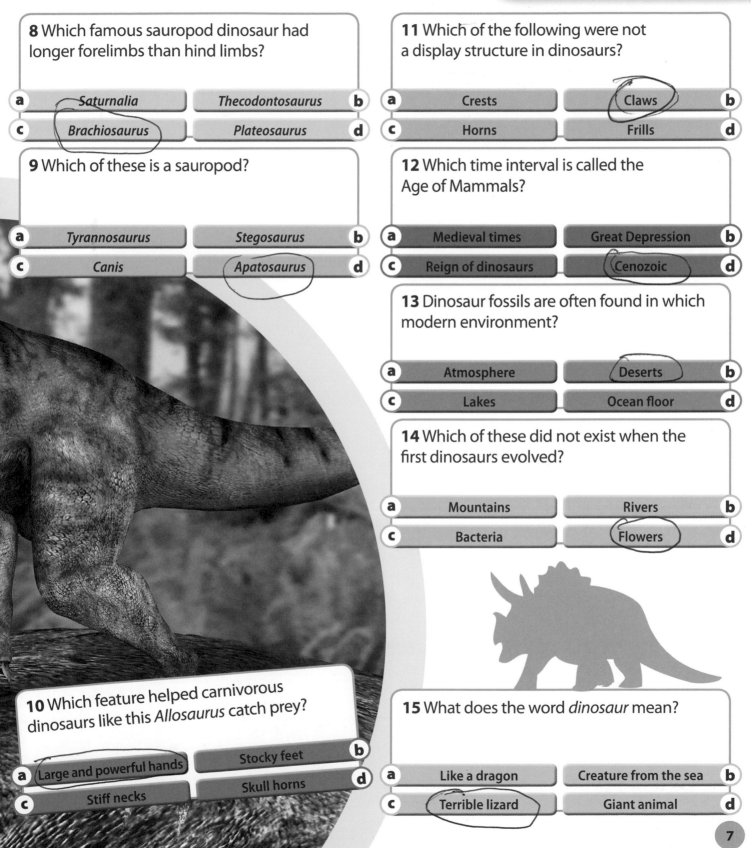

Fossils from Mount Kirkpatrick show that

1 The largest back plates of *Stegosaurus* are about the size of a…

a Car
b Small table
c Basketball
d Golf ball

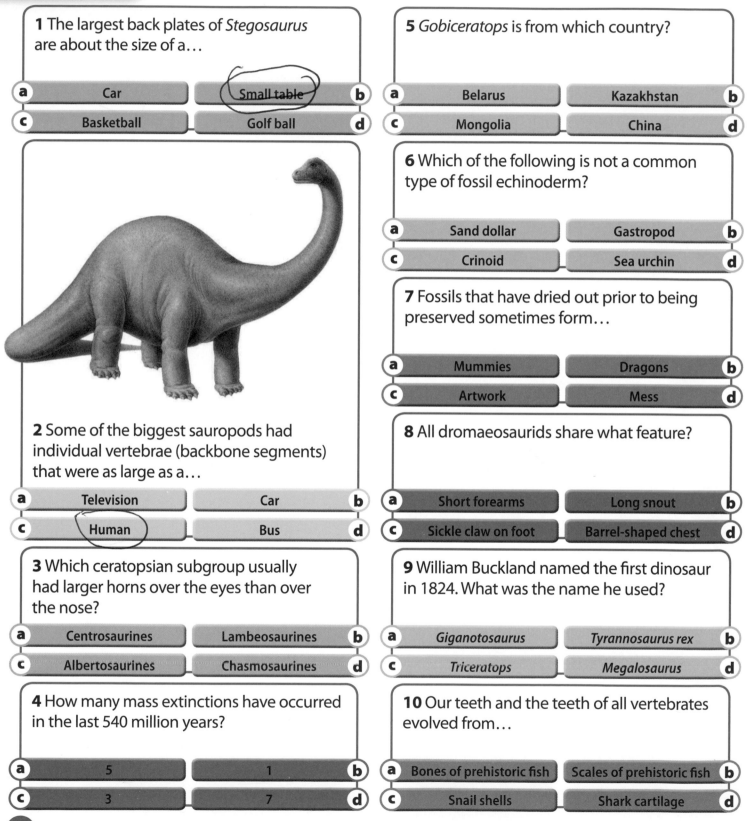

2 Some of the biggest sauropods had individual vertebrae (backbone segments) that were as large as a…

a Television
b Car
c Human
d Bus

3 Which ceratopsian subgroup usually had larger horns over the eyes than over the nose?

a Centrosaurines
b Lambeosaurines
c Albertosaurines
d Chasmosaurines

4 How many mass extinctions have occurred in the last 540 million years?

a 5
b 1
c 3
d 7

5 *Gobiceratops* is from which country?

a Belarus
b Kazakhstan
c Mongolia
d China

6 Which of the following is not a common type of fossil echinoderm?

a Sand dollar
b Gastropod
c Crinoid
d Sea urchin

7 Fossils that have dried out prior to being preserved sometimes form…

a Mummies
b Dragons
c Artwork
d Mess

8 All dromaeosaurids share what feature?

a Short forearms
b Long snout
c Sickle claw on foot
d Barrel-shaped chest

9 William Buckland named the first dinosaur in 1824. What was the name he used?

a *Giganotosaurus*
b *Tyrannosaurus rex*
c *Triceratops*
d *Megalosaurus*

10 Our teeth and the teeth of all vertebrates evolved from…

a Bones of prehistoric fish
b Scales of prehistoric fish
c Snail shells
d Shark cartilage

dinosaurs lived in Antarctica.

11 Which Chinese sauropod had perhaps the longest neck, in proportion to its body, of any animal that has ever lived?

- **a** Apatotitan
- **b** Diplodocus
- **c** Mussaurus
- **d** Mamenchisaurus

12 Which of these is not an ornithomimosaur, or "ostrich mimic" theropod?

- **a** Therizinosaurus
- **b** Ornithomimus
- **c** Gallimimus
- **d** Struthiomimus

13 In classification, there are at least how many animal phyla today?

- **a** 10
- **b** 23
- **c** 28
- **d** 2

14 The skulls of the largest ceratopsians were approximately how long, from the snout to the end of the frill?

- **a** 7ft (2m)
- **b** 16ft (5m)
- **c** 3ft (1m)
- **d** 33ft (10m)

15 The Triassic-Jurassic boundary is how old?

- **a** 20 million years
- **b** 2 million years
- **c** 50 years
- **d** 200 million years

16 Which of the following is not a gymnosperm?

- **a** Cycad
- **b** Ginkgo
- **c** Sunflower
- **d** Conifer

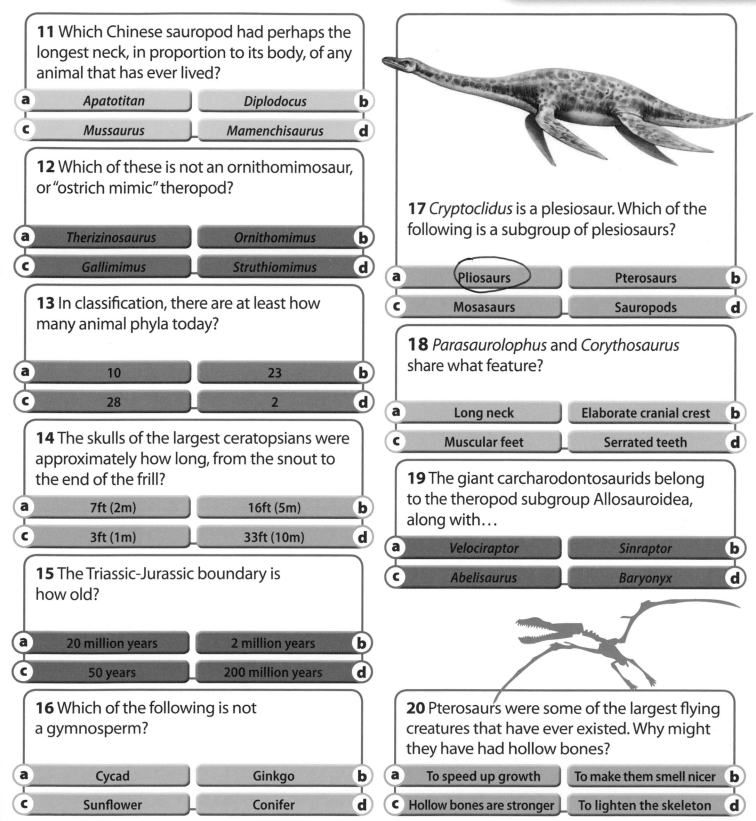

17 *Cryptoclidus* is a plesiosaur. Which of the following is a subgroup of plesiosaurs?

- **a** Pliosaurs
- **b** Pterosaurs
- **c** Mosasaurs
- **d** Sauropods

18 *Parasaurolophus* and *Corythosaurus* share what feature?

- **a** Long neck
- **b** Elaborate cranial crest
- **c** Muscular feet
- **d** Serrated teeth

19 The giant carcharodontosaurids belong to the theropod subgroup Allosauroidea, along with…

- **a** Velociraptor
- **b** Sinraptor
- **c** Abelisaurus
- **d** Baryonyx

20 Pterosaurs were some of the largest flying creatures that have ever existed. Why might they have had hollow bones?

- **a** To speed up growth
- **b** To make them smell nicer
- **c** Hollow bones are stronger
- **d** To lighten the skeleton

Kronosaurus's **skull** was nearly **twice** the

1 Which of these is a group of ocean-dwelling crocodiles that lived during the Mesozoic?

a Metriorhynchids
b Pristichampsids
c Spehnosuchians
d Mosasaurs

2 How did the shape of *Triceratops*'s nasal horn change during growth?

a It straightened out
b It became shorter
c It became less pointed
d It became thinner

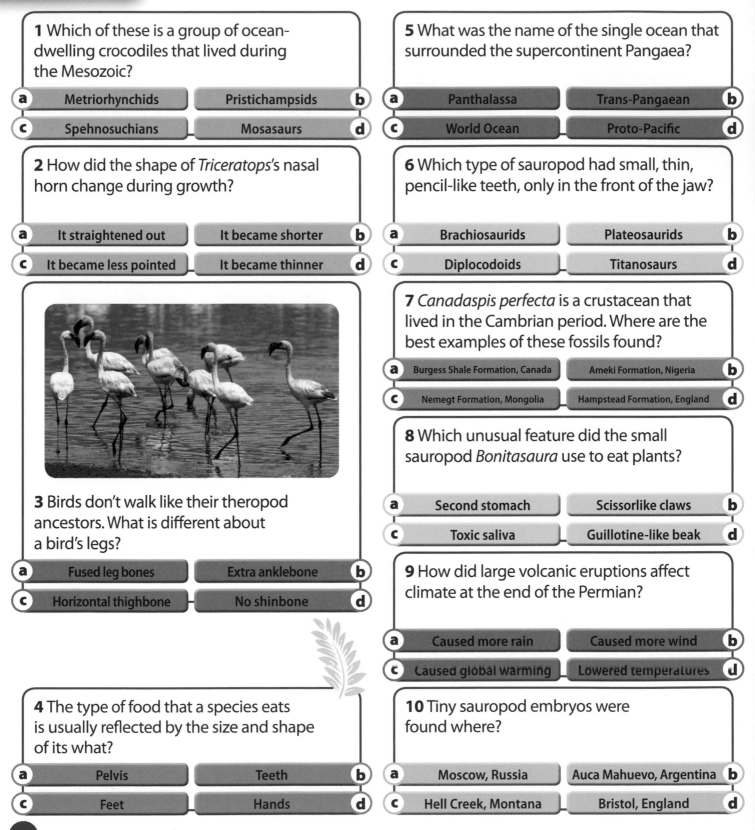

3 Birds don't walk like their theropod ancestors. What is different about a bird's legs?

a Fused leg bones
b Extra anklebone
c Horizontal thighbone
d No shinbone

4 The type of food that a species eats is usually reflected by the size and shape of its what?

a Pelvis
b Teeth
c Feet
d Hands

5 What was the name of the single ocean that surrounded the supercontinent Pangaea?

a Panthalassa
b Trans-Pangaean
c World Ocean
d Proto-Pacific

6 Which type of sauropod had small, thin, pencil-like teeth, only in the front of the jaw?

a Brachiosaurids
b Plateosaurids
c Diplocodoids
d Titanosaurs

7 *Canadaspis perfecta* is a crustacean that lived in the Cambrian period. Where are the best examples of these fossils found?

a Burgess Shale Formation, Canada
b Ameki Formation, Nigeria
c Nemegt Formation, Mongolia
d Hampstead Formation, England

8 Which unusual feature did the small sauropod *Bonitasaura* use to eat plants?

a Second stomach
b Scissorlike claws
c Toxic saliva
d Guillotine-like beak

9 How did large volcanic eruptions affect climate at the end of the Permian?

a Caused more rain
b Caused more wind
c Caused global warming
d Lowered temperatures

10 Tiny sauropod embryos were found where?

a Moscow, Russia
b Auca Mahuevo, Argentina
c Hell Creek, Montana
d Bristol, England

size of a **tyrannosaur's**.

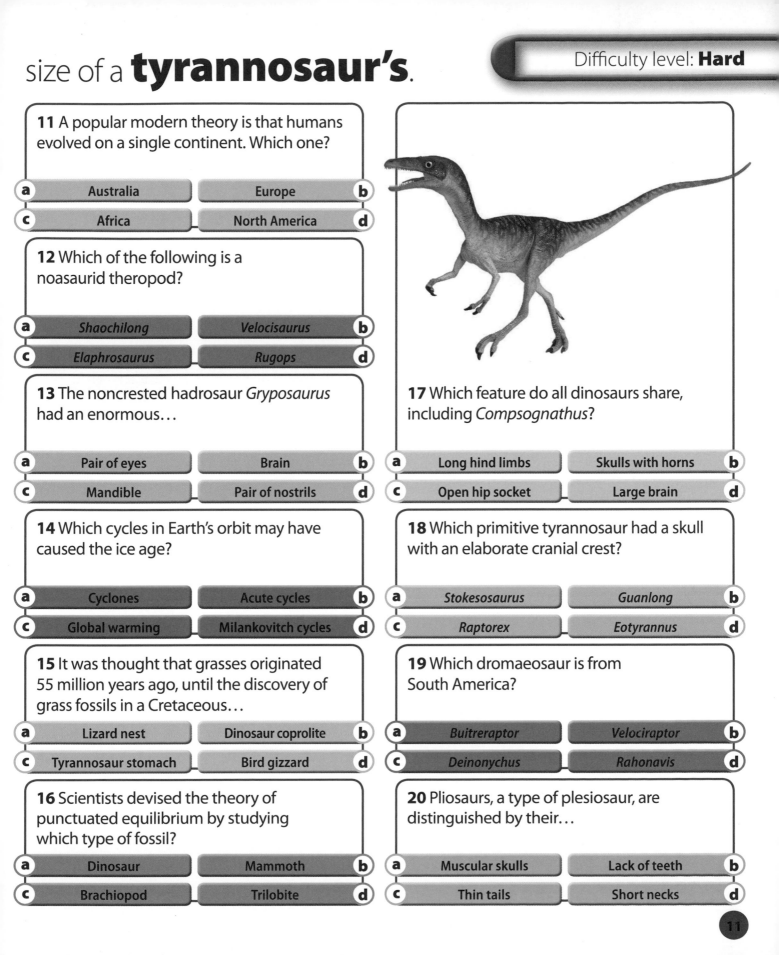

11 A popular modern theory is that humans evolved on a single continent. Which one?

a Australia	Europe **b**
c Africa	North America **d**

12 Which of the following is a noasaurid theropod?

a *Shaochilong*	*Velocisaurus* **b**
c *Elaphrosaurus*	*Rugops* **d**

13 The noncrested hadrosaur *Gryposaurus* had an enormous…

a Pair of eyes	Brain **b**
c Mandible	Pair of nostrils **d**

14 Which cycles in Earth's orbit may have caused the ice age?

a Cyclones	Acute cycles **b**
c Global warming	Milankovitch cycles **d**

15 It was thought that grasses originated 55 million years ago, until the discovery of grass fossils in a Cretaceous…

a Lizard nest	Dinosaur coprolite **b**
c Tyrannosaur stomach	Bird gizzard **d**

16 Scientists devised the theory of punctuated equilibrium by studying which type of fossil?

a Dinosaur	Mammoth **b**
c Brachiopod	Trilobite **d**

17 Which feature do all dinosaurs share, including *Compsognathus*?

a Long hind limbs	Skulls with horns **b**
c Open hip socket	Large brain **d**

18 Which primitive tyrannosaur had a skull with an elaborate cranial crest?

a *Stokesosaurus*	*Guanlong* **b**
c *Raptorex*	*Eotyrannus* **d**

19 Which dromaeosaur is from South America?

a *Buitreraptor*	*Velociraptor* **b**
c *Deinonychus*	*Rahonavis* **d**

20 Pliosaurs, a type of plesiosaur, are distinguished by their…

a Muscular skulls	Lack of teeth **b**
c Thin tails	Short necks **d**

Hadrosaurs had **hundreds**

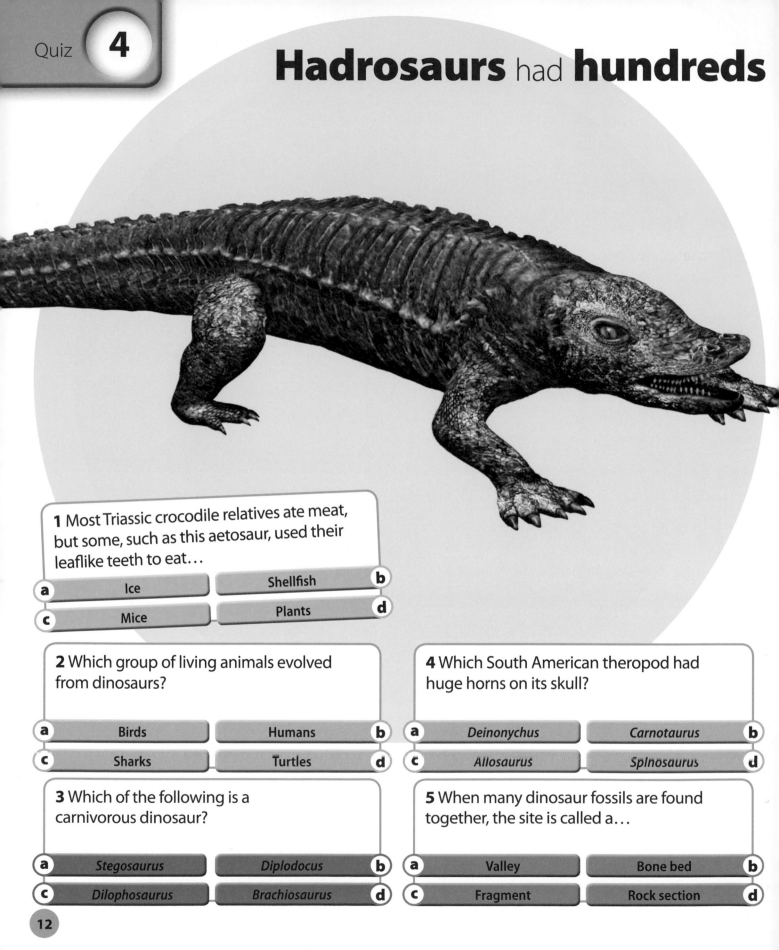

1 Most Triassic crocodile relatives ate meat, but some, such as this aetosaur, used their leaflike teeth to eat…

a   Ice

b   Shellfish

c   Mice

d   Plants

2 Which group of living animals evolved from dinosaurs?

a   Birds

b   Humans

c   Sharks

d   Turtles

3 Which of the following is a carnivorous dinosaur?

a   *Stegosaurus*

b   *Diplodocus*

c   *Dilophosaurus*

d   *Brachiosaurus*

4 Which South American theropod had huge horns on its skull?

a   *Deinonychus*

b   *Carnotaurus*

c   *Allosaurus*

d   *Spinosaurus*

5 When many dinosaur fossils are found together, the site is called a…

a   Valley

b   Bone bed

c   Fragment

d   Rock section

of **teeth** to chop up leaves.

6 What covered the land during the ice ages?

a Mines

b Buildings

c Volcanoes

d Glaciers

7 Dinosaurs that walked on two legs are called…

a Slow

b Fast

c Failures

d Bipedal

8 Which small, primitive ceratopsian had tiny horns?

a *Stegosaurus*

b *Megaraptor*

c *Protoceratops*

d *Triceratops*

9 Which of the following is a pterosaur?

a *Allosaurus*

b *Pteranodon*

c *Deinosuchus*

d *Parasaurolophus*

10 What do experts think might have brought about the end of the dinosaurs?

a Meteorite hitting Earth

b Humans

c Other animals

d Disease

11 Early cousins of sauropods are often called prosauropods. What is an example of one?

a *Brachiosaurus*

b *Apatosaurus*

c *Allosaurus*

d *Plateosaurus*

12 Which of the following is not a flowering plant?

a Conifer

b Rose

c Daffodil

d Sunflower

13 The theropod *Oviraptor* is bizarre because…

a It had no teeth

b It was larger than a bus

c It is still alive

d It had fur

14 What does an invertebrate paleontologist study?

a Plants

b Ancient maps

c Fossils without backbones

d Fossils with backbones

15 Which other group went extinct with the dinosaurs?

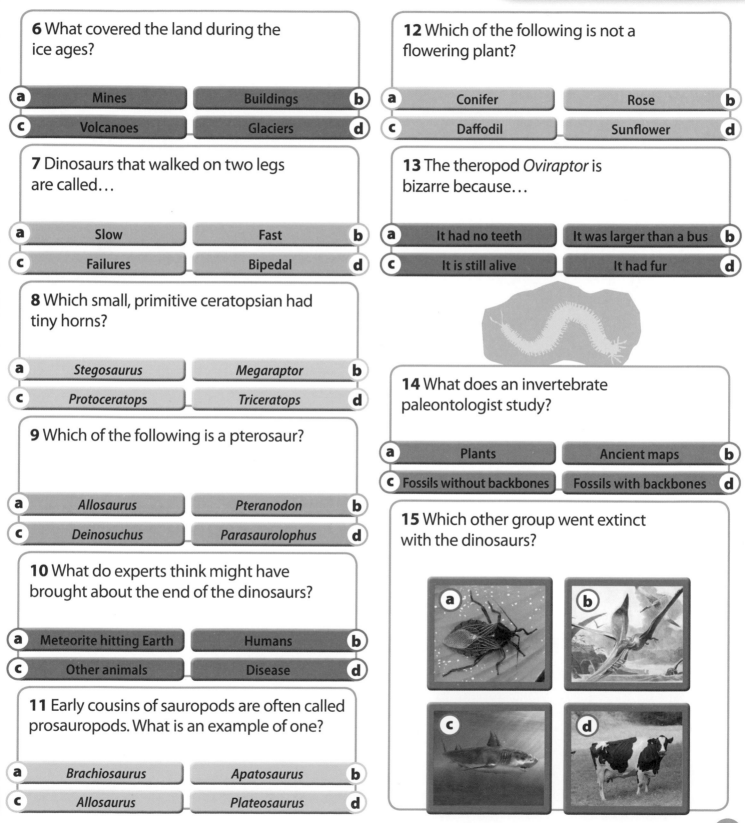

a

b

c

d

Tyrannosaurus had a **stronger**

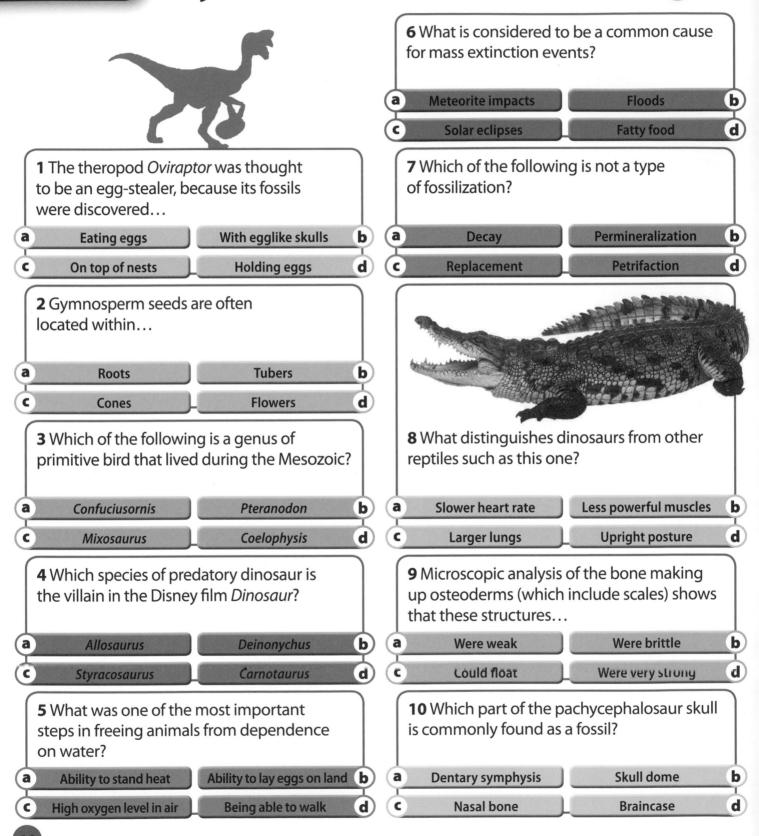

6 What is considered to be a common cause for mass extinction events?

- **a** Meteorite impacts
- **b** Floods
- **c** Solar eclipses
- **d** Fatty food

1 The theropod *Oviraptor* was thought to be an egg-stealer, because its fossils were discovered…

- **a** Eating eggs
- **b** With egglike skulls
- **c** On top of nests
- **d** Holding eggs

7 Which of the following is not a type of fossilization?

- **a** Decay
- **b** Permineralization
- **c** Replacement
- **d** Petrifaction

2 Gymnosperm seeds are often located within…

- **a** Roots
- **b** Tubers
- **c** Cones
- **d** Flowers

3 Which of the following is a genus of primitive bird that lived during the Mesozoic?

- **a** *Confuciusornis*
- **b** *Pteranodon*
- **c** *Mixosaurus*
- **d** *Coelophysis*

8 What distinguishes dinosaurs from other reptiles such as this one?

- **a** Slower heart rate
- **b** Less powerful muscles
- **c** Larger lungs
- **d** Upright posture

4 Which species of predatory dinosaur is the villain in the Disney film *Dinosaur*?

- **a** *Allosaurus*
- **b** *Deinonychus*
- **c** *Styracosaurus*
- **d** *Carnotaurus*

9 Microscopic analysis of the bone making up osteoderms (which include scales) shows that these structures…

- **a** Were weak
- **b** Were brittle
- **c** Could float
- **d** Were very strong

5 What was one of the most important steps in freeing animals from dependence on water?

- **a** Ability to stand heat
- **b** Ability to lay eggs on land
- **c** High oxygen level in air
- **d** Being able to walk

10 Which part of the pachycephalosaur skull is commonly found as a fossil?

- **a** Dentary symphysis
- **b** Skull dome
- **c** Nasal bone
- **d** Braincase

bite than **any** other animal.

11 In birds, which body part folds against the body when not in use?

| a | Skull | Tail | b |
| c | Wing | Foot | d |

12 Which scientist proposed the theory of continental drift?

| a | Jonas Salk | Aristotle | b |
| c | George Washington | Alfred Wegener | d |

13 Which of these is a primitive theropod that lived during the Triassic period?

| a | Abelisaurus | Herrerasaurus | b |
| c | Deinonychus | Ceratosaurus | d |

14 Which close relative of *Brachiosaurus*, found in Oklahoma, was one of the largest sauropods?

| a | Dicraeosaurus | Jobaria | b |
| c | Sauroposeidon | Camarasaurus | d |

15 The largest plesiosaurs were approximately how big?

| a | 7ft (2m) | 13ft (4m) | b |
| c | 300ft (92m) | 75ft (23m) | d |

16 Ceratopsian horns are usually located on which two bones?

| a | Nasal and postorbital | Frontal and parietal | b |
| c | Jugal and squamosal | Pterygoid and maxilla | d |

17 Some fossil sharks probably used their thick, broad tooth plates to crush…

| a | Seeds | Brachiopods | b |
| c | Eggs | Nuts | d |

18 Which dinosaur has a name that is a reference to the Harry Potter series?

| a | Rowlingraptor | Dracorex hogwartsia | b |
| c | Potterosaurus | Darosaurus radcliffei | d |

19 Primates originated approximately how long ago?

| a | 1 billion years | 5,000 years | b |
| c | 65 million years | 200 million years | d |

20 The Chinese theropod *Sinosauropteryx* was one of the first dinosaurs found preserved with…

| a | Feathers | Bones | b |
| c | Skin | Color | d |

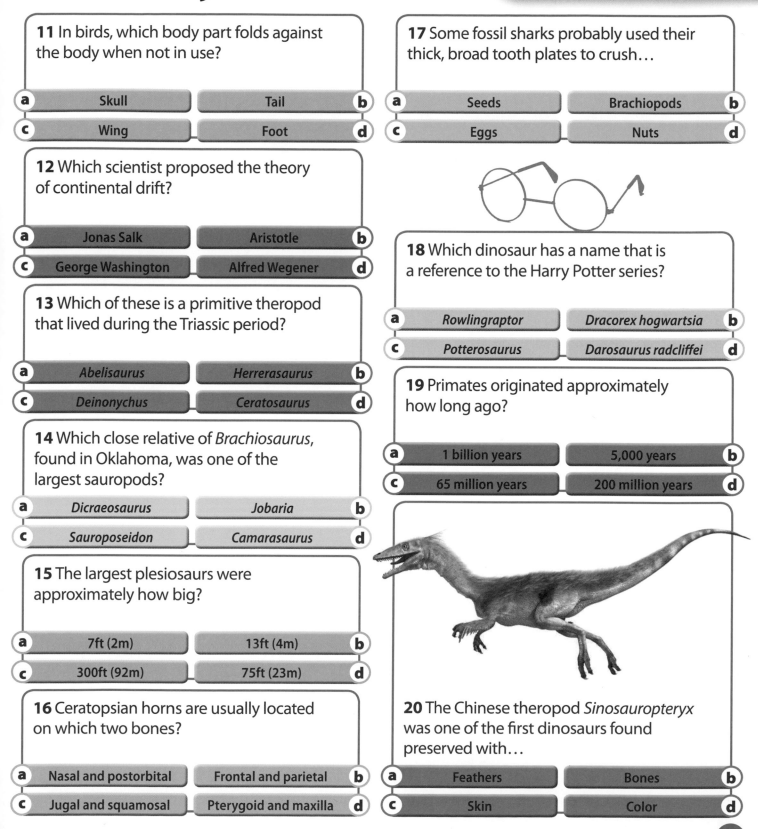

Tupandactylus's **crest** is the **largest**

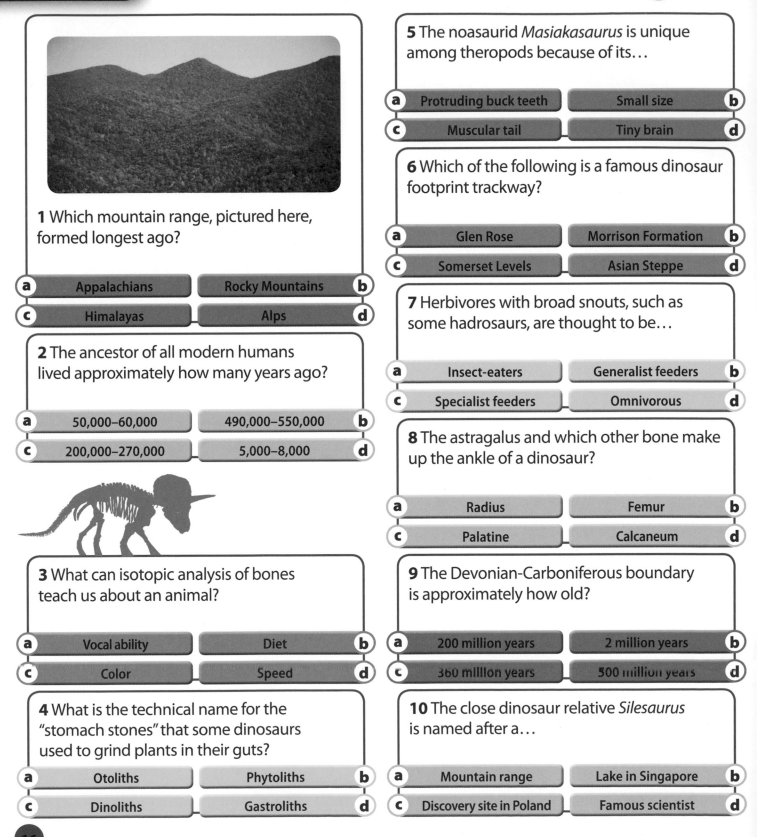

1 Which mountain range, pictured here, formed longest ago?

a Appalachians
b Rocky Mountains
c Himalayas
d Alps

2 The ancestor of all modern humans lived approximately how many years ago?

a 50,000–60,000
b 490,000–550,000
c 200,000–270,000
d 5,000–8,000

3 What can isotopic analysis of bones teach us about an animal?

a Vocal ability
b Diet
c Color
d Speed

4 What is the technical name for the "stomach stones" that some dinosaurs used to grind plants in their guts?

a Otoliths
b Phytoliths
c Dinoliths
d Gastroliths

5 The noasaurid *Masiakasaurus* is unique among theropods because of its…

a Protruding buck teeth
b Small size
c Muscular tail
d Tiny brain

6 Which of the following is a famous dinosaur footprint trackway?

a Glen Rose
b Morrison Formation
c Somerset Levels
d Asian Steppe

7 Herbivores with broad snouts, such as some hadrosaurs, are thought to be…

a Insect-eaters
b Generalist feeders
c Specialist feeders
d Omnivorous

8 The astragalus and which other bone make up the ankle of a dinosaur?

a Radius
b Femur
c Palatine
d Calcaneum

9 The Devonian-Carboniferous boundary is approximately how old?

a 200 million years
b 2 million years
c 360 million years
d 500 million years

10 The close dinosaur relative *Silesaurus* is named after a…

a Mountain range
b Lake in Singapore
c Discovery site in Poland
d Famous scientist

# of any known **pterosaur**.

11 What is in the middle of the frill of the ceratopsian *Torvosaurus*?

a Windowlike hole
b Spike
c Bump
d Gland

12 The species name of which dinosaur is named after scientist Jacques Gauthier?

a *Suuwassea*
b *Incisivosaurus*
c *Nomingia*
d *Parasaurolophus*

13 What is thought to have caused the end-Triassic extinction?

a Sea-level rise
b Ocean circulation changes
c Solar radiation
d Large volcanic eruptions

14 What made the dromaeosaurid *Balaur* unique?

a Its flamboyant head crest
b It ate plants
c Two sickle claws on its feet
d It was the largest theropod

15 What are large, fast-swimming ichthyosaurs like *Stenopterygius* called, because of their similarities to modern tuna?

a Thunnosaurs
b Azdharchids
c Tetanurans
d Fishosaurs

16 The nasal horns of juvenile *Triceratops* pointed in which direction?

a Forward
b Upward
c Downward
d Backward

17 Which microstructures helped scientists determine the color of the troodontid *Anchiornis*'s feathers?

a Filaments
b Melanosomes
c Mitochondria
d Barbules

18 Which of the following is a plesiosaur?

a *Ctenochasma*
b *Tylosaurus*
c *Geosaurus*
d *Liopleurodon*

19 Some plants store silica within what type of structure, which is a common fossil?

a Silicolith
b Phytolith
c Gastrolith
d Coprolite

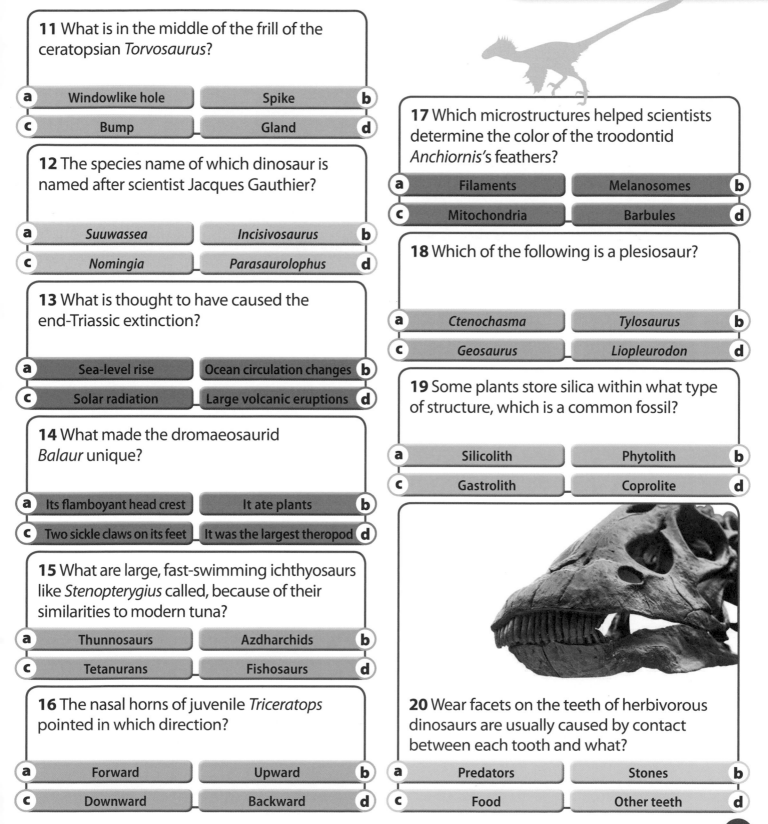

20 Wear facets on the teeth of herbivorous dinosaurs are usually caused by contact between each tooth and what?

a Predators
b Stones
c Food
d Other teeth

Maiasaura's name **means**

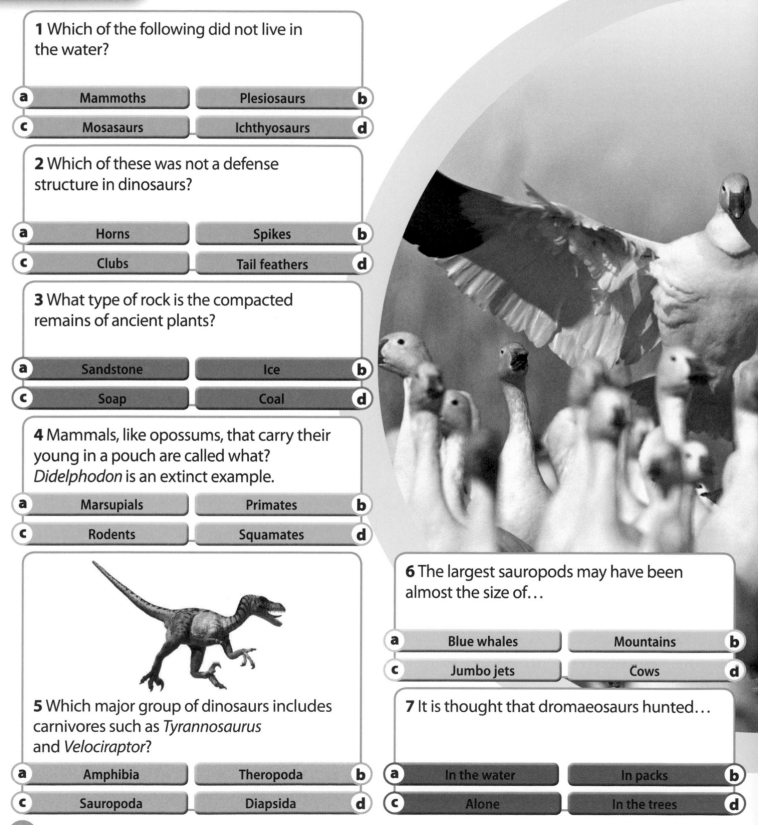

1 Which of the following did not live in the water?

a Mammoths	Plesiosaurs **b**
c Mosasaurs	Ichthyosaurs **d**

2 Which of these was not a defense structure in dinosaurs?

a Horns	Spikes **b**
c Clubs	Tail feathers **d**

3 What type of rock is the compacted remains of ancient plants?

a Sandstone	Ice **b**
c Soap	Coal **d**

4 Mammals, like opossums, that carry their young in a pouch are called what? *Didelphodon* is an extinct example.

a Marsupials	Primates **b**
c Rodents	Squamates **d**

5 Which major group of dinosaurs includes carnivores such as *Tyrannosaurus* and *Velociraptor*?

a Amphibia	Theropoda **b**
c Sauropoda	Diapsida **d**

6 The largest sauropods may have been almost the size of…

a Blue whales	Mountains **b**
c Jumbo jets	Cows **d**

7 It is thought that dromaeosaurs hunted…

a In the water	In packs **b**
c Alone	In the trees **d**

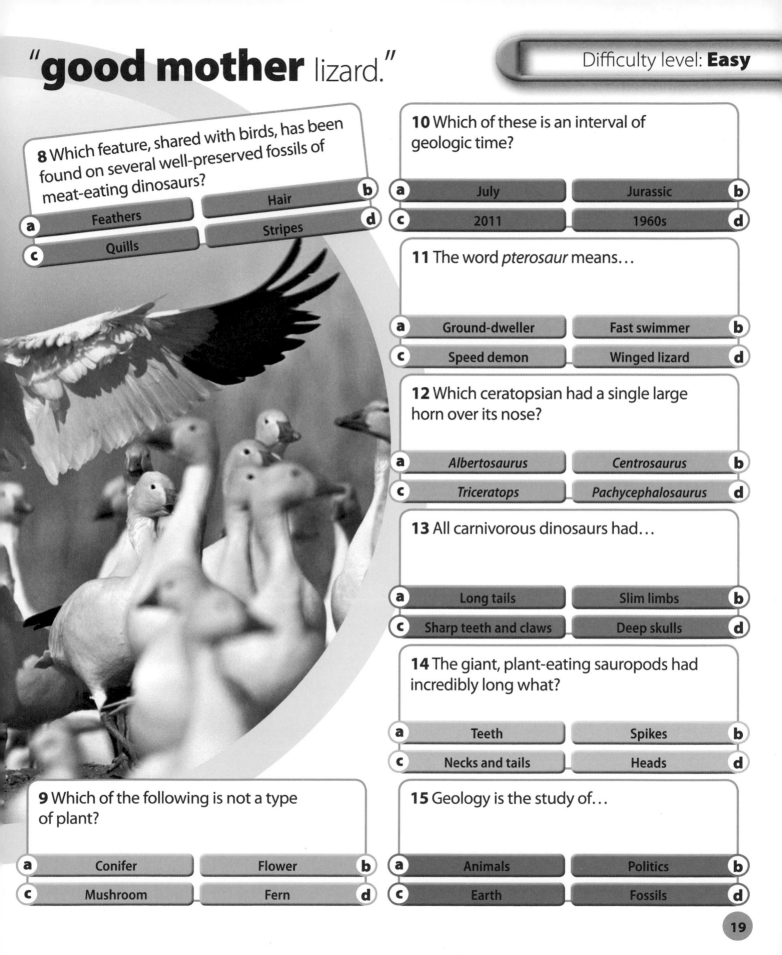

"**good mother** lizard."

8 Which feature, shared with birds, has been found on several well-preserved fossils of meat-eating dinosaurs?

- **a** Feathers
- **b** Hair
- **c** Quills
- **d** Stripes

9 Which of the following is not a type of plant?

- **a** Conifer
- **b** Flower
- **c** Mushroom
- **d** Fern

10 Which of these is an interval of geologic time?

- **a** July
- **b** Jurassic
- **c** 2011
- **d** 1960s

11 The word *pterosaur* means…

- **a** Ground-dweller
- **b** Fast swimmer
- **c** Speed demon
- **d** Winged lizard

12 Which ceratopsian had a single large horn over its nose?

- **a** *Albertosaurus*
- **b** *Centrosaurus*
- **c** *Triceratops*
- **d** *Pachycephalosaurus*

13 All carnivorous dinosaurs had…

- **a** Long tails
- **b** Slim limbs
- **c** Sharp teeth and claws
- **d** Deep skulls

14 The giant, plant-eating sauropods had incredibly long what?

- **a** Teeth
- **b** Spikes
- **c** Necks and tails
- **d** Heads

15 Geology is the study of…

- **a** Animals
- **b** Politics
- **c** Earth
- **d** Fossils

Unlike most **reptiles**,

1 The skulls of very young ceratopsians lacked…

- **a** Teeth
- **b** Nostrils
- **c** Horns
- **d** Eyes

2 Dinosaurs, birds, and crocodiles belong to which larger group?

- **a** Testudines
- **b** Aves
- **c** Theropoda
- **d** Archosauria

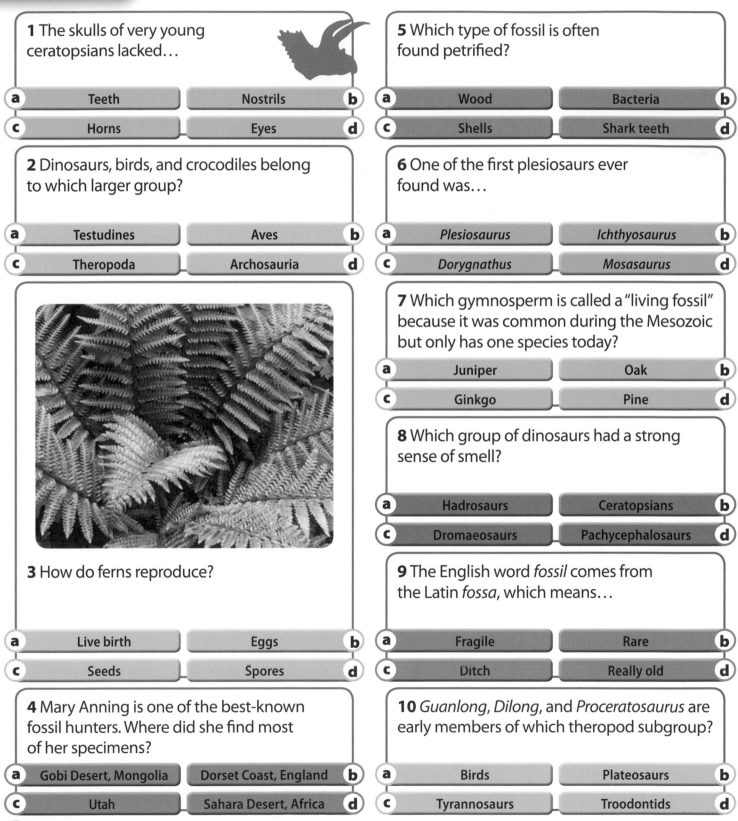

3 How do ferns reproduce?

- **a** Live birth
- **b** Eggs
- **c** Seeds
- **d** Spores

4 Mary Anning is one of the best-known fossil hunters. Where did she find most of her specimens?

- **a** Gobi Desert, Mongolia
- **b** Dorset Coast, England
- **c** Utah
- **d** Sahara Desert, Africa

5 Which type of fossil is often found petrified?

- **a** Wood
- **b** Bacteria
- **c** Shells
- **d** Shark teeth

6 One of the first plesiosaurs ever found was…

- **a** *Plesiosaurus*
- **b** *Ichthyosaurus*
- **c** *Dorygnathus*
- **d** *Mosasaurus*

7 Which gymnosperm is called a "living fossil" because it was common during the Mesozoic but only has one species today?

- **a** Juniper
- **b** Oak
- **c** Ginkgo
- **d** Pine

8 Which group of dinosaurs had a strong sense of smell?

- **a** Hadrosaurs
- **b** Ceratopsians
- **c** Dromaeosaurs
- **d** Pachycephalosaurs

9 The English word *fossil* comes from the Latin *fossa*, which means…

- **a** Fragile
- **b** Rare
- **c** Ditch
- **d** Really old

10 *Guanlong*, *Dilong*, and *Proceratosaurus* are early members of which theropod subgroup?

- **a** Birds
- **b** Plateosaurs
- **c** Tyrannosaurs
- **d** Troodontids

ornithischians had **cheeks**.

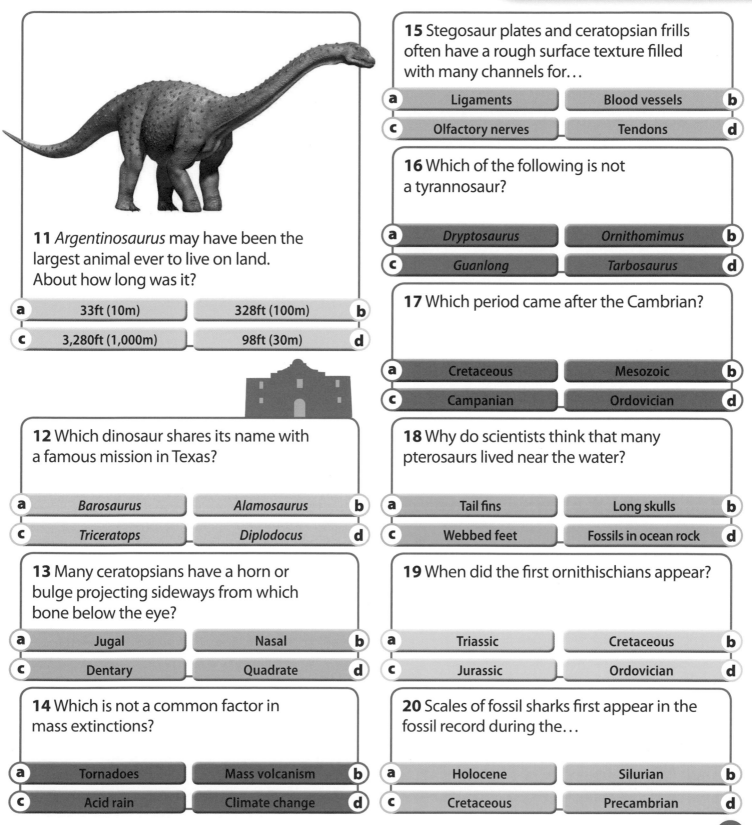

11 *Argentinosaurus* may have been the largest animal ever to live on land. About how long was it?

a 33ft (10m)
b 328ft (100m)
c 3,280ft (1,000m)
d 98ft (30m)

12 Which dinosaur shares its name with a famous mission in Texas?

a *Barosaurus*
b *Alamosaurus*
c *Triceratops*
d *Diplodocus*

13 Many ceratopsians have a horn or bulge projecting sideways from which bone below the eye?

a Jugal
b Nasal
c Dentary
d Quadrate

14 Which is not a common factor in mass extinctions?

a Tornadoes
b Mass volcanism
c Acid rain
d Climate change

15 Stegosaur plates and ceratopsian frills often have a rough surface texture filled with many channels for…

a Ligaments
b Blood vessels
c Olfactory nerves
d Tendons

16 Which of the following is not a tyrannosaur?

a *Dryptosaurus*
b *Ornithomimus*
c *Guanlong*
d *Tarbosaurus*

17 Which period came after the Cambrian?

a Cretaceous
b Mesozoic
c Campanian
d Ordovician

18 Why do scientists think that many pterosaurs lived near the water?

a Tail fins
b Long skulls
c Webbed feet
d Fossils in ocean rock

19 When did the first ornithischians appear?

a Triassic
b Cretaceous
c Jurassic
d Ordovician

20 Scales of fossil sharks first appear in the fossil record during the…

a Holocene
b Silurian
c Cretaceous
d Precambrian

Most **dinosaurs died**

1 What is it called when an organism dissolves, leaving a space in the surrounding rock, which is then filled?

- **a** Cast-and-mold
- **b** Permineralization
- **c** Petrifaction
- **d** Soft-tissue preservation

2 Which dinosaur is named after a Buddhist spiritual leader?

- **a** *Kryptops*
- **b** *Zanabazar*
- **c** *Acrocanthosaurus*
- **d** *Shaochilong*

3 Ichthyosaurs went extinct when, in relation to dinosaurs?

- **a** 20 million years before
- **b** At the same time
- **c** 20 million years after
- **d** 200 million years before

4 The most primitive prosauropods—cousins to the sauropods—were probably…

- **a** Herbivores
- **b** Carnivores
- **c** Insectivores
- **d** Omnivores

5 Which bizarre Asian hadrosaur had a single, unicorn-like crest on its skull?

- **a** *Shantungosaurus*
- **b** *Tanius*
- **c** *Olorotitan*
- **d** *Tsintaosaurus*

6 The Chinese carnivore *Anchiornis* is one of the…

- **a** Smallest dinosaurs
- **b** Ancestors of dinosaurs
- **c** Closest relatives to birds
- **d** Largest dinosaurs

7 Ammonites were named by Pliny the Elder, and their name denotes their resemblance to…

- **a** Spirals
- **b** A ram's horns
- **c** Coiled springs
- **d** Bullets

8 Which scientist first recognized that large periods of time are not preserved in the rock record?

- **a** James Hutton
- **b** Alfred Wegener
- **c** Plato
- **d** Graeme Lloyd

9 Which famous Italian scientist and artist observed fossil seashells on mountaintops?

- **a** Guglielmo Marconi
- **b** Leonardo da Vinci
- **c** Plato
- **d** Enrico Fermi

10 Which feature on the ulna of *Velociraptor* suggests that feathers were present?

- **a** Quill knobs
- **b** Muscular ridge
- **c** Pits and scratches
- **d** Double condyles

before the age of 30.

11 Which carnivorous dinosaur is named after rock musician Mark Knopfler?

- **a** *Majungasaurus*
- **b** *Metriocanthosaurus*
- **c** *Megalosaurus*
- **d** *Masiakasaurus*

12 Abelisaurid theropods have never been found where?

- **a** Madagascar
- **b** North America
- **c** Africa
- **d** South America

13 Wide-gauge trackways, with a wide distance between left and right footprints, were made by which sauropods?

- **a** Camarasaurids
- **b** Diplodocoids
- **c** Titanosaurs
- **d** Shunosaurids

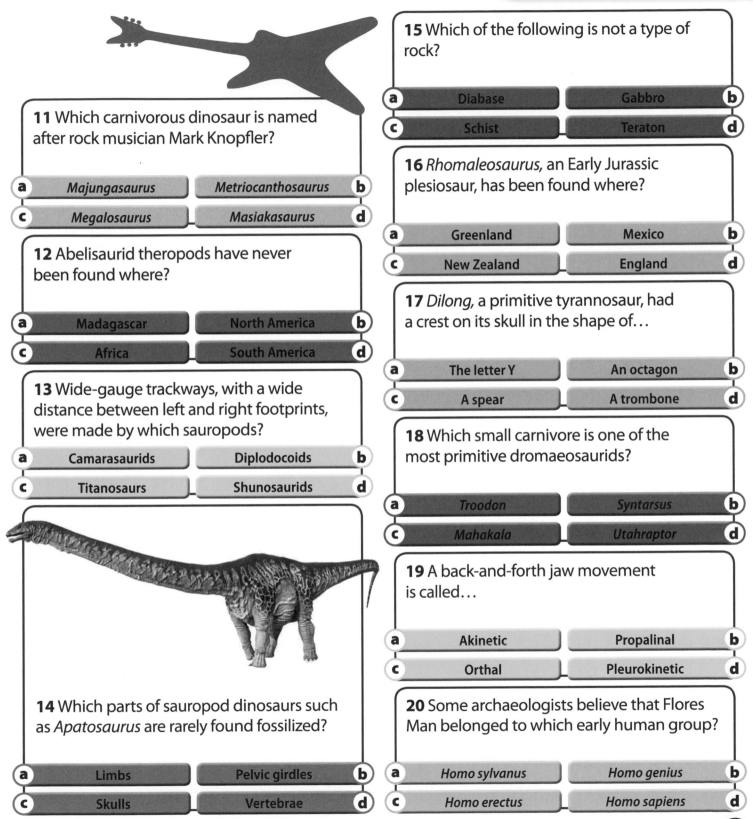

14 Which parts of sauropod dinosaurs such as *Apatosaurus* are rarely found fossilized?

- **a** Limbs
- **b** Pelvic girdles
- **c** Skulls
- **d** Vertebrae

15 Which of the following is not a type of rock?

- **a** Diabase
- **b** Gabbro
- **c** Schist
- **d** Teraton

16 *Rhomaleosaurus,* an Early Jurassic plesiosaur, has been found where?

- **a** Greenland
- **b** Mexico
- **c** New Zealand
- **d** England

17 *Dilong,* a primitive tyrannosaur, had a crest on its skull in the shape of…

- **a** The letter Y
- **b** An octagon
- **c** A spear
- **d** A trombone

18 Which small carnivore is one of the most primitive dromaeosaurids?

- **a** *Troodon*
- **b** *Syntarsus*
- **c** *Mahakala*
- **d** *Utahraptor*

19 A back-and-forth jaw movement is called…

- **a** Akinetic
- **b** Propalinal
- **c** Orthal
- **d** Pleurokinetic

20 Some archaeologists believe that Flores Man belonged to which early human group?

- **a** *Homo sylvanus*
- **b** *Homo genius*
- **c** *Homo erectus*
- **d** *Homo sapiens*

Tyrannosaurus rex's skeleton

1 What is it called when an organism or group completely dies out?

- **a** Revival
- **b** Origin
- **c** Celebration
- **d** Extinction

2 Humans, gorillas, chimps, and the extinct *Australopithecus* belong to which larger group of mammals?

- **a** Sirenians
- **b** Primates
- **c** Rodents
- **d** Ungulates

3 Hadrosaurs probably alternated between walking on two legs and walking on…

- **a** Four legs
- **b** One leg
- **c** Their tail
- **d** Their back

4 Ichthyosaurs used what structures to swim?

- **a** Scuba gear
- **b** Flippers
- **c** Cranial crests
- **d** Long skulls

5 What type of structure is rarely preserved in dinosaur fossils?

- **a** Internal organs
- **b** Bones
- **c** Teeth
- **d** Skulls

6 A good sense of smell is important for predators and…

- **a** Plant-eaters
- **b** Flying animals
- **c** Swimming animals
- **d** Scavengers

7 What common word is often used to describe pterosaurs?

- **a** Pterodactyls
- **b** Dinosaurs
- **c** Mammoths
- **d** Night hawks

8 A close relative of *Tyrannosaurus* is…

- **a** *Ichthyosaurus*
- **b** Mammoth
- **c** *Allosaurus*
- **d** *Stegosaurus*

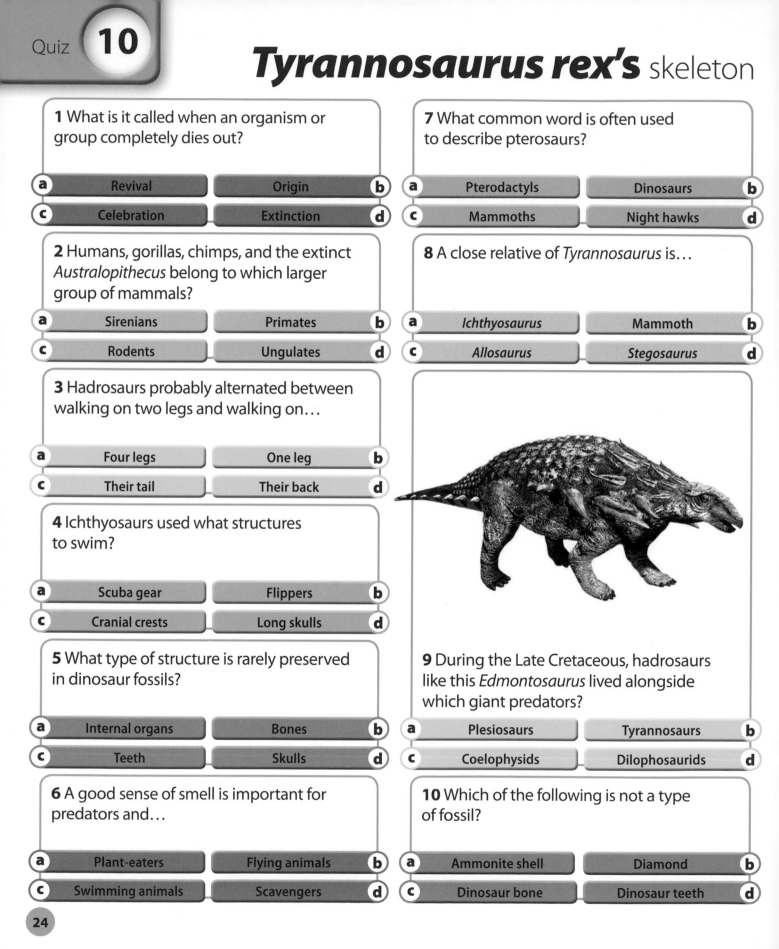

9 During the Late Cretaceous, hadrosaurs like this *Edmontosaurus* lived alongside which giant predators?

- **a** Plesiosaurs
- **b** Tyrannosaurs
- **c** Coelophysids
- **d** Dilophosaurids

10 Which of the following is not a type of fossil?

- **a** Ammonite shell
- **b** Diamond
- **c** Dinosaur bone
- **d** Dinosaur teeth

had more than **200 bones**.

11 Which chemical substance do plants release? There was less of this in the Triassic atmosphere than today.

a Mud
b Silicon
c Oxygen
d Oil

12 How many horns did *Triceratops* have?

a 2
b 6
c 9
d 3

13 Mammals originated at the same general time as what other group?

a Plants
b Bacteria
c Dinosaurs
d Humans

14 No theropod dinosaurs were able to…

a Run
b Fly
c Live in the ocean
d Walk

15 This dinosaur has a domed head. Which of these groups does it belong to?

a Allosaurs
b Raptors
c Avians
d Pachycephalosaurs

The **dinosaur** with the **shortest**

1 Many marine reptiles have the word *neustes* in their names, which means…

a Runner | Predator b
c Hunter | Swimmer d

2 The most recent ice age occurred during which formal time interval?

a Jurassic | Paleozoic b
c Victorian Age | Pleistocene d

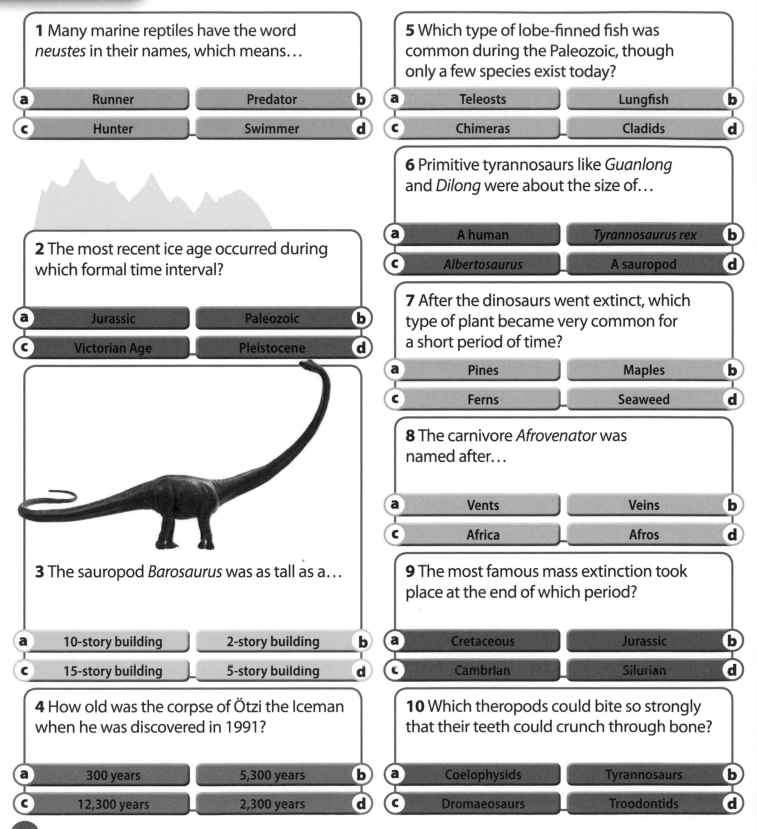

3 The sauropod *Barosaurus* was as tall as a…

a 10-story building | 2-story building b
c 15-story building | 5-story building d

4 How old was the corpse of Ötzi the Iceman when he was discovered in 1991?

a 300 years | 5,300 years b
c 12,300 years | 2,300 years d

5 Which type of lobe-finned fish was common during the Paleozoic, though only a few species exist today?

a Teleosts | Lungfish b
c Chimeras | Cladids d

6 Primitive tyrannosaurs like *Guanlong* and *Dilong* were about the size of…

a A human | *Tyrannosaurus rex* b
c *Albertosaurus* | A sauropod d

7 After the dinosaurs went extinct, which type of plant became very common for a short period of time?

a Pines | Maples b
c Ferns | Seaweed d

8 The carnivore *Afrovenator* was named after…

a Vents | Veins b
c Africa | Afros d

9 The most famous mass extinction took place at the end of which period?

a Cretaceous | Jurassic b
c Cambrian | Silurian d

10 Which theropods could bite so strongly that their teeth could crunch through bone?

a Coelophysids | Tyrannosaurs b
c Dromaeosaurs | Troodontids d

name is *Mei*.

11 Which group does this animal belong to?

a Pterosaurs	**b** Sauropods		
c Pliosaurs	**d** Theropods		

12 The famous "feathered dinosaurs" were found in which country?

a China	**b** Mexico
c Sudan	**d** Poland

13 In birds, which body part is reduced into a stubby structure called a pygostyle?

a Foot	**b** Hand
c Tail	**d** Neck

14 One famous fossil is the frill of a ceratopsian that was bitten by…

a *Brachiosaurus*	**b** *Tyrannosaurus*
c *Allosaurus*	**d** Another *Triceratops*

15 Which scientist, who also named Dinosauria, gave ichthyosaurs their name?

a Richard Owen	**b** James Hutton
c H. G. Seeley	**d** Josh Mathews

16 In addition to spikes on the back and tail, some stegosaurs have spikes…

a On the feet	**b** On the arms
c On the skull	**d** On the shoulders

17 Which branch of geology is the study of earthquakes?

a Chemistry	**b** Philosophy
c Seismology	**d** Paleontology

18 It has been suggested that hadrosaurs and ceratopsians were able to live side by side, because they…

a Drank different water	**b** Fought over territory
c Ate different plants	**d** Slept at different times

19 Which of the following ceratopsians did not have any horns?

a *Psittacosaurus*	**b** *Triceratops*
c *Styracosaurus*	**d** *Centrosaurus*

20 *Mantellisaurus* is named after which famous paleontologist?

a Mantel Harcourt-Smith	**b** Gideon Mantell
c William Tell	**d** Manuel Santos

Gasosaurus was **discovered**

1 Which carnivorous dinosaurs are often called "shark-tooth reptiles"?

- **a** Spinosaurids
- **b** Tyrannosaurids
- **c** Carcharodontosaurids
- **d** Megalosaurids

2 Hand-only trackways, in which no trace of footprints are present, may indicate that sauropods could do what?

- **a** Jump
- **b** Fly
- **c** Hop
- **d** Swim

3 What is the final substage division of the Cretaceous?

- **a** Maastrichtian
- **b** Campanian
- **c** Paleozoic
- **d** Olenekian

4 A scrap of eroded fossil is often referred to as what?

- **a** Garbage
- **b** Rubbish
- **c** Treasure
- **d** Float

5 Bite marks matching *Tyrannosaurus rex*'s teeth have been found on the facial bones of a *Tyrannosaurus*. What caused this?

- **a** Agonistic behavior
- **b** Omnivory
- **c** Niche partitioning
- **d** Diurnal behavior

6 When did the first ichthyosaurs evolve?

- **a** Early Triassic
- **b** Early Jurassic
- **c** Late Cretaceous
- **d** Cambrian

7 The outer surface of the pachycephalosaur dome consisted of which type of bone tissue?

- **a** Enameloid
- **b** Compact
- **c** Fluid
- **d** Cartilaginous

8 The jaws of some hadrosaurs like *Brachylophosaurus* contained up to how many teeth?

- **a** 60
- **b** 10
- **c** 5
- **d** 100

9 Dolomite is similar to limestone, but includes which additional mineral?

- **a** Iridium
- **b** Arsenic
- **c** Nitrogen
- **d** Magnesium

10 *Lourinhanosaurus* is named after a town in which European country?

- **a** Slovenia
- **b** Portugal
- **c** Spain
- **d** Scotland

by a natural **gas** company.

11 Dinosaur teeth are made of enamel and…

a | Dentine
b | Bone
c | Iridium
d | Muscle

12 The large theropod *Cryolophosaurus* was the first dinosaur from which continent to be officially named?

a | Greenland
b | Australia
c | Antarctica
d | North America

13 Which instrument measures the isotopic composition of rocks?

a | CT scanner
b | Supercomputer
c | Mass spectrometer
d | Microscope

14 Which hadrosaurid subgroup did not have elaborate cranial crests?

a | Iguanodontids
b | Scutellosaurids
c | Nodosaurids
d | Hadrosaurines

15 The abelisaurid *Majungasaurus* was once thought to be what?

a | Amphibian
b | Pachycephalosaur
c | Lizard
d | Mosasaur

16 Which types of ammonites are not spiraled?

a | Belemnites
b | Heteromorphs
c | Homomorphs
d | Nautiloids

17 Which of the following primates is the most distant relative of humans?

18 Which microscopic structures were controversially reported in the fossil bone of a *Tyrannosaurus rex*?

a | Tendons
b | Blood vessels
c | Nerves
d | Golgi apparatuses

19 Which scientist first classified dinosaurs into ornithischians and saurischians, and also named the Pliosauridae?

a | Hilary Ketchum
b | Adam Smith
c | William Buckland
d | H. G. Seeley

20 What do you call an animal that specializes in eating fruit?

a | Herbivore
b | Fruitivore
c | Berrivore
d | Frugivore

Euoplocephalus's **tailbones** were

1 Spinosaurids were not typical theropods. They probably ate what, in addition to meat?

- **a** Foliage
- **b** Fish
- **c** Insects
- **d** Salt

2 Many ocean-dwelling reptiles probably ate…

- **a** Dinosaurs
- **b** Mammoths
- **c** Insects
- **d** Fish

3 Ceratopsians are often found in bone beds that contain hundreds of individual skeletons. What does this indicate?

- **a** They died constantly
- **b** They lived in water
- **c** They ate meat
- **d** They lived in herds

4 The oldest primate fossils are found in rocks that formed…

- **a** In the deep ocean
- **b** In volcanoes
- **c** After the dinosaurs died
- **d** During the Cambrian

5 Sauropods had which of the following features?

- **a** Stubby tails
- **b** Only two limbs
- **c** Long necks
- **d** Huge skulls

6 In the largest ceratopsians, the horns over the eyes could reach what length?

- **a** 3ft (1m)
- **b** 4in (10cm)
- **c** 12in (30cm)
- **d** 33ft (10m)

7 Dinosaurs that walked on four legs are called…

- **a** Lazy
- **b** Quadrupedal
- **c** Slow
- **d** Fast

8 Which of the following is a type of rock?

- **a** Granite
- **b** Mud
- **c** Straw
- **d** Pottery

9 The ceratopsian dinosaurs used what structures for display?

- **a** Colorful tails
- **b** Horns and frills
- **c** Tail clubs
- **d** Big teeth

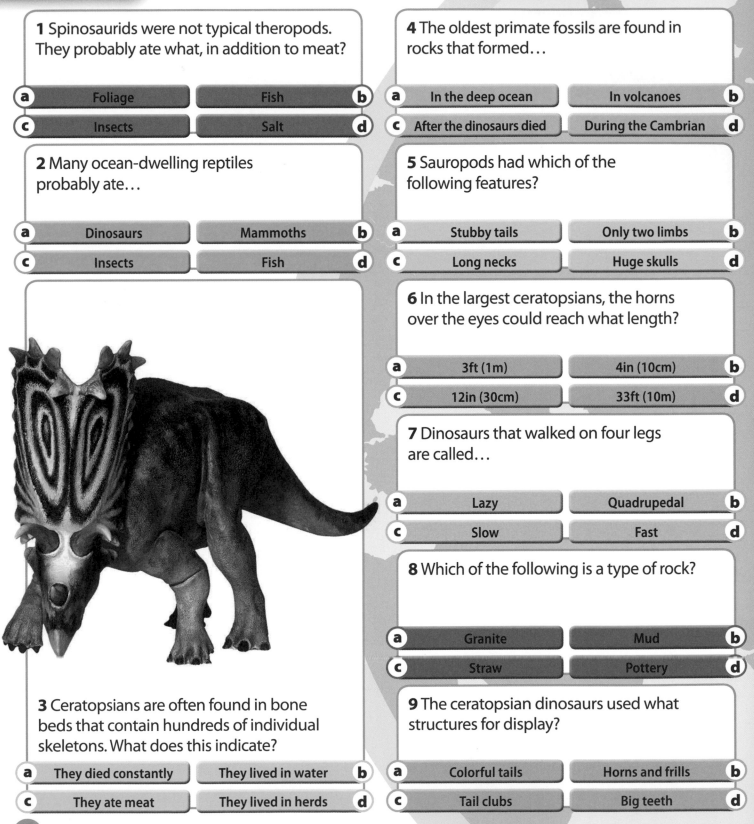

fused, forming a club.

10 Which feathered dinosaur has been found in Mongolia?

- **a** Velociraptor
- **b** Triceratops
- **c** Allosaurus
- **d** Brachiosaurus

13 Fossils of which of these dinosaurs have not been found in China?

- **a** Shunosaurus
- **b** Mamenchisaurus
- **c** Albertosaurus
- **d** Huayangosaurus

11 What greenhouse gas, increased quantities of which can cause climates to warm, do plants require for growth?

- **a** Oxygen
- **b** Salt
- **c** Flesh
- **d** Carbon dioxide

14 When they walked on land, pterosaurs moved in a similar way to…

- **a** Snakes
- **b** Prairie dogs
- **c** Dinosaurs
- **d** Frogs

12 The large claws of dromaeosaurs were used to…

- **a** Slash prey
- **b** Climb mountains
- **c** Nest in trees
- **d** Provide balance

15 Dinosaurs lived in which of these environments?

- **a** Oceans
- **b** Lakes
- **c** Outer space
- **d** Land

Ankylosaurus and *Euoplocephalus*

1 Many early cousins of sauropods had teeth that resembled the teeth of which living herbivorous reptile?

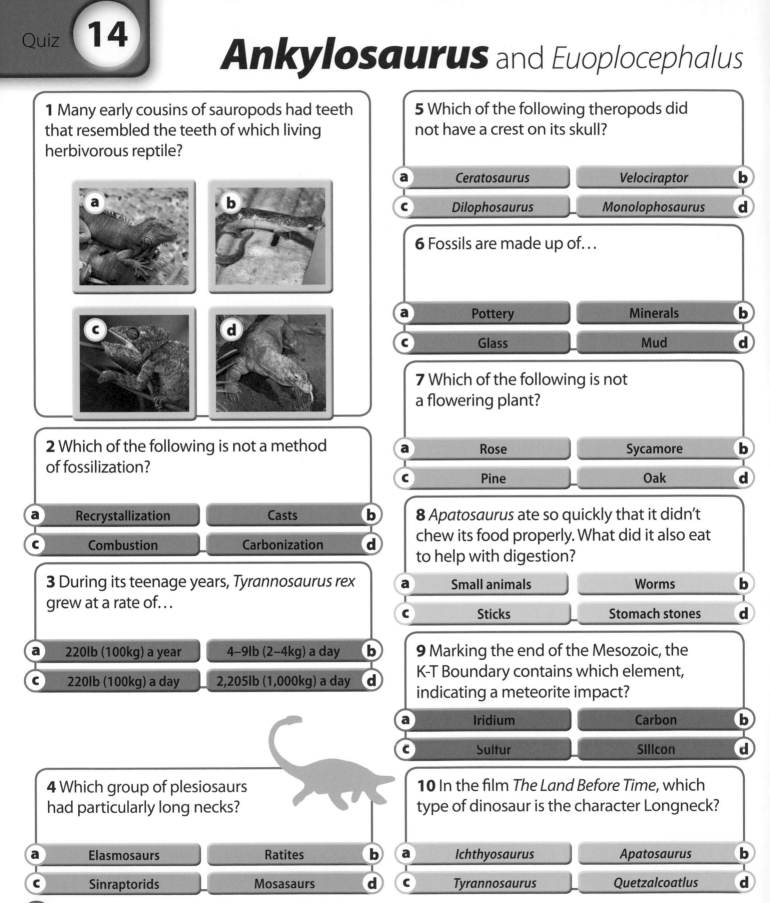

2 Which of the following is not a method of fossilization?

a Recrystallization	**b** Casts	
c Combustion	**d** Carbonization	

3 During its teenage years, *Tyrannosaurus rex* grew at a rate of…

a 220lb (100kg) a year	**b** 4–9lb (2–4kg) a day
c 220lb (100kg) a day	**d** 2,205lb (1,000kg) a day

4 Which group of plesiosaurs had particularly long necks?

a Elasmosaurs	**b** Ratites
c Sinraptorids	**d** Mosasaurs

5 Which of the following theropods did not have a crest on its skull?

a *Ceratosaurus*	**b** *Velociraptor*
c *Dilophosaurus*	**d** *Monolophosaurus*

6 Fossils are made up of…

a Pottery	**b** Minerals
c Glass	**d** Mud

7 Which of the following is not a flowering plant?

a Rose	**b** Sycamore
c Pine	**d** Oak

8 *Apatosaurus* ate so quickly that it didn't chew its food properly. What did it also eat to help with digestion?

a Small animals	**b** Worms
c Sticks	**d** Stomach stones

9 Marking the end of the Mesozoic, the K-T Boundary contains which element, indicating a meteorite impact?

a Iridium	**b** Carbon
c Sulfur	**d** Silicon

10 In the film *The Land Before Time*, which type of dinosaur is the character Longneck?

a *Ichthyosaurus*	**b** *Apatosaurus*
c *Tyrannosaurus*	**d** *Quetzalcoatlus*

11 Which of these is a famous pterosaur discovered in Jurassic rocks in England?

- **a** Monolophosaurus
- **b** Coelophysis
- **c** Nanotyrannus
- **d** Dimorphodon

12 A giant ceratopsian skull from New Mexico has recently been described as a new genus called…

- **a** Megaceratops
- **b** Einiosaurus
- **c** Pachyrhinosaurus
- **d** Titanoceratops

13 The Carboniferous period is divided into the Pennsylvanian and…

- **a** Triassic
- **b** Cold War
- **c** Devonian
- **d** Mississippian

14 Which dinosaur is named after paleontologist O. C. Marsh?

- **a** Ocsaurus
- **b** Marshtitan
- **c** Othnielosaurus
- **d** Marshraptor

15 One type of plant that sauropods probably ate was…

- **a** Wheat
- **b** Mushrooms
- **c** Cycads
- **d** Strawberries

16 Which American president enjoyed collecting fossils?

- **a** Thomas Jefferson
- **b** George W. Bush
- **c** Abraham Lincoln
- **d** Bill Clinton

17 Which is a species of primitive tetrapod that is probably one of the oldest vertebrates with limbs?

- **a** Ichthyosaurus
- **b** Acanthostega
- **c** Dimetrodon
- **d** Coelophysis

18 *Koreaceratops* is a close relative of…

- **a** Brontops
- **b** Deinonychus
- **c** Kentrosaurus
- **d** Triceratops

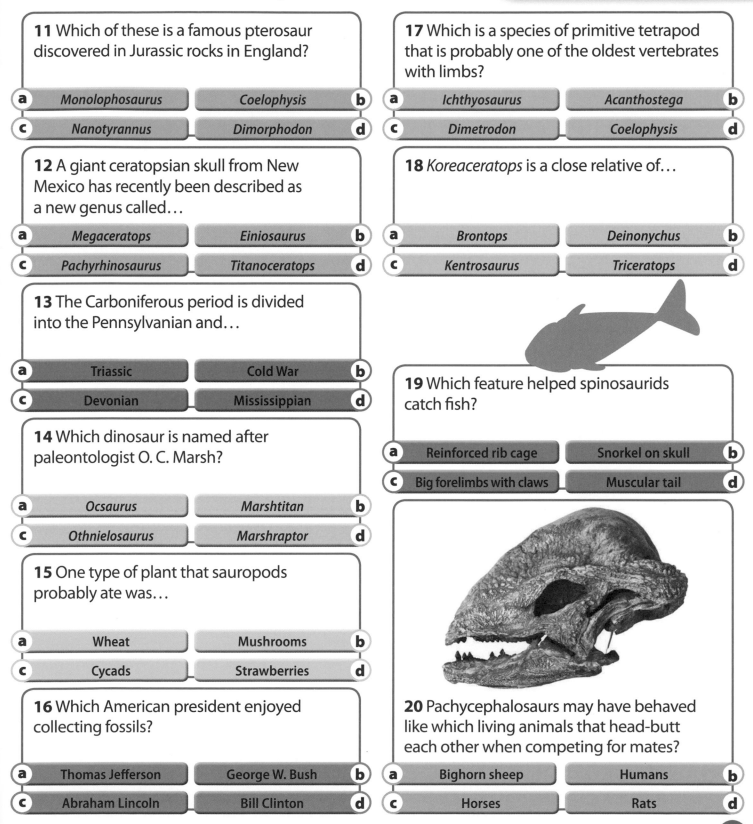

19 Which feature helped spinosaurids catch fish?

- **a** Reinforced rib cage
- **b** Snorkel on skull
- **c** Big forelimbs with claws
- **d** Muscular tail

20 Pachycephalosaurs may have behaved like which living animals that head-butt each other when competing for mates?

- **a** Bighorn sheep
- **b** Humans
- **c** Horses
- **d** Rats

1 What is located inside the cranial crest of many hadrosaurids?

a Nasal cavity **b** Brain

c Olfactory bulbs **d** Jaw-closing muscles

2 Which of the following is a primitive member of the tyrannosaur group?

a *Falcarius* **b** *Concavenator*

c *Dilong* **d** *Sinosauropteryx*

3 Which of the following is not a metamorphic rock?

a Schist **b** Slate

c Gneiss **d** Shale

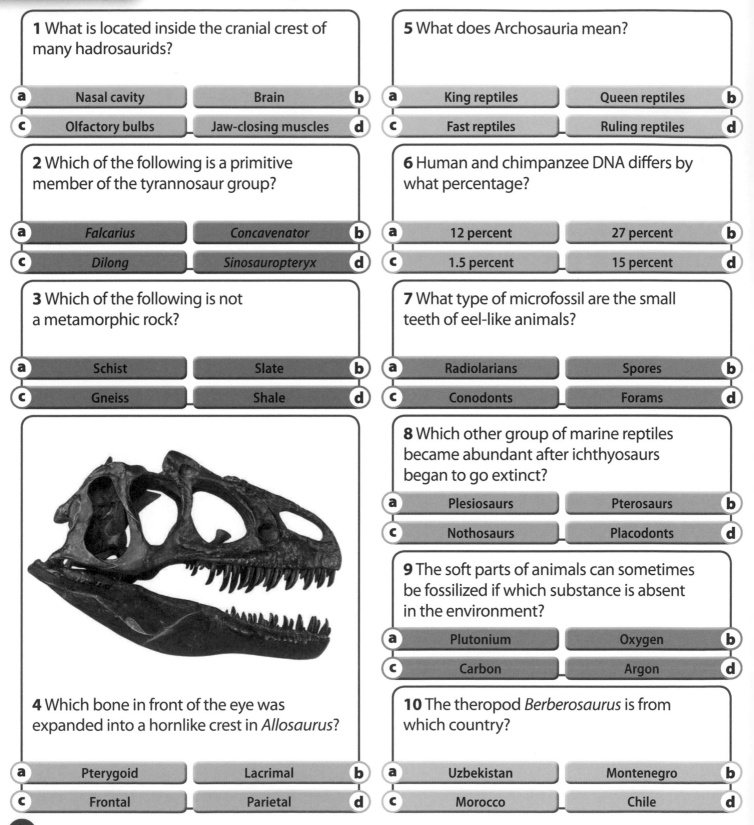

4 Which bone in front of the eye was expanded into a hornlike crest in *Allosaurus*?

a Pterygoid **b** Lacrimal

c Frontal **d** Parietal

5 What does Archosauria mean?

a King reptiles **b** Queen reptiles

c Fast reptiles **d** Ruling reptiles

6 Human and chimpanzee DNA differs by what percentage?

a 12 percent **b** 27 percent

c 1.5 percent **d** 15 percent

7 What type of microfossil are the small teeth of eel-like animals?

a Radiolarians **b** Spores

c Conodonts **d** Forams

8 Which other group of marine reptiles became abundant after ichthyosaurs began to go extinct?

a Plesiosaurs **b** Pterosaurs

c Nothosaurs **d** Placodonts

9 The soft parts of animals can sometimes be fossilized if which substance is absent in the environment?

a Plutonium **b** Oxygen

c Carbon **d** Argon

10 The theropod *Berberosaurus* is from which country?

a Uzbekistan **b** Montenegro

c Morocco **d** Chile

first complete ichthyosaur fossil.

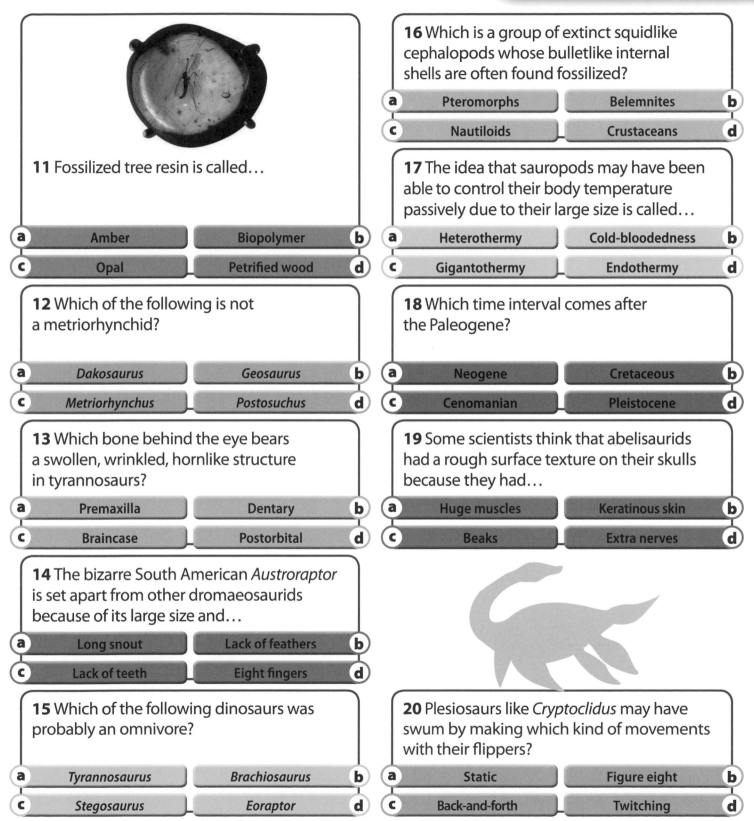

11 Fossilized tree resin is called…

a Amber
b Biopolymer
c Opal
d Petrified wood

16 Which is a group of extinct squidlike cephalopods whose bulletlike internal shells are often found fossilized?

a Pteromorphs
b Belemnites
c Nautiloids
d Crustaceans

17 The idea that sauropods may have been able to control their body temperature passively due to their large size is called…

a Heterothermy
b Cold-bloodedness
c Gigantothermy
d Endothermy

12 Which of the following is not a metriorhynchid?

a *Dakosaurus*
b *Geosaurus*
c *Metriorhynchus*
d *Postosuchus*

18 Which time interval comes after the Paleogene?

a Neogene
b Cretaceous
c Cenomanian
d Pleistocene

13 Which bone behind the eye bears a swollen, wrinkled, hornlike structure in tyrannosaurs?

a Premaxilla
b Dentary
c Braincase
d Postorbital

19 Some scientists think that abelisaurids had a rough surface texture on their skulls because they had…

a Huge muscles
b Keratinous skin
c Beaks
d Extra nerves

14 The bizarre South American *Austroraptor* is set apart from other dromaeosaurids because of its large size and…

a Long snout
b Lack of feathers
c Lack of teeth
d Eight fingers

15 Which of the following dinosaurs was probably an omnivore?

a *Tyrannosaurus*
b *Brachiosaurus*
c *Stegosaurus*
d *Eoraptor*

20 Plesiosaurs like *Cryptoclidus* may have swum by making which kind of movements with their flippers?

a Static
b Figure eight
c Back-and-forth
d Twitching

Gastonia used **spines** studded all

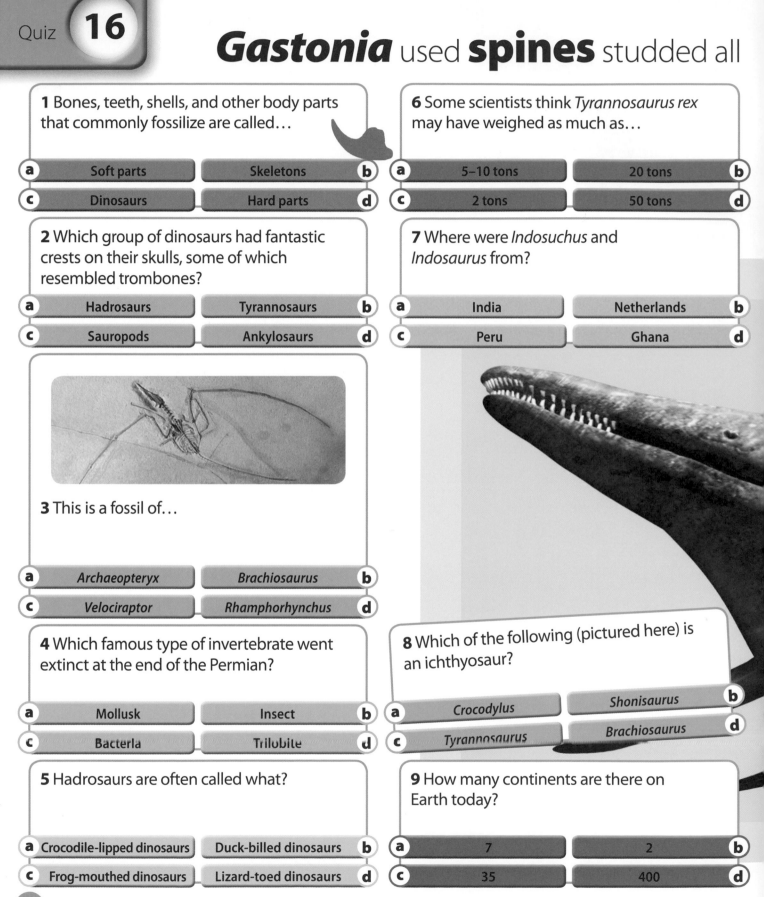

1 Bones, teeth, shells, and other body parts that commonly fossilize are called…

a Soft parts	Skeletons **b**
c Dinosaurs	Hard parts **d**

2 Which group of dinosaurs had fantastic crests on their skulls, some of which resembled trombones?

a Hadrosaurs	Tyrannosaurs **b**
c Sauropods	Ankylosaurs **d**

3 This is a fossil of…

a *Archaeopteryx*	*Brachiosaurus* **b**
c *Velociraptor*	*Rhamphorhynchus* **d**

4 Which famous type of invertebrate went extinct at the end of the Permian?

a Mollusk	Insect **b**
c Bacteria	Trilobite **d**

5 Hadrosaurs are often called what?

a Crocodile-lipped dinosaurs	Duck-billed dinosaurs **b**
c Frog-mouthed dinosaurs	Lizard-toed dinosaurs **d**

6 Some scientists think *Tyrannosaurus rex* may have weighed as much as…

a 5–10 tons	20 tons **b**
c 2 tons	50 tons **d**

7 Where were *Indosuchus* and *Indosaurus* from?

a India	Netherlands **b**
c Peru	Ghana **d**

8 Which of the following (pictured here) is an ichthyosaur?

a *Crocodylus*	*Shonisaurus* **b**
c *Tyrannosaurus*	*Brachiosaurus* **d**

9 How many continents are there on Earth today?

a 7	2 **b**
c 35	400 **d**

over its body to **defend** itself.

10 What type of extinct animal was once found with a pterosaur fossil in its stomach?

a Tiger	Shark **b**
c Dinosaur	Mammoth **d**

11 Why do dinosaurs and birds both have wishbones?

a Random chance	No reason **b**
c Birds come from dinosaurs	They are the same **d**

12 The two major subgroups of dinosaurs are ornithischians and…

a Tortoises	Saurischians **b**
c Sauropods	Crocodiles **d**

13 A famous fossil specimen shows the dromaeosaurid *Velociraptor* fighting with…

a *Tyrannosaurus rex*	*Allosaurus* **b**
c A turtle	*Protoceratops* **d**

14 Which feature helped sauropods support their huge weight?

a Reduced tail	Lack of bones **b**
c Sturdy, columnar limbs	Extra back muscles **d**

15 What causes mountains to form?

a Ocean currents	Continents colliding **b**
c Thunder	Rain **d**

Early **Triassic** conditions were **dry**,

1 The Jurassic period ended how many million years ago?

a 145.5 million
b 64.2 million
c 203.6 million
d 85.8 million

2 How can fossils in one rock unit be used to link that unit to another set of rocks of similar age?

a Geological dating
b Faunal similarity
c Absolute dating
d Radiometric dating

3 The name of one dinosaur comes from its parenting skills. What does *Maiasaura* mean?

a Good mother lizard
b Bad mother lizard
c Good father lizard
d Bad father lizard

4 What is it called when an animal uses its skull to strike the side, not the head, of a rival?

a Tail-butting
b Flank-butting
c Head-butting
d Skull-butting

5 The vast stretch of time before the Cambrian is called…

a Noncambrian
b Jurassic
c Ice age
d Precambrian

6 Which type of egg is protected by several membranes, allowing it to develop on land without drying out?

a Terrestrial
b Amniotic
c Placental
d Amphibic

7 The order name *Ichthyosauria* means…

a Sea reptile
b Fish lizard
c Fast lizard
d Fast fish

8 *Teratophoneus curriei* is named after which paleontologist?

a Terrence Terato
b Billy Phoneus
c Jack Horner
d Philip Currie

9 The skulls of spinosaurids generally resemble the skulls of which living animal?

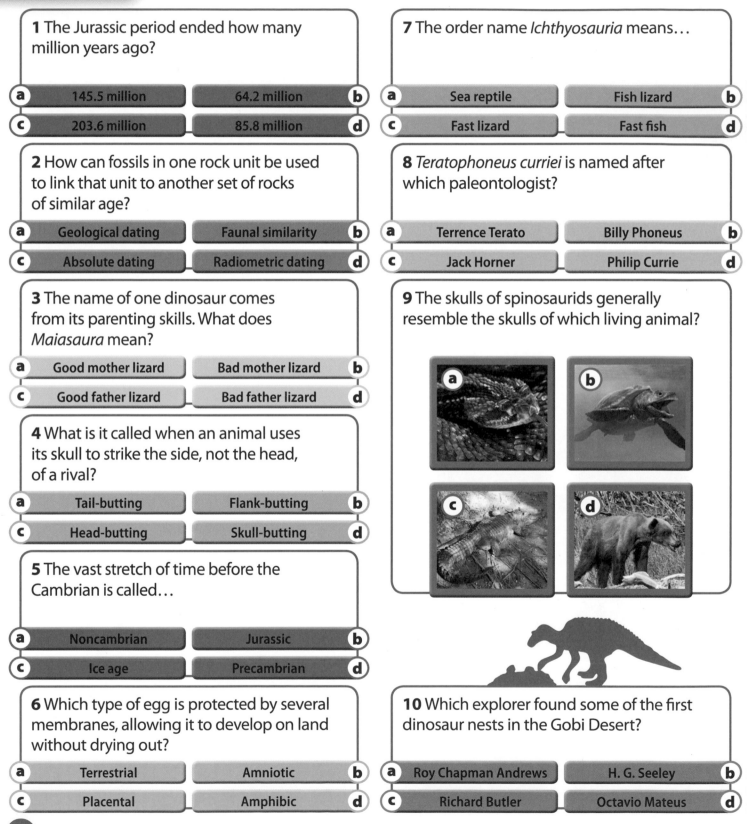

10 Which explorer found some of the first dinosaur nests in the Gobi Desert?

a Roy Chapman Andrews
b H. G. Seeley
c Richard Butler
d Octavio Mateus

11 Which animal, like *Dimetrodon*, is an ancient reptile with a sail on its back?

a | Acanthostega
b | Eoraptor
c | Carcharodon
d | Edaphosaurus

12 Sauropods probably walked in a similar way to…

a | Pigeons
b | Frogs
c | Wolves
d | Elephants

13 Which animals survived the end-Triassic extinction?

a | Trilobites
b | Monkeys
c | Dinosaurs
d | Pigs

14 The Burgess Shale Formation is one of the most important fossil locations in the world. Where is it located?

a | Xinjiang, China
b | British Columbia, Canada
c | Arizona, US
d | New South Wales, Australia

15 How many spikes did *Stegosaurus* have on its tail?

a | 4
b | 1
c | 7
d | 15

16 Fossils of the small ceratopsian *Protoceratops* are commonly found where, alongside *Oviraptor* and *Velociraptor*?

a | Mojave Desert
b | Atacama Desert
c | Gobi Desert
d | Sahara Desert

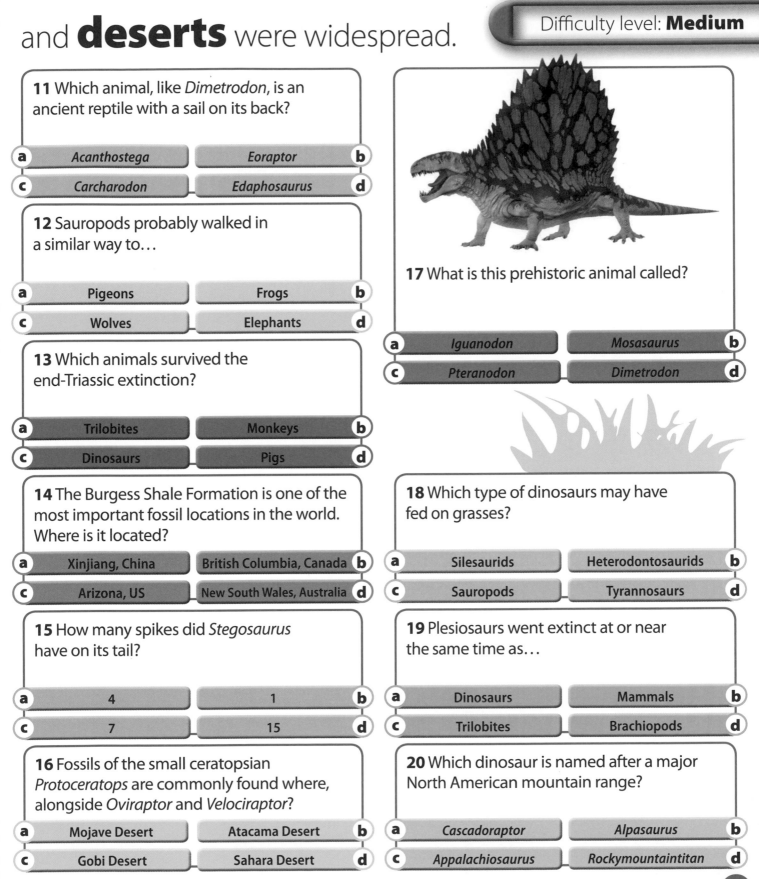

17 What is this prehistoric animal called?

a | Iguanodon
b | Mosasaurus
c | Pteranodon
d | Dimetrodon

18 Which type of dinosaurs may have fed on grasses?

a | Silesaurids
b | Heterodontosaurids
c | Sauropods
d | Tyrannosaurs

19 Plesiosaurs went extinct at or near the same time as…

a | Dinosaurs
b | Mammals
c | Trilobites
d | Brachiopods

20 Which dinosaur is named after a major North American mountain range?

a | Cascadoraptor
b | Alpasaurus
c | Appalachiosaurus
d | Rockymountaintitan

The pterosaur **Pterodactylus's** name

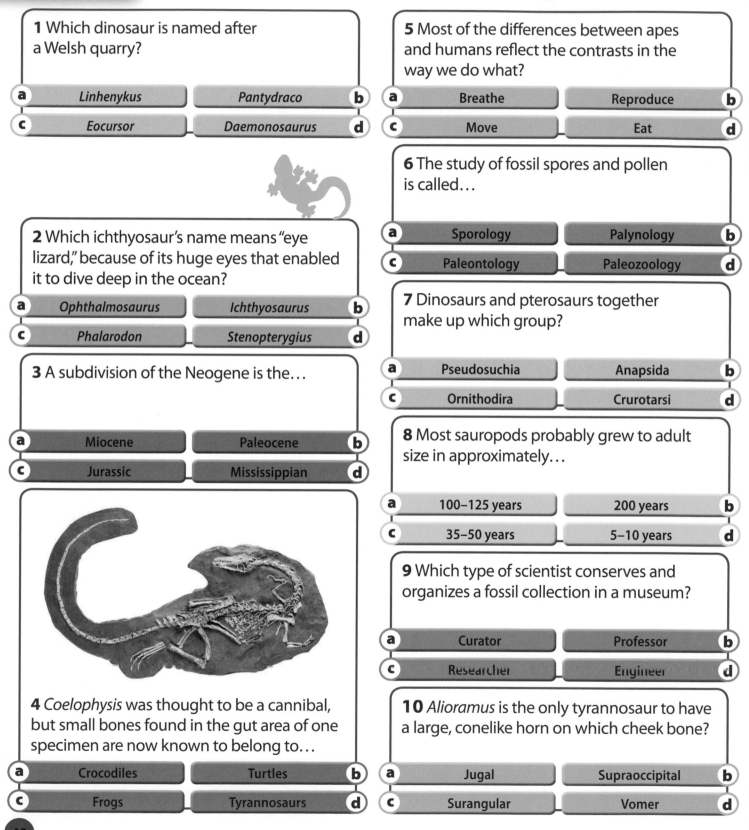

1 Which dinosaur is named after a Welsh quarry?

a | Linhenykus
b | Pantydraco
c | Eocursor
d | Daemonosaurus

2 Which ichthyosaur's name means "eye lizard," because of its huge eyes that enabled it to dive deep in the ocean?

a | Ophthalmosaurus
b | Ichthyosaurus
c | Phalarodon
d | Stenopterygius

3 A subdivision of the Neogene is the…

a | Miocene
b | Paleocene
c | Jurassic
d | Mississippian

4 *Coelophysis* was thought to be a cannibal, but small bones found in the gut area of one specimen are now known to belong to…

a | Crocodiles
b | Turtles
c | Frogs
d | Tyrannosaurs

5 Most of the differences between apes and humans reflect the contrasts in the way we do what?

a | Breathe
b | Reproduce
c | Move
d | Eat

6 The study of fossil spores and pollen is called…

a | Sporology
b | Palynology
c | Paleontology
d | Paleozoology

7 Dinosaurs and pterosaurs together make up which group?

a | Pseudosuchia
b | Anapsida
c | Ornithodira
d | Crurotarsi

8 Most sauropods probably grew to adult size in approximately…

a | 100–125 years
b | 200 years
c | 35–50 years
d | 5–10 years

9 Which type of scientist conserves and organizes a fossil collection in a museum?

a | Curator
b | Professor
c | Researcher
d | Engineer

10 *Alioramus* is the only tyrannosaur to have a large, conelike horn on which cheek bone?

a | Jugal
b | Supraoccipital
c | Surangular
d | Vomer

means "**wing-finger**."

11 Which crocodilian feature did metriorhynchids lose, in order to streamline their bodies for swimming?

- **a** Hands
- **b** Tails
- **c** Teeth
- **d** Body armor

12 Surprisingly, a coprolite (fossilized dung) showed that some hadrosaurs ate…

- **a** Flesh
- **b** Decaying wood
- **c** Bones
- **d** Mud

13 What happens when two continental plates meet?

- **a** One overrides the other
- **b** One plate disappears
- **c** An ocean forms
- **d** Mountains form

14 The skull of *Lambeosaurus* is often described as resembling a…

- **a** Helmet
- **b** Tuba
- **c** Teapot
- **d** Hatchet

15 Which principle describes the decay of one isotope into another, allowing scientists to date rocks?

- **a** Evolution
- **b** Magnetism
- **c** Radioactivity
- **d** Decomposition

16 According to scientists, which sauropod may have held its neck horizontally, not vertically?

- **a** *Brachiosaurus*
- **b** *Dromaeosaurus*
- **c** *Plateosaurus*
- **d** *Diplodocus*

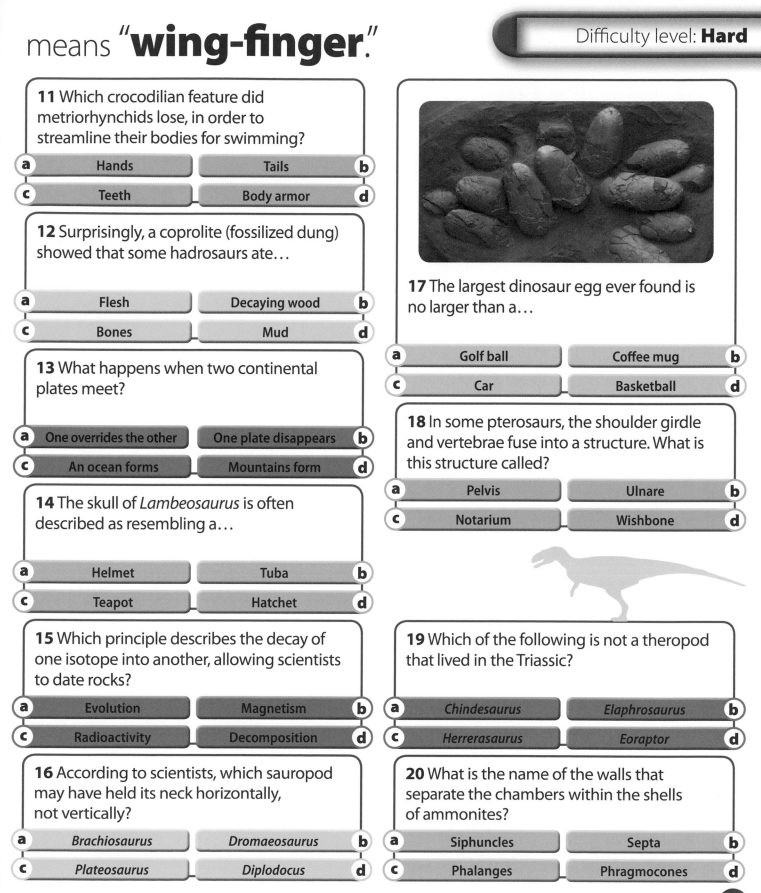

17 The largest dinosaur egg ever found is no larger than a…

- **a** Golf ball
- **b** Coffee mug
- **c** Car
- **d** Basketball

18 In some pterosaurs, the shoulder girdle and vertebrae fuse into a structure. What is this structure called?

- **a** Pelvis
- **b** Ulnare
- **c** Notarium
- **d** Wishbone

19 Which of the following is not a theropod that lived in the Triassic?

- **a** *Chindesaurus*
- **b** *Elaphrosaurus*
- **c** *Herrerasaurus*
- **d** *Eoraptor*

20 What is the name of the walls that separate the chambers within the shells of ammonites?

- **a** Siphuncles
- **b** Septa
- **c** Phalanges
- **d** Phragmocones

Small dinosaurs like **Deinonychus**

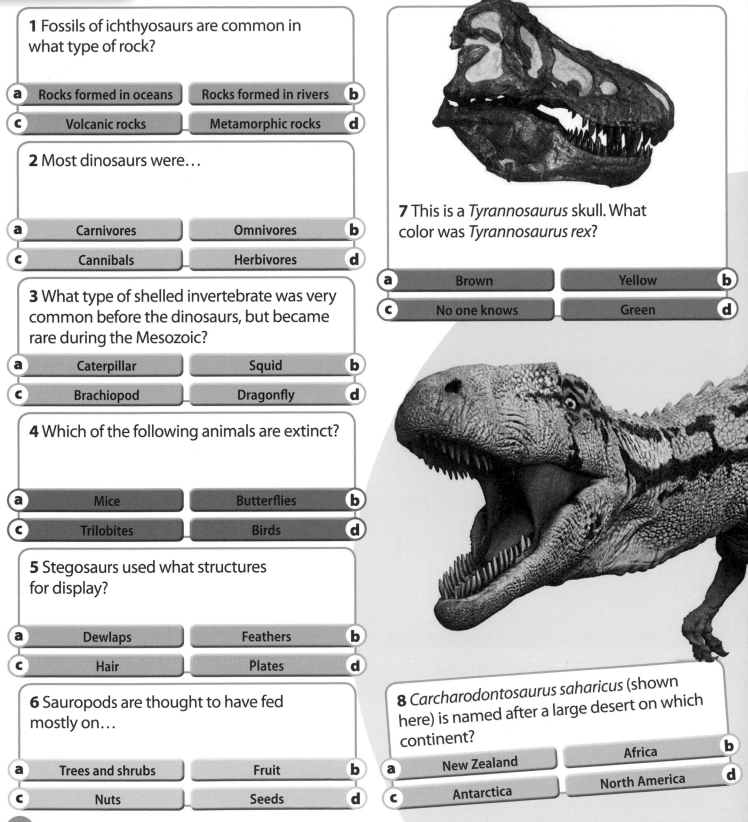

1 Fossils of ichthyosaurs are common in what type of rock?

a Rocks formed in oceans
b Rocks formed in rivers
c Volcanic rocks
d Metamorphic rocks

2 Most dinosaurs were…

a Carnivores
b Omnivores
c Cannibals
d Herbivores

3 What type of shelled invertebrate was very common before the dinosaurs, but became rare during the Mesozoic?

a Caterpillar
b Squid
c Brachiopod
d Dragonfly

4 Which of the following animals are extinct?

a Mice
b Butterflies
c Trilobites
d Birds

5 Stegosaurs used what structures for display?

a Dewlaps
b Feathers
c Hair
d Plates

6 Sauropods are thought to have fed mostly on…

a Trees and shrubs
b Fruit
c Nuts
d Seeds

7 This is a *Tyrannosaurus* skull. What color was *Tyrannosaurus rex*?

a Brown
b Yellow
c No one knows
d Green

8 *Carcharodontosaurus saharicus* (shown here) is named after a large desert on which continent?

a New Zealand
b Africa
c Antarctica
d North America

hunted in **packs**, like lions.

9 Which famous scientist came up with the theory of evolution?

- **a** Charles Darwin
- **b** Abraham Lincoln
- **c** William Herschel
- **d** Mike Benton

10 Pterosaurs could not swim, but lived near the water and ate…

- **a** Plants
- **b** Plankton
- **c** Seeds
- **d** Fish

11 Modern humans evolved approximately how long ago?

- **a** 200 years
- **b** 200,000 years
- **c** 1 billion years
- **d** 5 years

12 Most mammals that lived during the Age of Dinosaurs were about the same size as, or smaller than…

- **a** A cat
- **b** A horse
- **c** A mouse
- **d** An elephant

13 *Texacephale* was found in which US state?

- **a** South Carolina
- **b** Delaware
- **c** Texas
- **d** Tennessee

14 The theropod *Ceratosaurus* was about the same size as…

- **a** A mammoth
- **b** *Allosaurus*
- **c** A dog
- **d** *Diplodocus*

15 Which of the following was not a hadrosaur with a crest?

- **a** *Corythosaurus*
- **b** *Iguanodon*
- **c** *Parasaurolophus*
- **d** *Lambeosaurus*

The ankylosaur *Edmontonia*

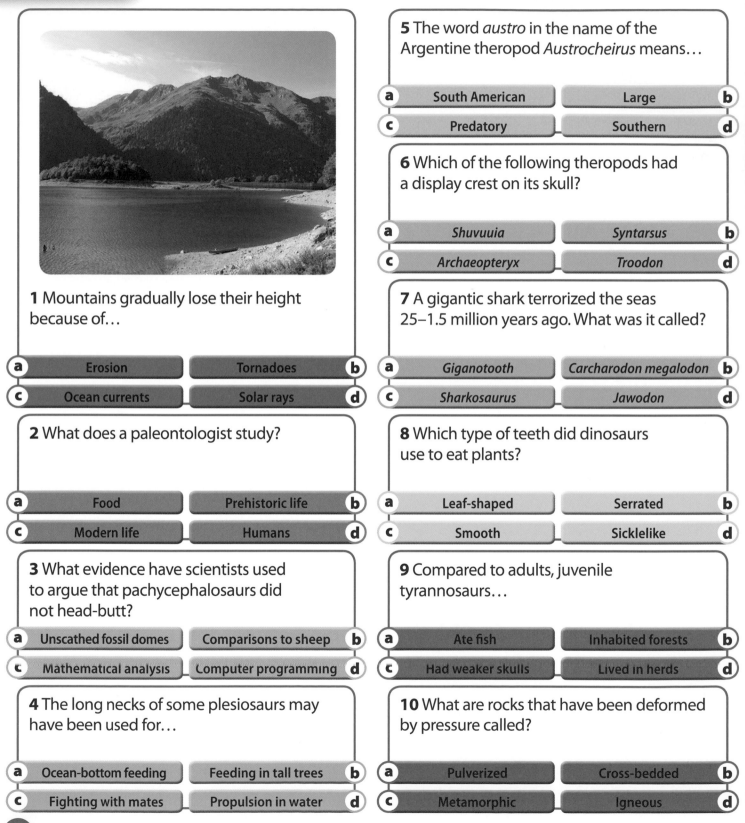

1 Mountains gradually lose their height because of…

a	Erosion	Tornadoes	**b**
c	Ocean currents	Solar rays	**d**

2 What does a paleontologist study?

a	Food	Prehistoric life	**b**
c	Modern life	Humans	**d**

3 What evidence have scientists used to argue that pachycephalosaurs did not head-butt?

a	Unscathed fossil domes	Comparisons to sheep	**b**
c	Mathematical analysis	Computer programming	**d**

4 The long necks of some plesiosaurs may have been used for…

a	Ocean-bottom feeding	Feeding in tall trees	**b**
c	Fighting with mates	Propulsion in water	**d**

5 The word *austro* in the name of the Argentine theropod *Austrocheirus* means…

a	South American	Large	**b**
c	Predatory	Southern	**d**

6 Which of the following theropods had a display crest on its skull?

a	*Shuvuuia*	*Syntarsus*	**b**
c	*Archaeopteryx*	*Troodon*	**d**

7 A gigantic shark terrorized the seas 25–1.5 million years ago. What was it called?

a	*Giganotooth*	*Carcharodon megalodon*	**b**
c	*Sharkosaurus*	*Jawodon*	**d**

8 Which type of teeth did dinosaurs use to eat plants?

a	Leaf-shaped	Serrated	**b**
c	Smooth	Sicklelike	**d**

9 Compared to adults, juvenile tyrannosaurs…

a	Ate fish	Inhabited forests	**b**
c	Had weaker skulls	Lived in herds	**d**

10 What are rocks that have been deformed by pressure called?

a	Pulverized	Cross-bedded	**b**
c	Metamorphic	Igneous	**d**

had **forked spikes**.

11 A trackway in Texas seems to show a theropod chasing which kind of dinosaur?

a Hypsilophodontid **b** Sauropod

c Dromaeosaur **d** Silesaurid

12 Some dwarf sauropods, which lived on European islands in the Late Cretaceous, were about the size of…

a Sparrows **b** Humans

c Cows **d** Dogs

13 *Hungarosaurus* is named after a country on which continent?

a Antarctica **b** Greenland

c Europe **d** North America

14 The change between a tadpole and frog is an example of…

a Genesis **b** Metamorphosis

c Evolution **d** Extinction

15 When did life begin on Earth?

a 3.8 trillion years ago **b** 6 million years ago

c 6 billion years ago **d** 3.8 billion years ago

16 Scientists think that the long and thin tail of *Diplodocus* may have been used…

a To grasp branches **b** To gather food

c To support the body **d** As a whip

17 Some pachycephalosaurs did not have convex skull domes, but instead had…

a Triangular skulls **b** No skulls

c Hollow skulls **d** Flat skulls

18 Which feature, connected to the lungs, has helped pterosaurs and birds breathe efficiently?

a Liver **b** Blood vessels

c Large nerves **d** Air sacs

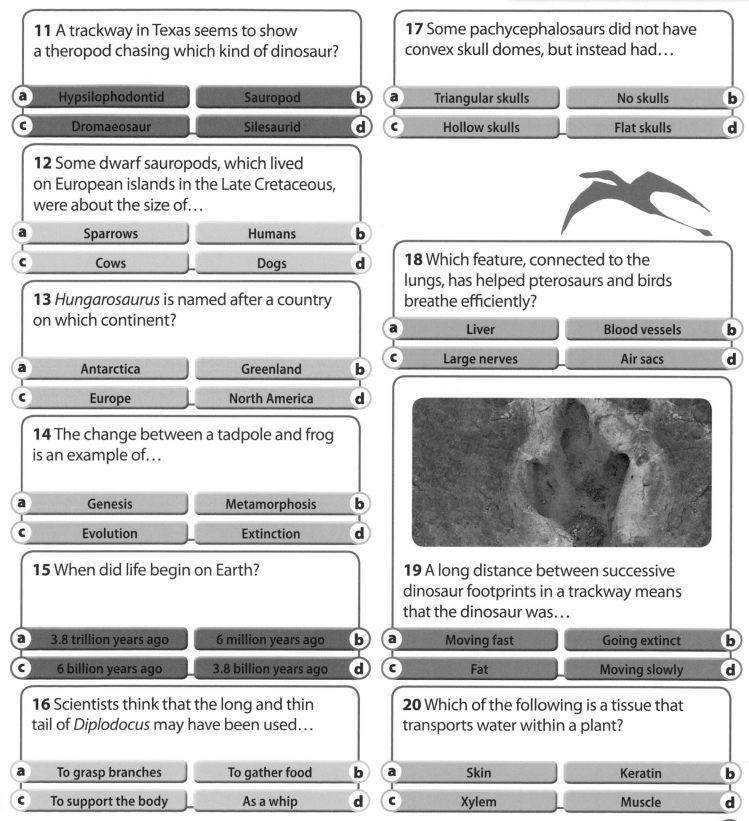

19 A long distance between successive dinosaur footprints in a trackway means that the dinosaur was…

a Moving fast **b** Going extinct

c Fat **d** Moving slowly

20 Which of the following is a tissue that transports water within a plant?

a Skin **b** Keratin

c Xylem **d** Muscle

The Late **Jurassic** is often called the

1 What is the name of the circular series of bones surrounding the eyes of ichthyosaurs?

- **a** Sclerotic ring
- **b** Bony circle
- **c** Osteological ring
- **d** Furcula

2 Which of the following scientists has never studied dinosaurs?

- **a** Stephen Hawking
- **b** Henry Fairfield Osborn
- **c** Robert Bakker
- **d** Jack Horner

3 A spot where an oceanic plate dives beneath a continental plate is called a…

- **a** Meeting zone
- **b** Transform boundary
- **c** Trench
- **d** Canyon

4 Which hadrosaur subgroup is known for its remarkable cranial crests?

- **a** Allosauridae
- **b** Titanosauridae
- **c** Heterodontosauridae
- **d** Lambeosaurinae

5 A close relative of the Triassic theropod *Coelophysis* is…

- **a** *Euparkeria*
- **b** *Alxasaurus*
- **c** *Camposaurus*
- **d** *Carnotaurus*

6 Which dinosaur from Antarctica was nearly named after Elvis Presley before scientists reconsidered?

- **a** *Elmisaurus*
- **b** *Cryolophosaurus*
- **c** *Antarctopelta*
- **d** *Eocarcharia*

7 Which is the closest-known relative to the South American *Piatnitzkysaurus*?

- **a** *Adasaurus*
- **b** *Condorraptor*
- **c** *Megalosaurus*
- **d** *Carnotaurus*

8 The positioning of which body feature is unique to humans compared to other primates?

- **a** Thumb
- **b** Little finger
- **c** Big toe
- **d** Little toe

9 The bizarre sauropod *Nigersaurus* may have eaten which particular type of plant food?

- **a** Nuts
- **b** Berries
- **c** Sunflowers
- **d** Ferns

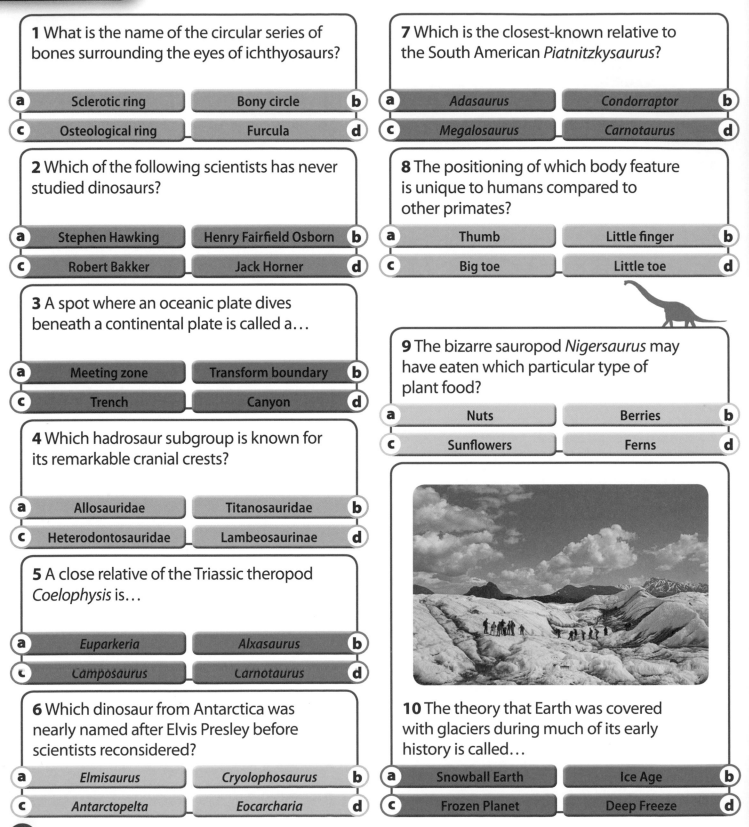

10 The theory that Earth was covered with glaciers during much of its early history is called…

- **a** Snowball Earth
- **b** Ice Age
- **c** Frozen Planet
- **d** Deep Freeze

"**age** of dinosaur **giants**."

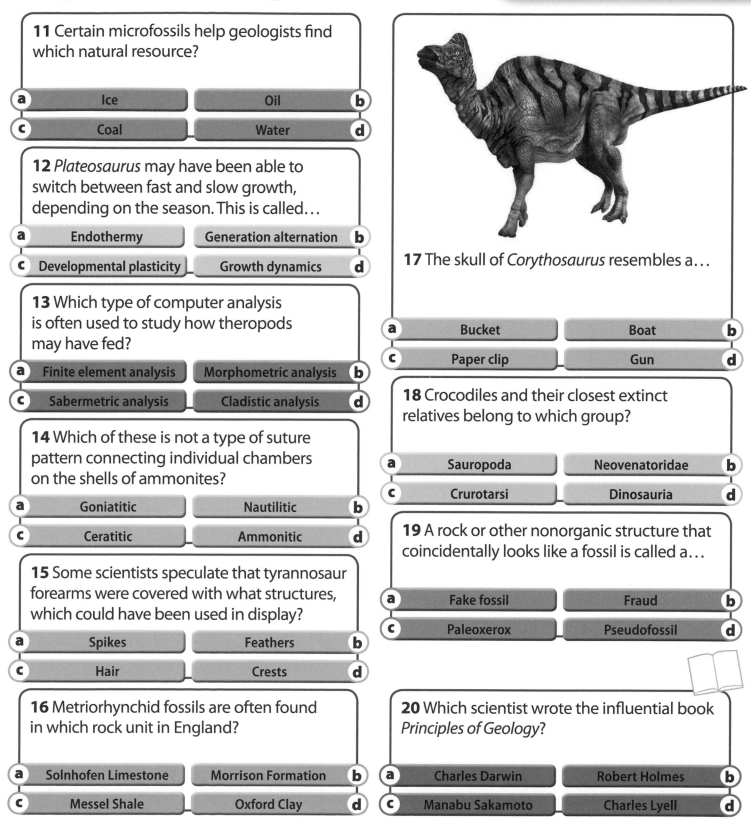

11 Certain microfossils help geologists find which natural resource?

a. Ice
b. Oil
c. Coal
d. Water

12 *Plateosaurus* may have been able to switch between fast and slow growth, depending on the season. This is called…

a. Endothermy
b. Generation alternation
c. Developmental plasticity
d. Growth dynamics

13 Which type of computer analysis is often used to study how theropods may have fed?

a. Finite element analysis
b. Morphometric analysis
c. Sabermetric analysis
d. Cladistic analysis

14 Which of these is not a type of suture pattern connecting individual chambers on the shells of ammonites?

a. Goniatitic
b. Nautilitic
c. Ceratitic
d. Ammonitic

15 Some scientists speculate that tyrannosaur forearms were covered with what structures, which could have been used in display?

a. Spikes
b. Feathers
c. Hair
d. Crests

16 Metriorhynchid fossils are often found in which rock unit in England?

a. Solnhofen Limestone
b. Morrison Formation
c. Messel Shale
d. Oxford Clay

17 The skull of *Corythosaurus* resembles a…

a. Bucket
b. Boat
c. Paper clip
d. Gun

18 Crocodiles and their closest extinct relatives belong to which group?

a. Sauropoda
b. Neovenatoridae
c. Crurotarsi
d. Dinosauria

19 A rock or other nonorganic structure that coincidentally looks like a fossil is called a…

a. Fake fossil
b. Fraud
c. Paleoxerox
d. Pseudofossil

20 Which scientist wrote the influential book *Principles of Geology*?

a. Charles Darwin
b. Robert Holmes
c. Manabu Sakamoto
d. Charles Lyell

Giganotosaurus **hid** in trees to **ambush**

1 Which of the following is not a sauropod?

a *Ornitholestes*
b *Camarasaurus*
c *Brachiosaurus*
d *Diplodocus*

2 What is it called when Earth gets very cold for a long time?

a Mass extinction
b Summer
c Mesozoic
d Ice age

3 How did ichthyosaurs and plesiosaurs move?

a By jogging
b By swimming
c By flying
d By running

4 The giant abelisaurid *Carnotaurus* was similar to *Tyrannosaurus* because both theropods…

a Ate plants
b Could fly
c Were the size of a fox
d Had small arms

5 What type of coiled invertebrate, similar to today's nautilus, was common during the age of dinosaurs?

a Bivalve
b Shark
c Ammonite
d Pterosaur

6 Which scientist founded the modern system of biological classification?

a Carl Linnaeus
b The Pope
c Elvis Presley
d Barack Obama

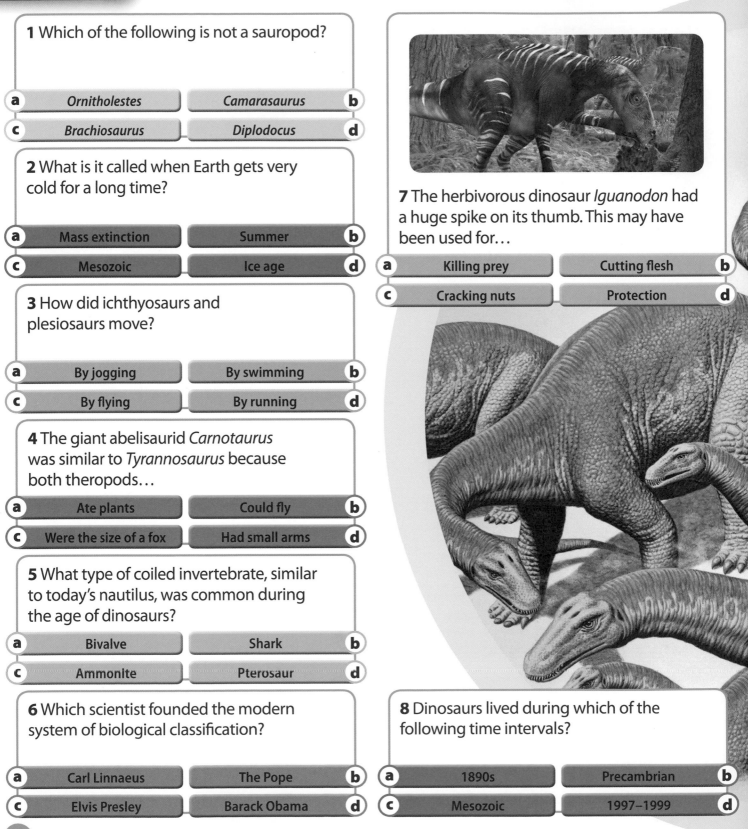

7 The herbivorous dinosaur *Iguanodon* had a huge spike on its thumb. This may have been used for…

a Killing prey
b Cutting flesh
c Cracking nuts
d Protection

8 Dinosaurs lived during which of the following time intervals?

a 1890s
b Precambrian
c Mesozoic
d 1997–1999

slow-moving **herbivores**.

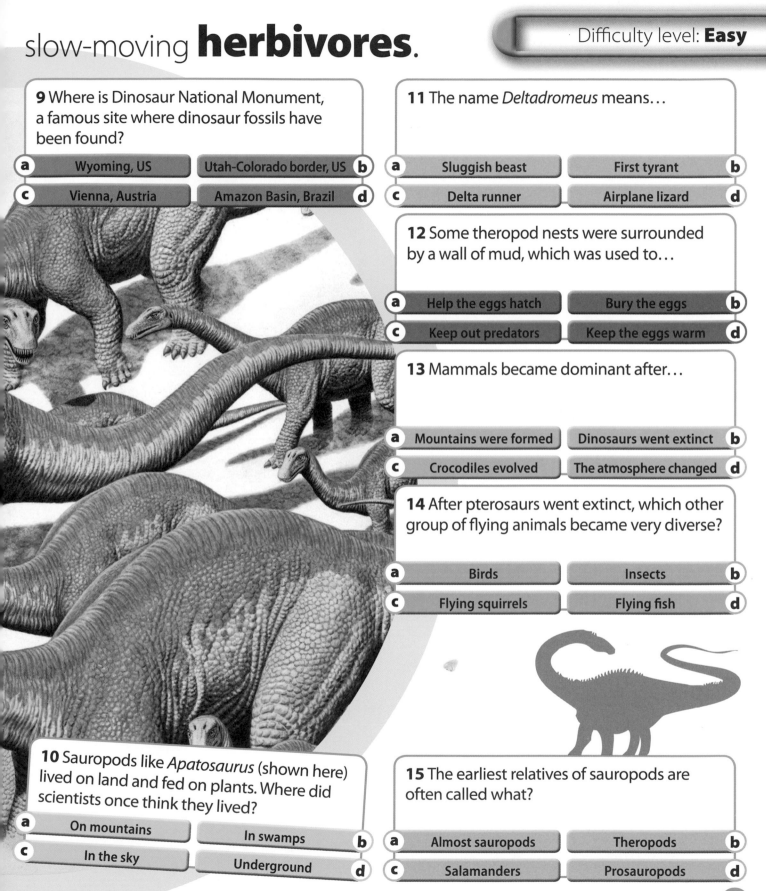

9 Where is Dinosaur National Monument, a famous site where dinosaur fossils have been found?

a Wyoming, US

b Utah-Colorado border, US

c Vienna, Austria

d Amazon Basin, Brazil

10 Sauropods like *Apatosaurus* (shown here) lived on land and fed on plants. Where did scientists once think they lived?

a On mountains

b In swamps

c In the sky

d Underground

11 The name *Deltadromeus* means…

a Sluggish beast

b First tyrant

c Delta runner

d Airplane lizard

12 Some theropod nests were surrounded by a wall of mud, which was used to…

a Help the eggs hatch

b Bury the eggs

c Keep out predators

d Keep the eggs warm

13 Mammals became dominant after…

a Mountains were formed

b Dinosaurs went extinct

c Crocodiles evolved

d The atmosphere changed

14 After pterosaurs went extinct, which other group of flying animals became very diverse?

a Birds

b Insects

c Flying squirrels

d Flying fish

15 The earliest relatives of sauropods are often called what?

a Almost sauropods

b Theropods

c Salamanders

d Prosauropods

49

Some sauropod **necks** were 10 times

1 Earth's history is divided into long stretches of time called periods. Which period came before the Jurassic?

- **a** Triassic
- **b** Cretaceous
- **c** Carboniferous
- **d** Cambrian

2 What does the name *Deinonychus* mean?

- **a** Many-toothed
- **b** Giant meat-eater
- **c** Flying monster
- **d** Terrible claw

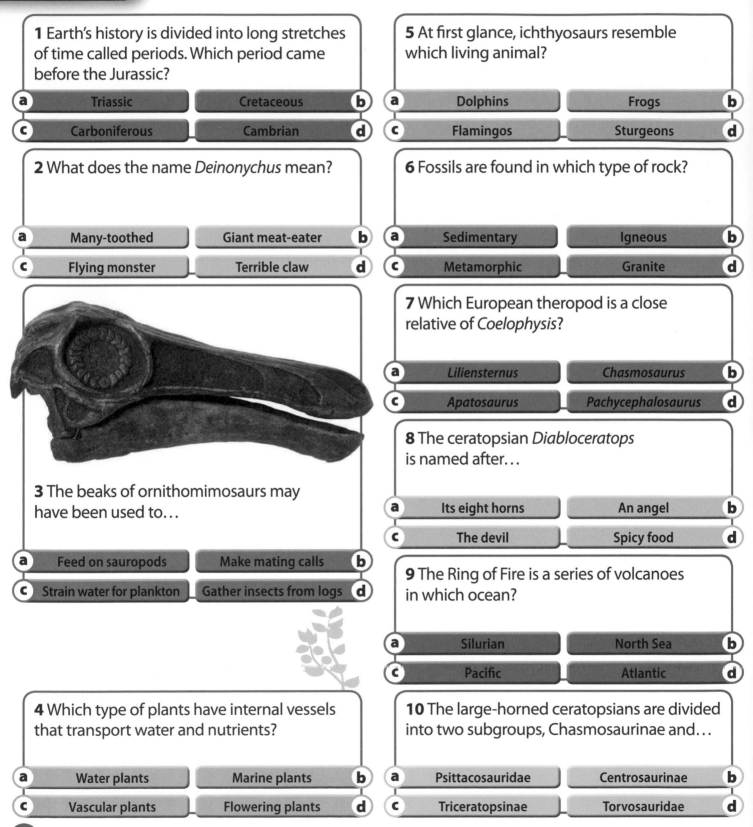

3 The beaks of ornithomimosaurs may have been used to…

- **a** Feed on sauropods
- **b** Make mating calls
- **c** Strain water for plankton
- **d** Gather insects from logs

4 Which type of plants have internal vessels that transport water and nutrients?

- **a** Water plants
- **b** Marine plants
- **c** Vascular plants
- **d** Flowering plants

5 At first glance, ichthyosaurs resemble which living animal?

- **a** Dolphins
- **b** Frogs
- **c** Flamingos
- **d** Sturgeons

6 Fossils are found in which type of rock?

- **a** Sedimentary
- **b** Igneous
- **c** Metamorphic
- **d** Granite

7 Which European theropod is a close relative of *Coelophysis*?

- **a** *Liliensternus*
- **b** *Chasmosaurus*
- **c** *Apatosaurus*
- **d** *Pachycephalosaurus*

8 The ceratopsian *Diabloceratops* is named after…

- **a** Its eight horns
- **b** An angel
- **c** The devil
- **d** Spicy food

9 The Ring of Fire is a series of volcanoes in which ocean?

- **a** Silurian
- **b** North Sea
- **c** Pacific
- **d** Atlantic

10 The large-horned ceratopsians are divided into two subgroups, Chasmosaurinae and…

- **a** Psittacosauridae
- **b** Centrosaurinae
- **c** Triceratopsinae
- **d** Torvosauridae

longer than that of a giraffe.

11 It is thought that the dromaeosaurid *Deinonychus* preyed on which herbivorous dinosaur?

- **a** *Brachiosaurus*
- **b** *Ornitholestes*
- **c** *Valdosaurus*
- **d** *Tenontosaurus*

12 What is the term for an animal that eats plants and meat?

- **a** Carnivore
- **b** Frugivore
- **c** Omnivore
- **d** Herbivore

13 Which of these is not a group of close crocodile relatives that lived during the Triassic?

- **a** Rauisuchians
- **b** Ichthyostegids
- **c** Phytosaurs
- **d** Aetosaurs

14 Which paleontologist coined the term *dinosaur*?

- **a** Roger Benson
- **b** Richard Owen
- **c** E. D. Cope
- **d** Charles Darwin

15 Which tooth-bearing bone often forms part of the crest in hadrosaurids?

- **a** Premaxilla
- **b** Dentary
- **c** Femur
- **d** Humerus

16 Which of the following is a dinosaur?

- **a** *Steneosaurus*
- **b** *Parasaurolophus*
- **c** *Batrachotomus*
- **d** *Felis*

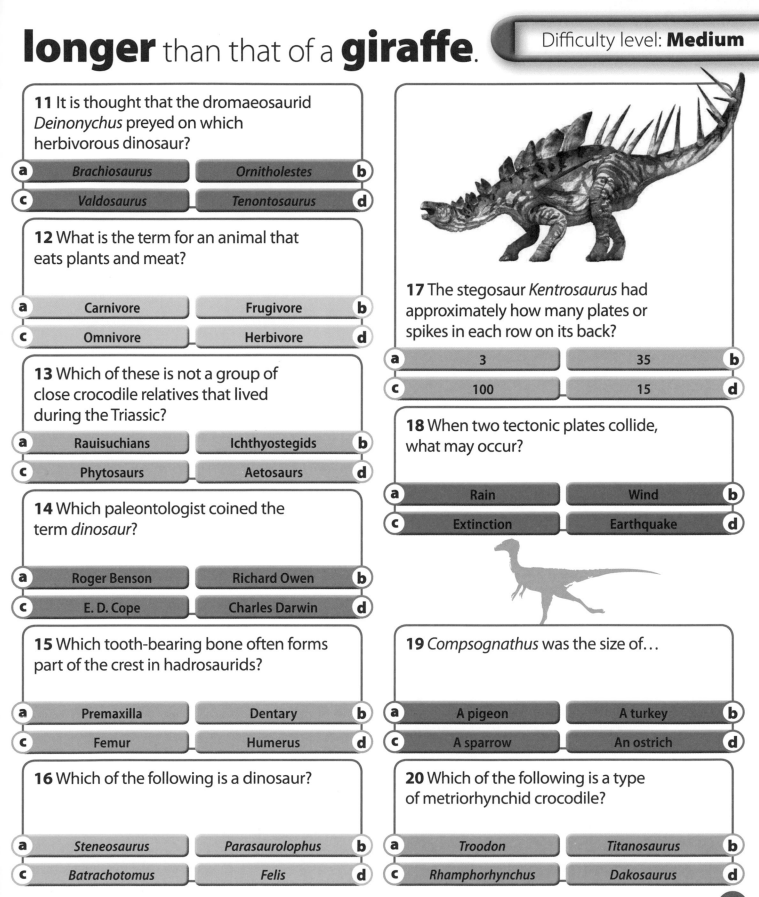

17 The stegosaur *Kentrosaurus* had approximately how many plates or spikes in each row on its back?

- **a** 3
- **b** 35
- **c** 100
- **d** 15

18 When two tectonic plates collide, what may occur?

- **a** Rain
- **b** Wind
- **c** Extinction
- **d** Earthquake

19 *Compsognathus* was the size of…

- **a** A pigeon
- **b** A turkey
- **c** A sparrow
- **d** An ostrich

20 Which of the following is a type of metriorhynchid crocodile?

- **a** *Troodon*
- **b** *Titanosaurus*
- **c** *Rhamphorhynchus*
- **d** *Dakosaurus*

Diplodocus's tail made up about

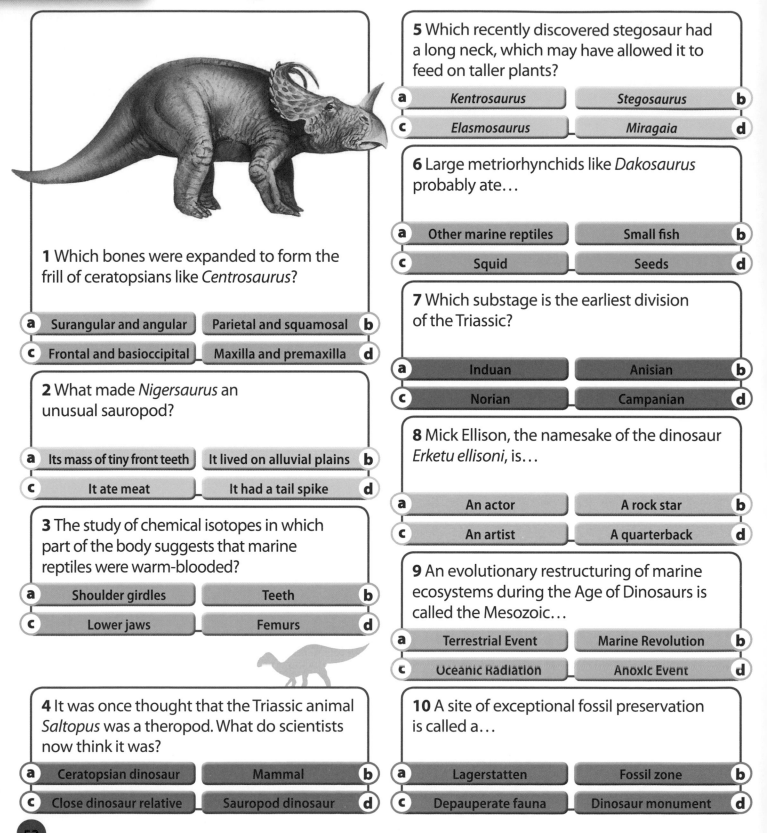

1 Which bones were expanded to form the frill of ceratopsians like *Centrosaurus*?

- **a** Surangular and angular
- **b** Parietal and squamosal
- **c** Frontal and basioccipital
- **d** Maxilla and premaxilla

2 What made *Nigersaurus* an unusual sauropod?

- **a** Its mass of tiny front teeth
- **b** It lived on alluvial plains
- **c** It ate meat
- **d** It had a tail spike

3 The study of chemical isotopes in which part of the body suggests that marine reptiles were warm-blooded?

- **a** Shoulder girdles
- **b** Teeth
- **c** Lower jaws
- **d** Femurs

4 It was once thought that the Triassic animal *Saltopus* was a theropod. What do scientists now think it was?

- **a** Ceratopsian dinosaur
- **b** Mammal
- **c** Close dinosaur relative
- **d** Sauropod dinosaur

5 Which recently discovered stegosaur had a long neck, which may have allowed it to feed on taller plants?

- **a** *Kentrosaurus*
- **b** *Stegosaurus*
- **c** *Elasmosaurus*
- **d** *Miragaia*

6 Large metriorhynchids like *Dakosaurus* probably ate…

- **a** Other marine reptiles
- **b** Small fish
- **c** Squid
- **d** Seeds

7 Which substage is the earliest division of the Triassic?

- **a** Induan
- **b** Anisian
- **c** Norian
- **d** Campanian

8 Mick Ellison, the namesake of the dinosaur *Erketu ellisoni*, is…

- **a** An actor
- **b** A rock star
- **c** An artist
- **d** A quarterback

9 An evolutionary restructuring of marine ecosystems during the Age of Dinosaurs is called the Mesozoic…

- **a** Terrestrial Event
- **b** Marine Revolution
- **c** Oceanic Radiation
- **d** Anoxic Event

10 A site of exceptional fossil preservation is called a…

- **a** Lagerstatten
- **b** Fossil zone
- **c** Depauperate fauna
- **d** Dinosaur monument

11 In 1973, what name was given to an *Australopithecus afarensis* skeleton?

a Kate

b Molly

c Dora

d Lucy

12 The Romanian dinosaur *Balaur bondoc* was named in which year?

a 1908

b 1812

c 1945

d 2010

13 *Monolophosaurus* was once thought to be a close relative of *Allosaurus*, but is now considered…

a More derived

b More primitive

c Closer to *Coelophysis*

d Closer to *Tyrannosaurus*

14 One theory linked hadrosaurid crests to a good sense of smell. What disproved this idea?

a Small olfactory system

b Wounds found on a crest

c Studying living animals

d Computer modeling

15 What is it called where two ocean plates diverge and form new rocks?

a Slip zone

b Convergent zone

c Ocean plain

d Mid-ocean ridge

16 In some pterosaurs, which skull opening is combined with the nostril to form a single large opening?

a Eye socket

b Brain cavity

c Lateral temporal fenestra

d Antorbital fenestra

17 Which of these is not a substage of the Cretaceous?

a Aptian

b Barremian

c Tithonian

d Campanian

18 Which small marine animals were very diverse in the Cretaceous but nearly went extinct with the dinosaurs?

a Pollen

b Forams

c Trilobites

d Crinoids

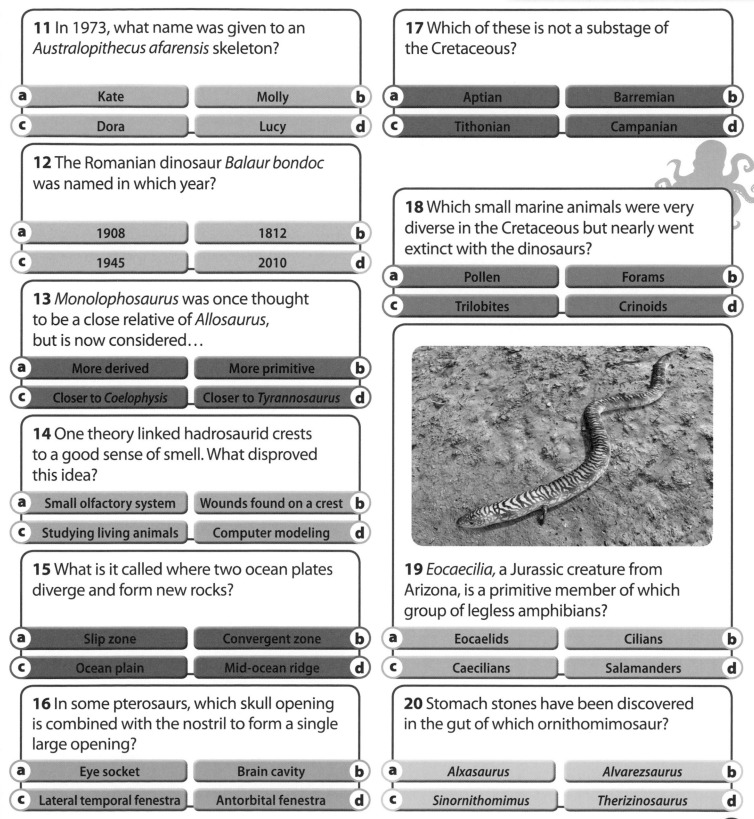

19 *Eocaecilia,* a Jurassic creature from Arizona, is a primitive member of which group of legless amphibians?

a Eocaelids

b Cilians

c Caecilians

d Salamanders

20 Stomach stones have been discovered in the gut of which ornithomimosaur?

a *Alxasaurus*

b *Alvarezsaurus*

c *Sinornithomimus*

d *Therizinosaurus*

The paleontologist **Richard Owen**

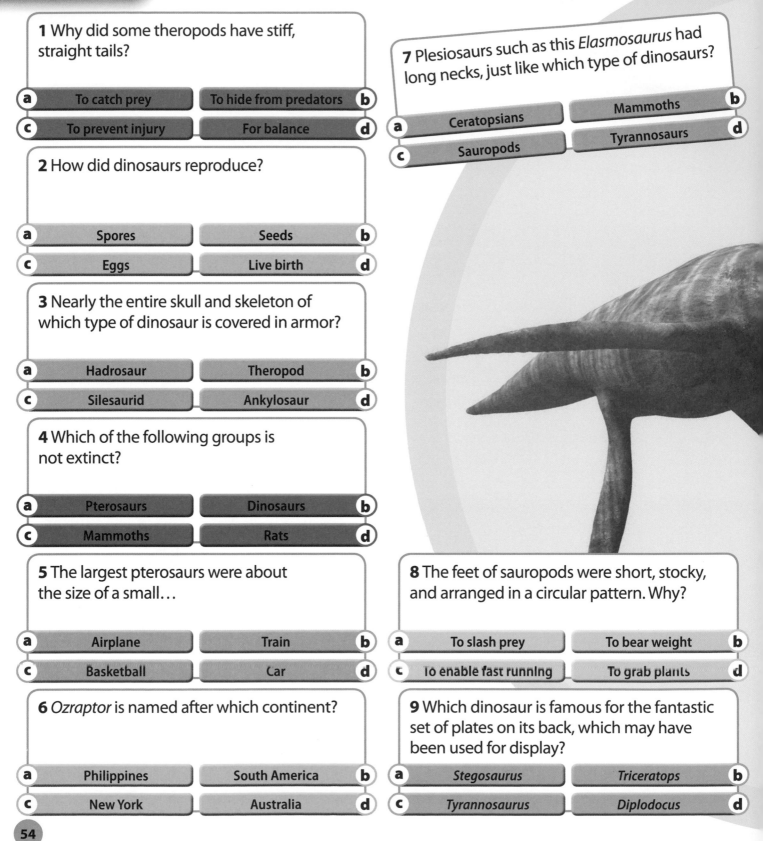

1 Why did some theropods have stiff, straight tails?

a To catch prey	To hide from predators **b**
c To prevent injury	For balance **d**

2 How did dinosaurs reproduce?

a Spores	Seeds **b**
c Eggs	Live birth **d**

3 Nearly the entire skull and skeleton of which type of dinosaur is covered in armor?

a Hadrosaur	Theropod **b**
c Silesaurid	Ankylosaur **d**

4 Which of the following groups is not extinct?

a Pterosaurs	Dinosaurs **b**
c Mammoths	Rats **d**

5 The largest pterosaurs were about the size of a small…

a Airplane	Train **b**
c Basketball	Car **d**

6 *Ozraptor* is named after which continent?

a Philippines	South America **b**
c New York	Australia **d**

7 Plesiosaurs such as this *Elasmosaurus* had long necks, just like which type of dinosaurs?

	Mammoths **b**
a Ceratopsians	Tyrannosaurs **d**
c Sauropods	

8 The feet of sauropods were short, stocky, and arranged in a circular pattern. Why?

a To slash prey	To bear weight **b**
c To enable fast running	To grab plants **d**

9 Which dinosaur is famous for the fantastic set of plates on its back, which may have been used for display?

a *Stegosaurus*	*Triceratops* **b**
c *Tyrannosaurus*	*Diplodocus* **d**

gave **dinosaurs** their **name**.

10 What do volcanoes release?

a Lava	Salt **b**
c Milk	Sand **d**

14 Ocean-dwelling ammonites were preyed upon by which type of animal?

a Mammals	Trilobites **b**
c Marine reptiles	Dinosaurs **d**

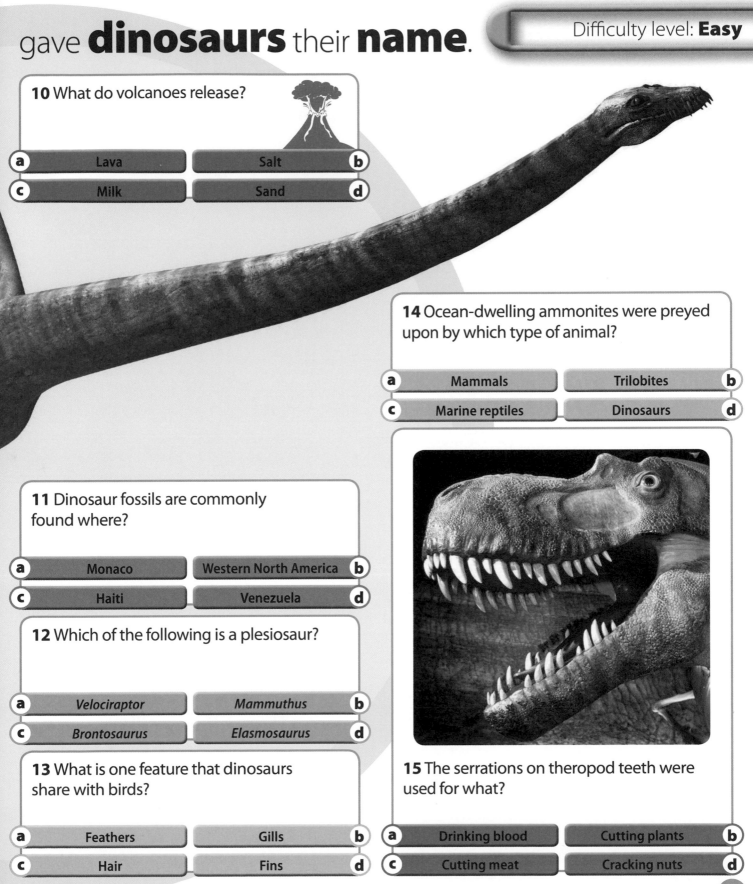

11 Dinosaur fossils are commonly found where?

a Monaco	Western North America **b**
c Haiti	Venezuela **d**

12 Which of the following is a plesiosaur?

a *Velociraptor*	*Mammuthus* **b**
c *Brontosaurus*	*Elasmosaurus* **d**

13 What is one feature that dinosaurs share with birds?

a Feathers	Gills **b**
c Hair	Fins **d**

15 The serrations on theropod teeth were used for what?

a Drinking blood	Cutting plants **b**
c Cutting meat	Cracking nuts **d**

Archaeopteryx, the **first bird**,

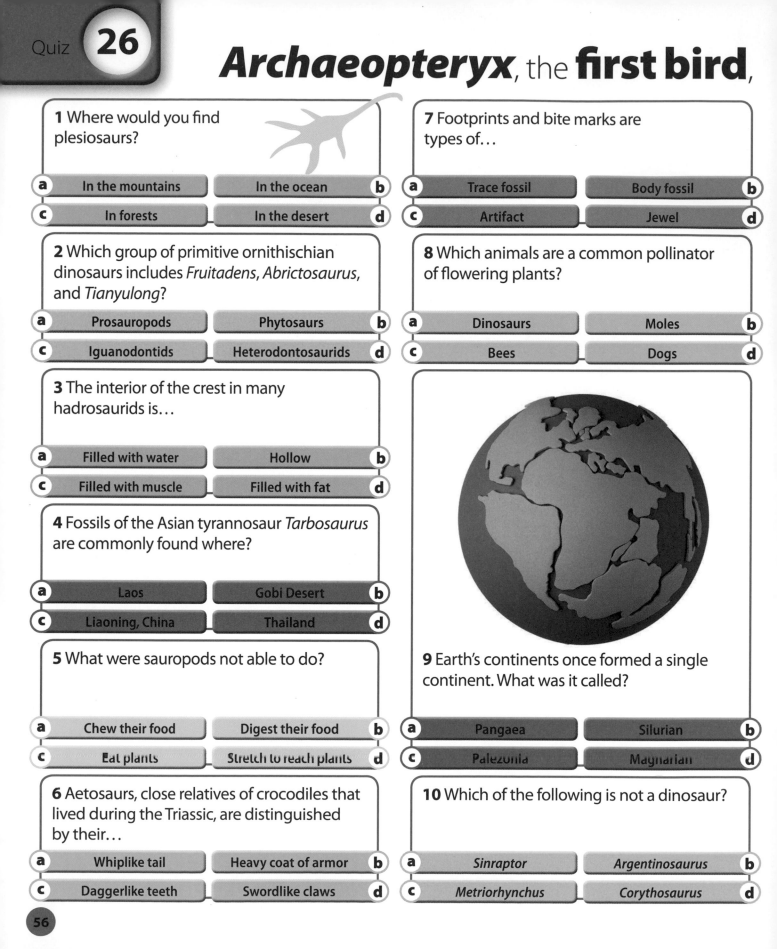

1 Where would you find plesiosaurs?

a In the mountains
b In the ocean
c In forests
d In the desert

2 Which group of primitive ornithischian dinosaurs includes *Fruitadens*, *Abrictosaurus*, and *Tianyulong*?

a Prosauropods
b Phytosaurs
c Iguanodontids
d Heterodontosaurids

3 The interior of the crest in many hadrosaurids is…

a Filled with water
b Hollow
c Filled with muscle
d Filled with fat

4 Fossils of the Asian tyrannosaur *Tarbosaurus* are commonly found where?

a Laos
b Gobi Desert
c Liaoning, China
d Thailand

5 What were sauropods not able to do?

a Chew their food
b Digest their food
c Eat plants
d Stretch to reach plants

6 Aetosaurs, close relatives of crocodiles that lived during the Triassic, are distinguished by their…

a Whiplike tail
b Heavy coat of armor
c Daggerlike teeth
d Swordlike claws

7 Footprints and bite marks are types of…

a Trace fossil
b Body fossil
c Artifact
d Jewel

8 Which animals are a common pollinator of flowering plants?

a Dinosaurs
b Moles
c Bees
d Dogs

9 Earth's continents once formed a single continent. What was it called?

a Pangaea
b Silurian
c Palezonia
d Magnarian

10 Which of the following is not a dinosaur?

a *Sinraptor*
b *Argentinosaurus*
c *Metriorhynchus*
d *Corythosaurus*

11 The Early Jurassic theropod *Syntarsus* is known from both North America and Africa because it…

a Flew between them
b Evolved in both places
c Lived on a supercontinent
d Swam between them

12 Which of the following is not a type of rock?

a Sandstone
b Basalt
c Slate
d Crystal

13 Some sauropods made their nests…

a In lakes
b On cliffs
c In burrows
d On beaches

14 The bizarre tyrannosaur *Alioramus* had five or six hornlike bumps on which bone of the snout?

a Frontal
b Laterosphenoid
c Nasal
d Maxilla

15 Which of these is not part of the fossilization process?

a Death
b Burial
c Digestion
d Decay

16 Living crocodiles use their limbs to walk on land. In ocean-dwelling metriorhynchids, these limbs evolved into…

a Flippers
b Clubs
c Fins
d Spikes

17 Which is an example of a noncrested hadrosaur?

a *Edmontosaurus*
b *Parasaurolophus*
c *Corythosaurus*
d *Hypacrosaurus*

18 Pterosaurs reproduced by…

a Giving birth to live young
b Spawning
c Seeds
d Laying eggs

19 Which part of dinosaur teeth is often used to study chemical isotopes?

a Striations
b Enamel
c Cells
d Serrations

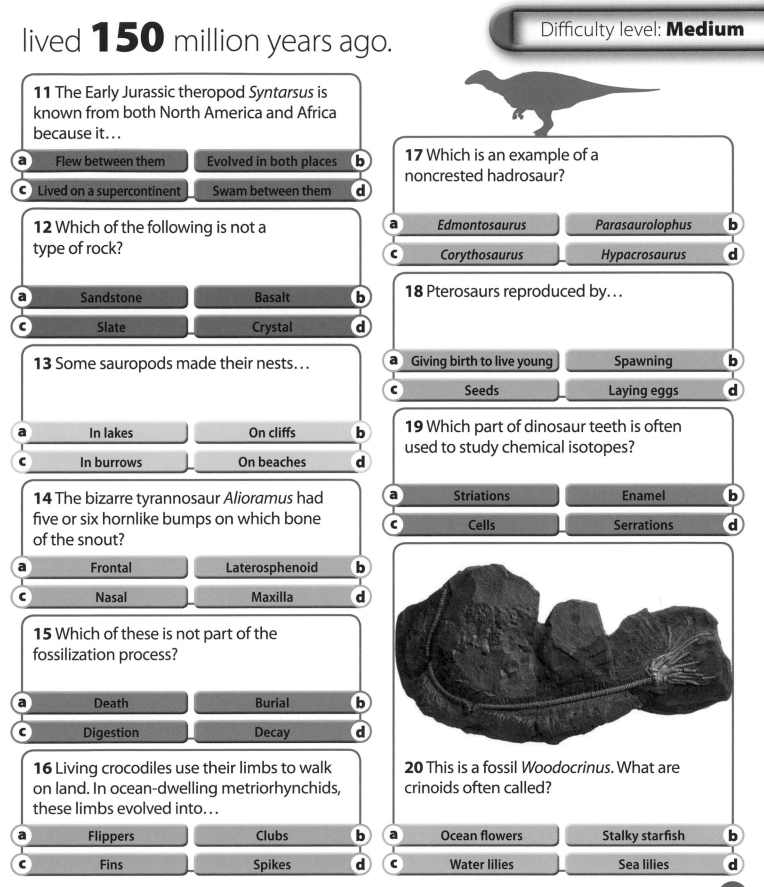

20 This is a fossil *Woodocrinus*. What are crinoids often called?

a Ocean flowers
b Stalky starfish
c Water lilies
d Sea lilies

The group of **spikes** on a stegosaur tail is

1 A close relative of metriorhynchids, which was also a crocodile that lived in the oceans, was…

- **a** Sphenosuchus
- **b** Terrestrisuchus
- **c** Batrachotomus
- **d** Teleosaurus

2 Which tool do paleontologists use to clean small bits of rock from dinosaur fossils?

- **a** Syringe
- **b** Magnetometer
- **c** Air scribe
- **d** Hose

3 Osteoderms, spikes, and scutes are examples of what type of bone, which forms in the skin?

- **a** Dermal
- **b** Endochondral
- **c** Enameloid
- **d** Cartilaginous

4 What does the Romanian word *balaur* mean?

- **a** Dragon
- **b** Monster
- **c** Vampire
- **d** Politician

5 The fragmentary Triassic genus *Guaibasaurus* may be either a theropod or a…

- **a** Silesaurid
- **b** Crurotarsan
- **c** Sauropodomorph
- **d** Ceratopsian

6 *Saurosuchus* from the Late Triassic of Argentina is one of the closest relatives of…

- **a** Pterosaurs
- **b** Crocodiles
- **c** Dinosaurs
- **d** Birds

7 A mass extinction occurred between which two substages of the Devonian?

- **a** Famennian-Frasnian
- **b** Campanian-Maastrichtian
- **c** Paleogene-Neogene
- **d** Ordovician-Silurian

8 What allowed *Homo habilis* to develop a larger brain?

- **a** Water
- **b** Shelter
- **c** Fire
- **d** Different food types

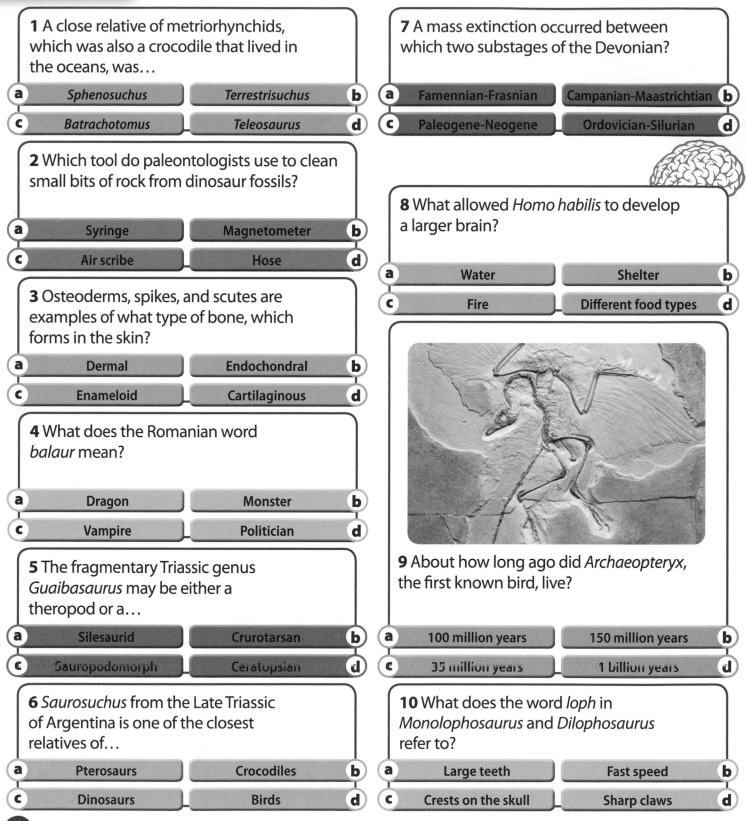

9 About how long ago did *Archaeopteryx*, the first known bird, live?

- **a** 100 million years
- **b** 150 million years
- **c** 35 million years
- **d** 1 billion years

10 What does the word *loph* in *Monolophosaurus* and *Dilophosaurus* refer to?

- **a** Large teeth
- **b** Fast speed
- **c** Crests on the skull
- **d** Sharp claws

11 The skulls of stegosaurs are…

a Big relative to the body
b Lacking teeth
c Long and narrow
d Short and deep

12 *Mapusaurus* is named after a word from the Mapuche language, which is indigenous to…

a Australia
b Spain
c Hong Kong
d South America

13 *Siamotyrannus* was first described as a primitive tyrannosaur. What is it now thought to be closely related to?

a Mammals
b *Allosaurus*
c Dromaeosaurs
d Birds

14 Most of a pachycephalosaur skull dome consists of the frontal and which other bone?

a Tuberculum
b Parietal
c Palatine
d Prootic

15 How long ago did North and South America collide and form the Isthmus of Panama?

a 30 million years
b 300 million years
c 3 billion years
d 3 million years

16 Which types of fossils are often found in the Holzmaden Shale in Germany?

a Trilobites
b Ichthyosaurs
c Dinosaurs
d Mammoths

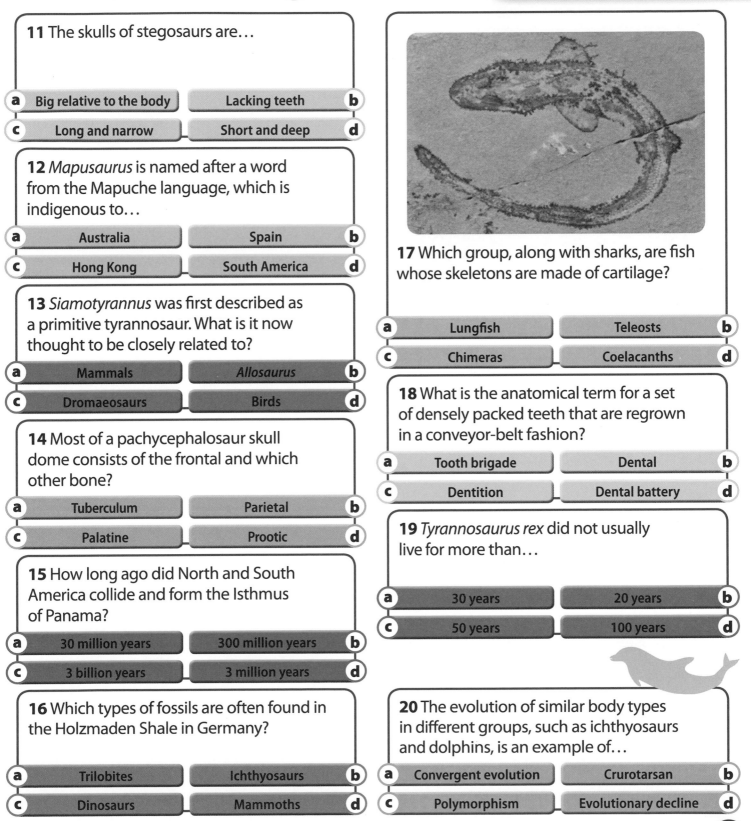

17 Which group, along with sharks, are fish whose skeletons are made of cartilage?

a Lungfish
b Teleosts
c Chimeras
d Coelacanths

18 What is the anatomical term for a set of densely packed teeth that are regrown in a conveyor-belt fashion?

a Tooth brigade
b Dental
c Dentition
d Dental battery

19 *Tyrannosaurus rex* did not usually live for more than…

a 30 years
b 20 years
c 50 years
d 100 years

20 The evolution of similar body types in different groups, such as ichthyosaurs and dolphins, is an example of…

a Convergent evolution
b Crurotarsan
c Polymorphism
d Evolutionary decline

Maiasaura covered its **eggs** with **rotten**

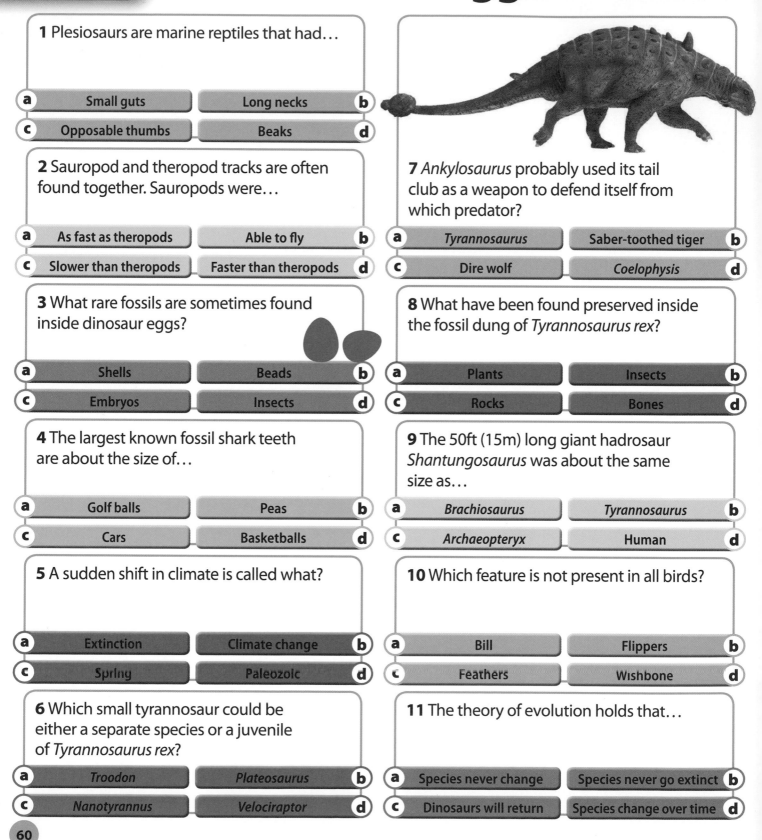

1 Plesiosaurs are marine reptiles that had…

a Small guts

b Long necks

c Opposable thumbs

d Beaks

2 Sauropod and theropod tracks are often found together. Sauropods were…

a As fast as theropods

b Able to fly

c Slower than theropods

d Faster than theropods

3 What rare fossils are sometimes found inside dinosaur eggs?

a Shells

b Beads

c Embryos

d Insects

4 The largest known fossil shark teeth are about the size of…

a Golf balls

b Peas

c Cars

d Basketballs

5 A sudden shift in climate is called what?

a Extinction

b Climate change

c Spring

d Paleozoic

6 Which small tyrannosaur could be either a separate species or a juvenile of *Tyrannosaurus rex*?

a *Troodon*

b *Plateosaurus*

c *Nanotyrannus*

d *Velociraptor*

7 *Ankylosaurus* probably used its tail club as a weapon to defend itself from which predator?

a *Tyrannosaurus*

b Saber-toothed tiger

c Dire wolf

d *Coelophysis*

8 What have been found preserved inside the fossil dung of *Tyrannosaurus rex*?

a Plants

b Insects

c Rocks

d Bones

9 The 50ft (15m) long giant hadrosaur *Shantungosaurus* was about the same size as…

a *Brachiosaurus*

b *Tyrannosaurus*

c *Archaeopteryx*

d Human

10 Which feature is not present in all birds?

a Bill

b Flippers

c Feathers

d Wishbone

11 The theory of evolution holds that…

a Species never change

b Species never go extinct

c Dinosaurs will return

d Species change over time

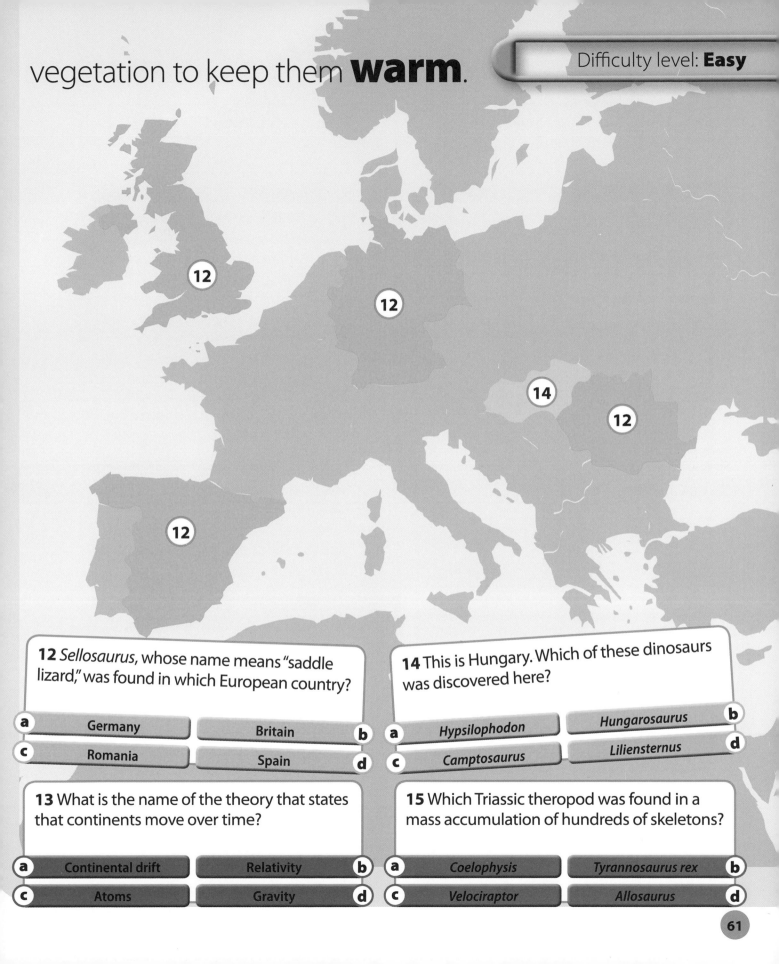

vegetation to keep them **warm**.

Difficulty level: **Easy**

12 *Sellosaurus*, whose name means "saddle lizard," was found in which European country?

a Germany
b Britain
c Romania
d Spain

13 What is the name of the theory that states that continents move over time?

a Continental drift
b Relativity
c Atoms
d Gravity

14 This is Hungary. Which of these dinosaurs was discovered here?

a *Hypsilophodon*
b *Hungarosaurus*
c *Camptosaurus*
d *Liliensternus*

15 Which Triassic theropod was found in a mass accumulation of hundreds of skeletons?

a *Coelophysis*
b *Tyrannosaurus rex*
c *Velociraptor*
d *Allosaurus*

Mesozoic Earth had **warm** climates

1 *Sanjuansaurus*, a Triassic theropod, is named after the province of San Juan in which country?

- **a** Czech Republic
- **b** Laos
- **c** Nigeria
- **d** Argentina

2 *Ctenosauriscus* and *Lotosaurus* are Triassic crocodile relatives that had…

- **a** A stubby tail
- **b** Sails on their backs
- **c** No front legs
- **d** Two sets of arms

3 How were sauropods able to grow to larger sizes than their ancestors?

- **a** They grew more slowly
- **b** They lived much longer
- **c** They were cold-blooded
- **d** They grew faster

4 The skull of the large carnivorous metriorhynchid *Dakosaurus* looks similar to that of which dinosaur?

- **a** *Tyrannosaurus*
- **b** *Coelophysis*
- **c** *Velociraptor*
- **d** *Barosaurus*

5 Dinosaurs survived for an astounding…

- **a** 160 million years
- **b** 50 million years
- **c** 16 million years
- **d** 6 billion years

6 A small fossil that cannot usually be seen by the naked eye is called what?

- **a** Shell
- **b** Microfossil
- **c** Macrofossil
- **d** Bone

7 Which type of dinosaur was able to chew its food with complex motions of its jaws?

- **a** Hadrosaur
- **b** Sauropod
- **c** Theropod
- **d** Pterosaur

8 The largest carnivorous dinosaur, slightly bigger than *Tyrannosaurus rex*, was thought to be…

- **a** *Argentinosaurus*
- **b** *Saltasaurus*
- **c** *Gallimimus*
- **d** *Giganotosaurus*

9 It has been suggested that the plates of stegosaurs helped warm their bodies by acting like…

- **a** Windsocks
- **b** Tanning lotion
- **c** A microwave
- **d** Solar panels

10 Most of the Middle East is located on which tectonic plate?

- **a** Australian
- **b** Eurasian
- **c** Arabian
- **d** North American

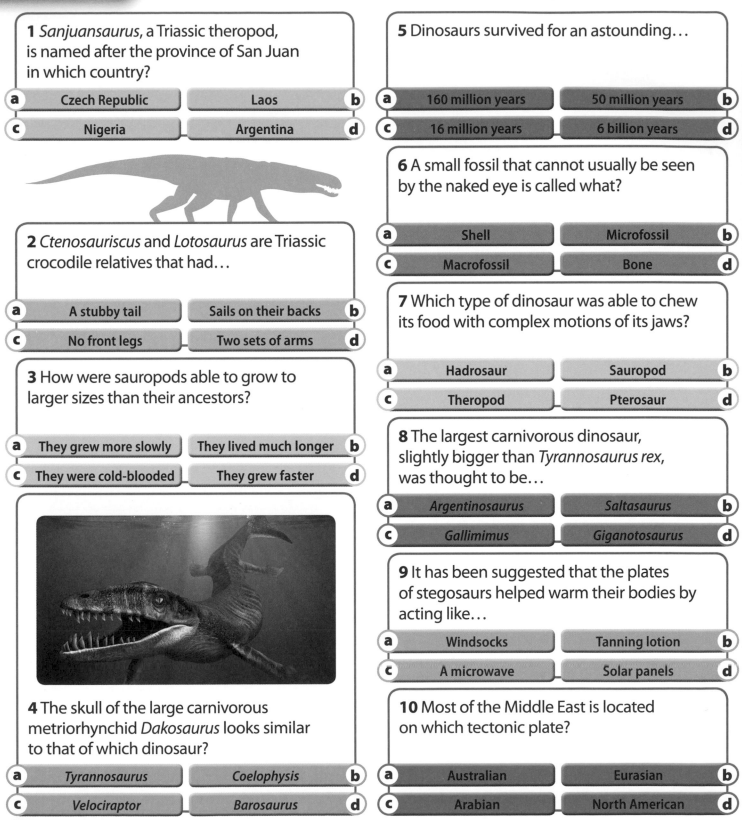

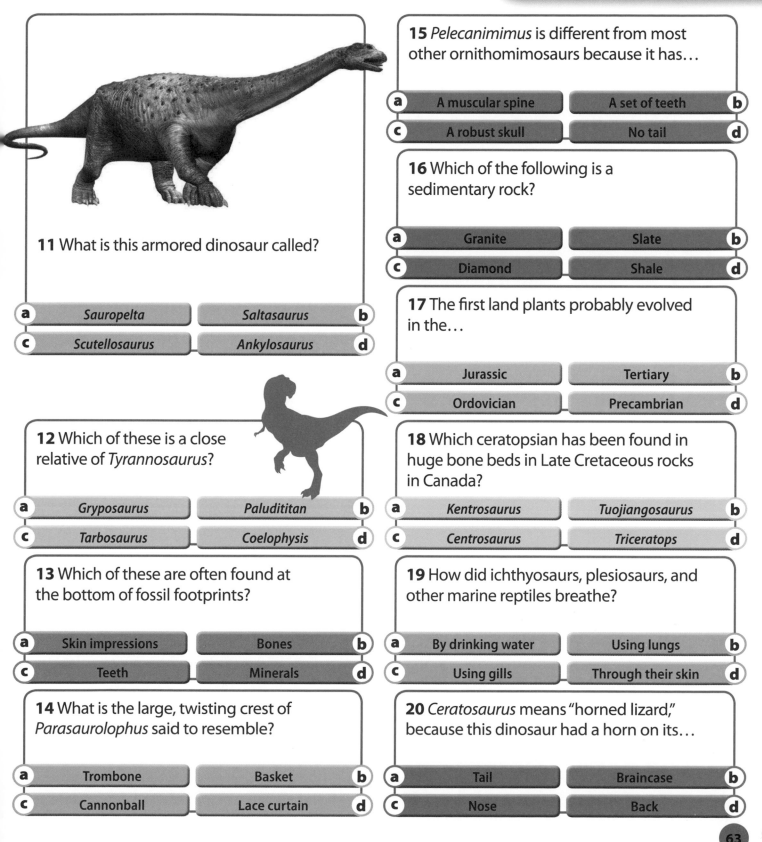

11 What is this armored dinosaur called?

a Sauropelta	**b** Saltasaurus	
c Scutellosaurus	**d** Ankylosaurus	

12 Which of these is a close relative of *Tyrannosaurus*?

a Gryposaurus	**b** Paludititan	
c Tarbosaurus	**d** Coelophysis	

13 Which of these are often found at the bottom of fossil footprints?

a Skin impressions	**b** Bones	
c Teeth	**d** Minerals	

14 What is the large, twisting crest of *Parasaurolophus* said to resemble?

a Trombone	**b** Basket	
c Cannonball	**d** Lace curtain	

15 *Pelecanimimus* is different from most other ornithomimosaurs because it has…

a A muscular spine	**b** A set of teeth	
c A robust skull	**d** No tail	

16 Which of the following is a sedimentary rock?

a Granite	**b** Slate	
c Diamond	**d** Shale	

17 The first land plants probably evolved in the…

a Jurassic	**b** Tertiary	
c Ordovician	**d** Precambrian	

18 Which ceratopsian has been found in huge bone beds in Late Cretaceous rocks in Canada?

a Kentrosaurus	**b** Tuojiangosaurus	
c Centrosaurus	**d** Triceratops	

19 How did ichthyosaurs, plesiosaurs, and other marine reptiles breathe?

a By drinking water	**b** Using lungs	
c Using gills	**d** Through their skin	

20 *Ceratosaurus* means "horned lizard," because this dinosaur had a horn on its…

a Tail	**b** Braincase	
c Nose	**d** Back	

More than **900** *Kentrosaurus* **bones** were

1 The vertebrae of stegosaurs are unique because they…

- **a** Lack ribs
- **b** Have two spinal openings
- **c** Are made of cartilage
- **d** Are stretched vertically

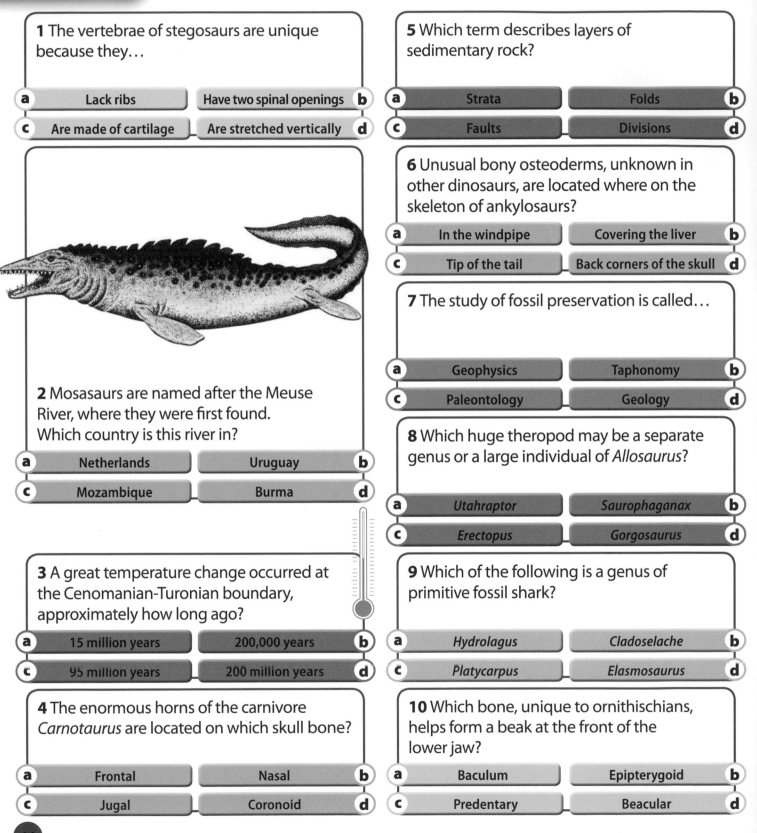

2 Mosasaurs are named after the Meuse River, where they were first found. Which country is this river in?

- **a** Netherlands
- **b** Uruguay
- **c** Mozambique
- **d** Burma

3 A great temperature change occurred at the Cenomanian-Turonian boundary, approximately how long ago?

- **a** 15 million years
- **b** 200,000 years
- **c** 95 million years
- **d** 200 million years

4 The enormous horns of the carnivore *Carnotaurus* are located on which skull bone?

- **a** Frontal
- **b** Nasal
- **c** Jugal
- **d** Coronoid

5 Which term describes layers of sedimentary rock?

- **a** Strata
- **b** Folds
- **c** Faults
- **d** Divisions

6 Unusual bony osteoderms, unknown in other dinosaurs, are located where on the skeleton of ankylosaurs?

- **a** In the windpipe
- **b** Covering the liver
- **c** Tip of the tail
- **d** Back corners of the skull

7 The study of fossil preservation is called…

- **a** Geophysics
- **b** Taphonomy
- **c** Paleontology
- **d** Geology

8 Which huge theropod may be a separate genus or a large individual of *Allosaurus*?

- **a** *Utahraptor*
- **b** *Saurophaganax*
- **c** *Erectopus*
- **d** *Gorgosaurus*

9 Which of the following is a genus of primitive fossil shark?

- **a** *Hydrolagus*
- **b** *Cladoselache*
- **c** *Platycarpus*
- **d** *Elasmosaurus*

10 Which bone, unique to ornithischians, helps form a beak at the front of the lower jaw?

- **a** Baculum
- **b** Epipterygoid
- **c** Predentary
- **d** Beacular

11 Human competition was predominantly responsible for Neanderthal extinction. What was another factor?

- **a** Fire
- **b** House prices
- **c** Unstable climate
- **d** Water

12 Among theropods, which subgroup had a particularly strong sense of smell?

- **a** Ceratosaurs
- **b** Allosaurs
- **c** Tyrannosaurs
- **d** Therizinosaurs

13 A group that appears to go extinct but later turns up in the fossil record is called a…

- **a** Near-extinct species
- **b** Living fossil
- **c** Resurrected species
- **d** Lazarus species

14 Dental batteries are present in which group of dinosaurs?

- **a** Hadrosaurs
- **b** Pachycephalosaurs
- **c** Theropods
- **d** Heterodontosaurids

15 Famous specimens of ichthyosaurs with well-preserved skin have been found where?

- **a** Morrison Formation, US
- **b** Holzmaden, Germany
- **c** Mazon Creek, US
- **d** Burgess Shale, Canada

16 More than 10 new species of which type of dinosaur were named in 2010?

- **a** Dromaeosaur
- **b** Troodontid
- **c** Alvarezsaur
- **d** Ceratopsian

17 Which of these is a subgroup of giant pterosaurs that may not have been able to fly?

- **a** Pterodactyls
- **b** Anurognathids
- **c** Neotheropods
- **d** Azdarchids

18 *Rajasaurus* is from which country?

- **a** Ukraine
- **b** Thailand
- **c** India
- **d** Estonia

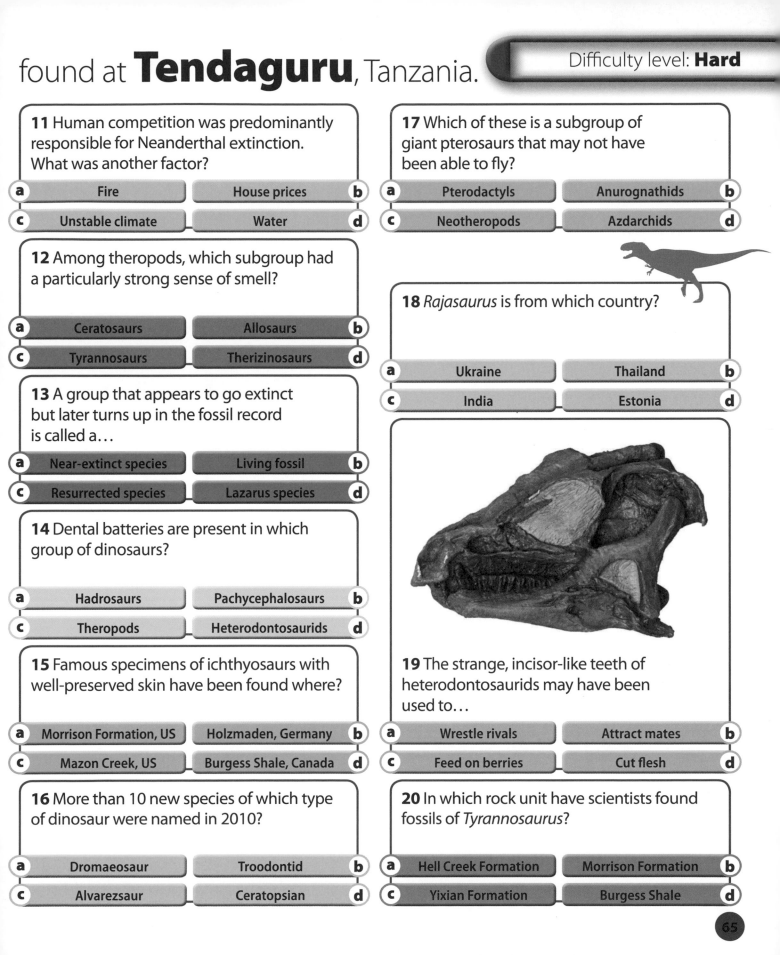

19 The strange, incisor-like teeth of heterodontosaurids may have been used to…

- **a** Wrestle rivals
- **b** Attract mates
- **c** Feed on berries
- **d** Cut flesh

20 In which rock unit have scientists found fossils of *Tyrannosaurus*?

- **a** Hell Creek Formation
- **b** Morrison Formation
- **c** Yixian Formation
- **d** Burgess Shale

Quetzalcoatlus was the **biggest**

1 The bony plates of ankylosaurs are sometimes compared to…

a Window glass
b Medieval armor
c Flags
d Fingernails

2 What is an organism that has existed unchanged for a long time called?

a Tiger
b Living fossil
c Lucky
d Dinosaur

3 Which of these is a small species of dromaeosaur?

a *Allosaurus*
b *Microraptor*
c *Megatyrant*
d *Tyrannosaurus*

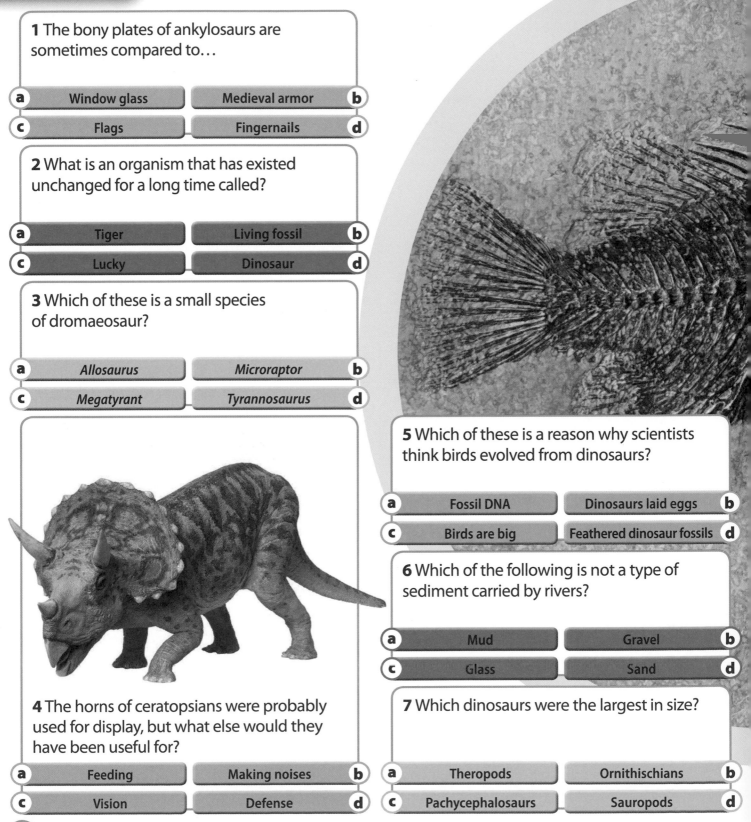

4 The horns of ceratopsians were probably used for display, but what else would they have been useful for?

a Feeding
b Making noises
c Vision
d Defense

5 Which of these is a reason why scientists think birds evolved from dinosaurs?

a Fossil DNA
b Dinosaurs laid eggs
c Birds are big
d Feathered dinosaur fossils

6 Which of the following is not a type of sediment carried by rivers?

a Mud
b Gravel
c Glass
d Sand

7 Which dinosaurs were the largest in size?

a Theropods
b Ornithischians
c Pachycephalosaurs
d Sauropods

creature **ever** to **fly**.

8 This is a well-preserved fossil fish. Most fish breathe using…

a Skin

b Tendons

c Gills

d Lungs

11 *Attenborosaurus*, a genus of plesiosaur, is named after which famous natural history television personality?

a David Attenborough

b Richard Attenborough

c Terence Attenborough

d Atten Borovic

12 Which of the following is one of the famous feathered theropods of China?

a *Kentrosaurus*

b *Microraptor*

c *Tyrannosaurus rex*

d *Stegosaurus*

13 The limbs of stegosaurs were short. This means that they probably ate plants that grew…

a Near the ground

b High in the canopy

c On cliffs

d In swamps

14 Which dinosaur is named after a continent?

a *Francorex*

b *Brachiosaurus*

c *Europasaurus*

d *Canadaraptor*

9 Some spinosaurids had…

a Webbed feet

b Human-sized brains

c A sail on their back

d No teeth

10 Darwin originally studied evolution by observing birds on which island(s)?

a Galapagos Islands

b Antarctica

c Greenland

d Isle of Wight

15 Sharks do not have bones. Instead, their skeleton is made of…

a Cartilage

b Muscle

c Paper

d Wood

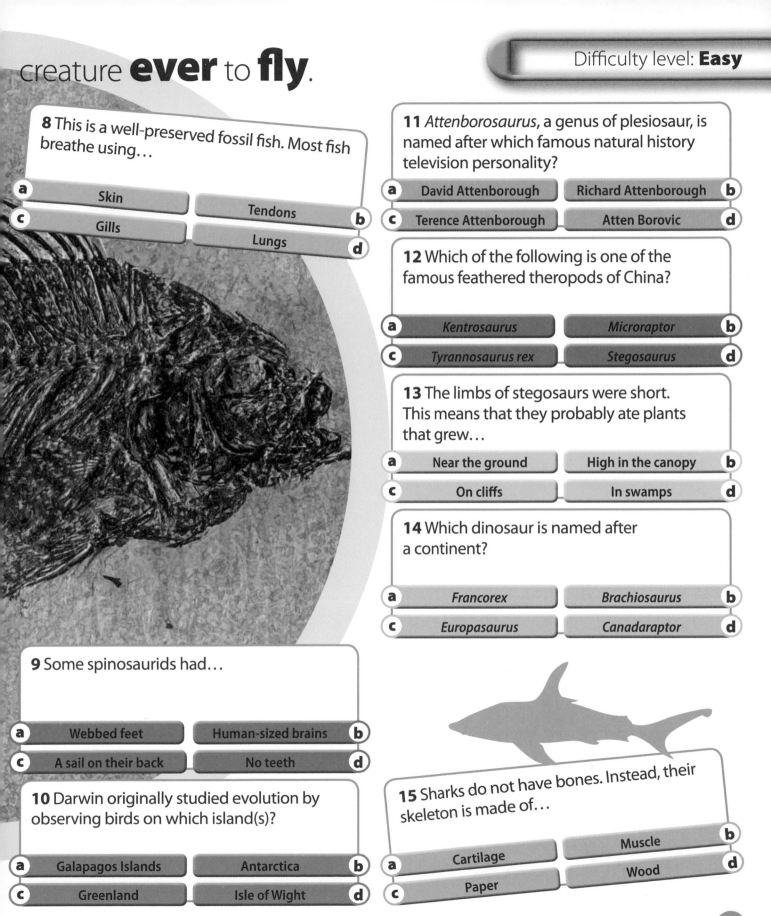

Fossils reveal that some prehistoric **fish**

1 The biggest flying animal that ever lived was found in the Late Cretaceous period. What was its name?

- **a** Quetzalcoatlus
- **b** Archaeopteryx
- **c** Pteranodon
- **d** Dimorphodon

2 Scientists once incorrectly thought that the crests of hadrosaurs were used as…

- **a** Snorkels
- **b** Battering rams
- **c** Navigation devices
- **d** Predatory weapons

3 Dinosaurs are most closely related to which of the following organisms?

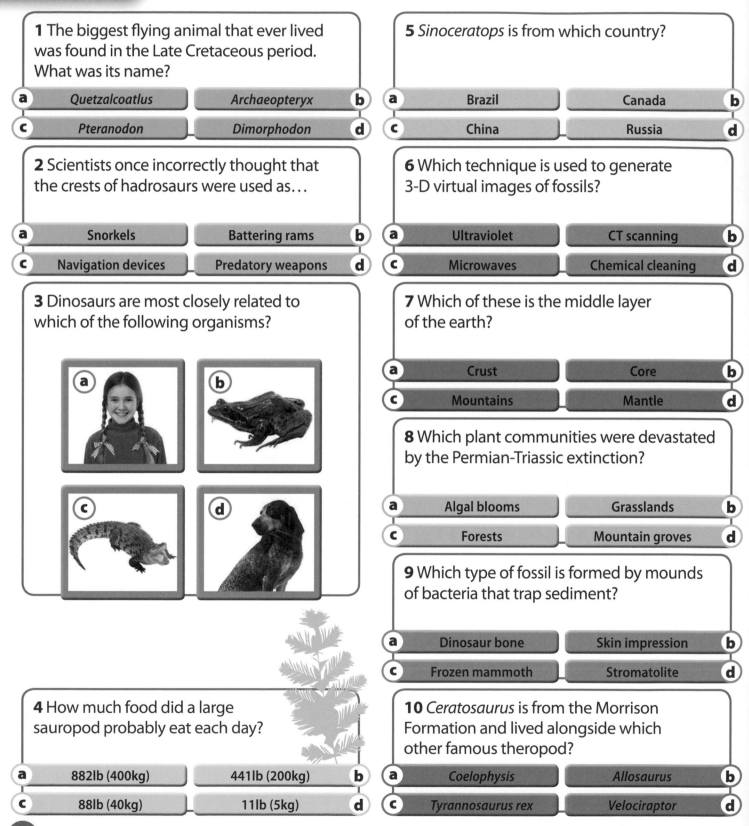

4 How much food did a large sauropod probably eat each day?

- **a** 882lb (400kg)
- **b** 441lb (200kg)
- **c** 88lb (40kg)
- **d** 11lb (5kg)

5 Sinoceratops is from which country?

- **a** Brazil
- **b** Canada
- **c** China
- **d** Russia

6 Which technique is used to generate 3-D virtual images of fossils?

- **a** Ultraviolet
- **b** CT scanning
- **c** Microwaves
- **d** Chemical cleaning

7 Which of these is the middle layer of the earth?

- **a** Crust
- **b** Core
- **c** Mountains
- **d** Mantle

8 Which plant communities were devastated by the Permian-Triassic extinction?

- **a** Algal blooms
- **b** Grasslands
- **c** Forests
- **d** Mountain groves

9 Which type of fossil is formed by mounds of bacteria that trap sediment?

- **a** Dinosaur bone
- **b** Skin impression
- **c** Frozen mammoth
- **d** Stromatolite

10 Ceratosaurus is from the Morrison Formation and lived alongside which other famous theropod?

- **a** Coelophysis
- **b** Allosaurus
- **c** Tyrannosaurus rex
- **d** Velociraptor

11 The skull domes of pachycephalosaurs are often surrounded by small…

a Claws
b Horns and swellings
c Circular depressions
d Nerves

12 Pterosaurs belong to which major vertebrate group, which also includes dinosaurs?

a Anapsids
b Amphibians
c Archosaurs
d Ichthyosaurs

13 Which process is important in exposing fossils so that paleontologists can find them?

a Erosion
b Compaction
c Degradation
d Global warming

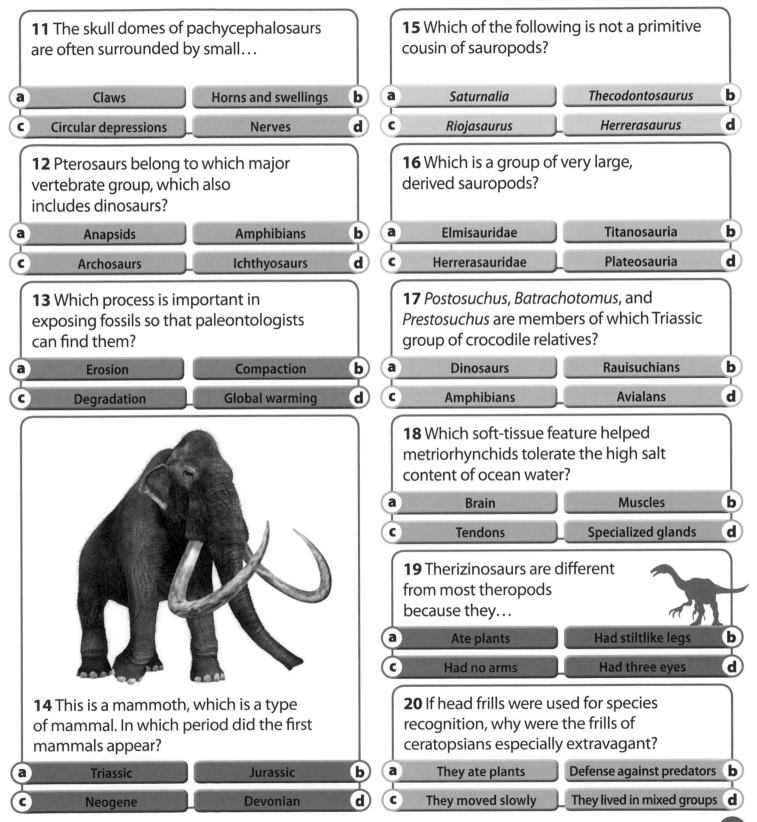

14 This is a mammoth, which is a type of mammal. In which period did the first mammals appear?

a Triassic
b Jurassic
c Neogene
d Devonian

15 Which of the following is not a primitive cousin of sauropods?

a *Saturnalia*
b *Thecodontosaurus*
c *Riojasaurus*
d *Herrerasaurus*

16 Which is a group of very large, derived sauropods?

a Elmisauridae
b Titanosauria
c Herrerasauridae
d Plateosauria

17 *Postosuchus*, *Batrachotomus*, and *Prestosuchus* are members of which Triassic group of crocodile relatives?

a Dinosaurs
b Rauisuchians
c Amphibians
d Avialans

18 Which soft-tissue feature helped metriorhynchids tolerate the high salt content of ocean water?

a Brain
b Muscles
c Tendons
d Specialized glands

19 Therizinosaurs are different from most theropods because they…

a Ate plants
b Had stiltlike legs
c Had no arms
d Had three eyes

20 If head frills were used for species recognition, why were the frills of ceratopsians especially extravagant?

a They ate plants
b Defense against predators
c They moved slowly
d They lived in mixed groups

Sinosauropteryx, the first *"**feathered**"*

1 Which fossils may have inspired the Ancient Greek legend of the one-eyed cyclops?

a Dinosaurs	Trilobites **b**
c Elephants	Rodents **d**

2 The name of the dromaeosaurid *Tsaagan mangas* means…

a Killer claw	Tyrant king **b**
c Mountain roamer	White monster **d**

3 A specialized type of hadrosaur jaw motion, in which the upper jaw rotated outward against the lower jaw, is called…

a Statokinesis	Hadrokinesis **b**
c Akinesis	Pleurokinesis **d**

4 The center of the supercontinent Pangaea was…

a Rainy	Humid **b**
c Flat	A giant desert **d**

5 What find in Blombos Cave, South Africa, indicated advanced behavior by early *Homo sapiens*?

a Poetry	Songs **b**
c Stone radios	Geometric patterns **d**

6 The eyes of *Tyrannosaurus rex* had partially overlapping fields of vision, which gave them…

a Color vision	Sepia vision **b**
c Binocular vision	Night vision **d**

7 An ichthyosaur's tail was divided into how many lobes?

a 2	7 **b**
c 19	1 **d**

8 What surprising hypothesis about theropods was recently proposed?

a Fathers cared for eggs	They lived in deep oceans **b**
c They grew very slowly	None of them ate meat **d**

9 What is the name of a large, fused set of osteoderms covering the pelvis of some ankylosaurs?

a Sacral shield	Pelvic plate **b**
c Back armor	Osteojacket **d**

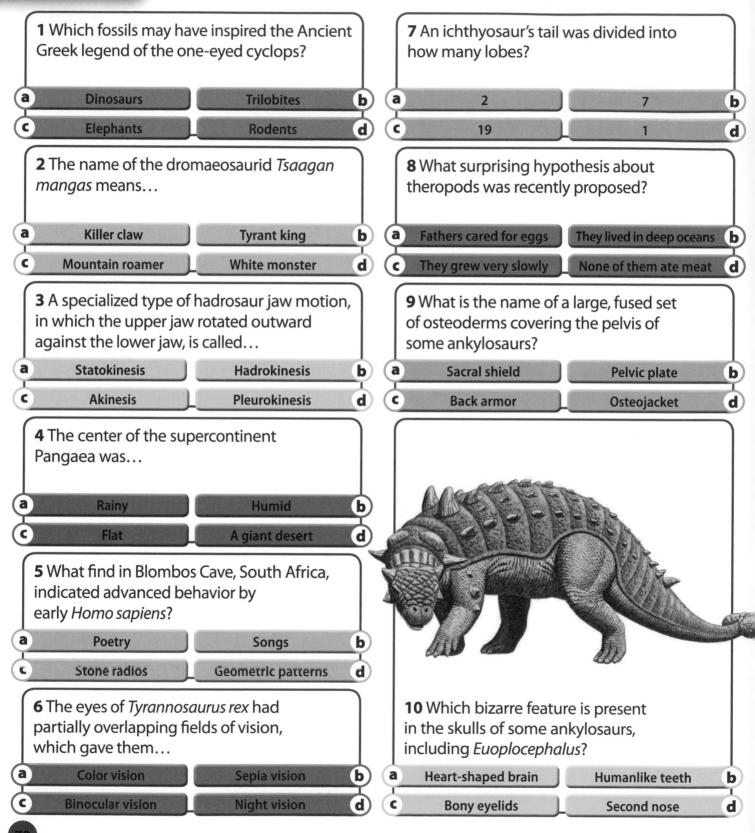

10 Which bizarre feature is present in the skulls of some ankylosaurs, including *Euoplocephalus*?

a Heart-shaped brain	Humanlike teeth **b**
c Bony eyelids	Second nose **d**

dinosaur, was found in **1996**.

11 Which genus of Mesozoic mammal was found with a dinosaur fossil preserved in its stomach?

a *Mus*

b *Repenomamus*

c *Purgatorius*

d *Taeniolabis*

12 The Chinle Formation, which has yielded fossils of Triassic dinosaurs, is located where?

a Cambodia

b United States

c France

d Angola

13 Which feature of the teeth is commonly seen in carchardontosaurids?

a Cingula

b Enamel wrinkles

c Color bands

d Smooth carinae

14 The substance covering the horns of dinosaurs is the same substance that forms…

a Muscles

b Fingernails

c Teeth

d Bones

15 Mosasaur fossils are very common in Cretaceous rock units formed where in North America?

a Deep seas

b Rivers

c Lakes

d Shallow seas

16 Which artist is the Triassic crocodile relative *Effigia okeeffeae* named after?

a Georgia O'Keeffe

b Pablo Picasso

c Frank Effigens

d Anne Curthoys

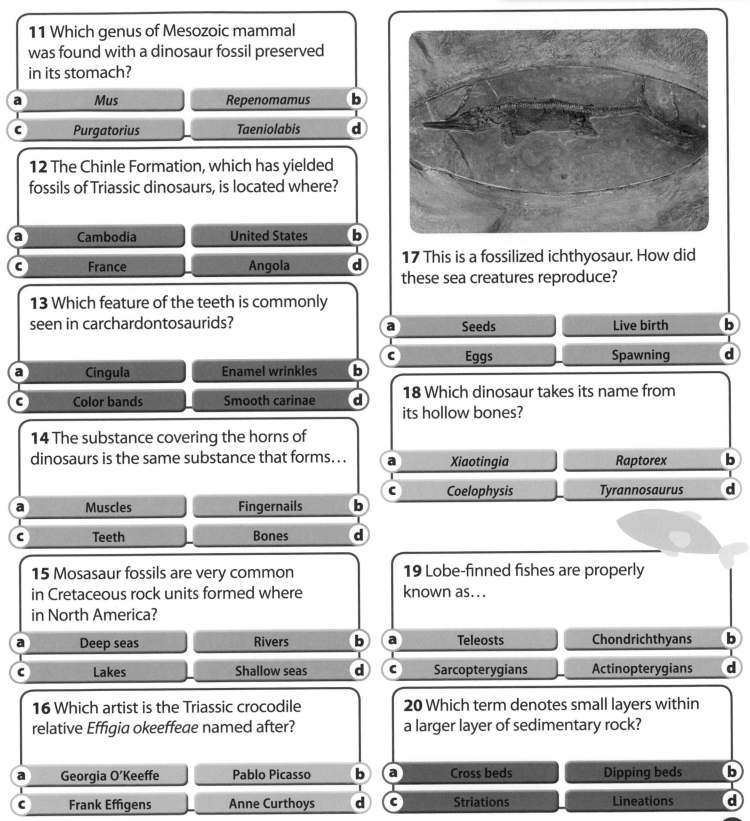

17 This is a fossilized ichthyosaur. How did these sea creatures reproduce?

a Seeds

b Live birth

c Eggs

d Spawning

18 Which dinosaur takes its name from its hollow bones?

a *Xiaotingia*

b *Raptorex*

c *Coelophysis*

d *Tyrannosaurus*

19 Lobe-finned fishes are properly known as…

a Teleosts

b Chondrichthyans

c Sarcopterygians

d Actinopterygians

20 Which term denotes small layers within a larger layer of sedimentary rock?

a Cross beds

b Dipping beds

c Striations

d Lineations

Ichthyosaurus females gave

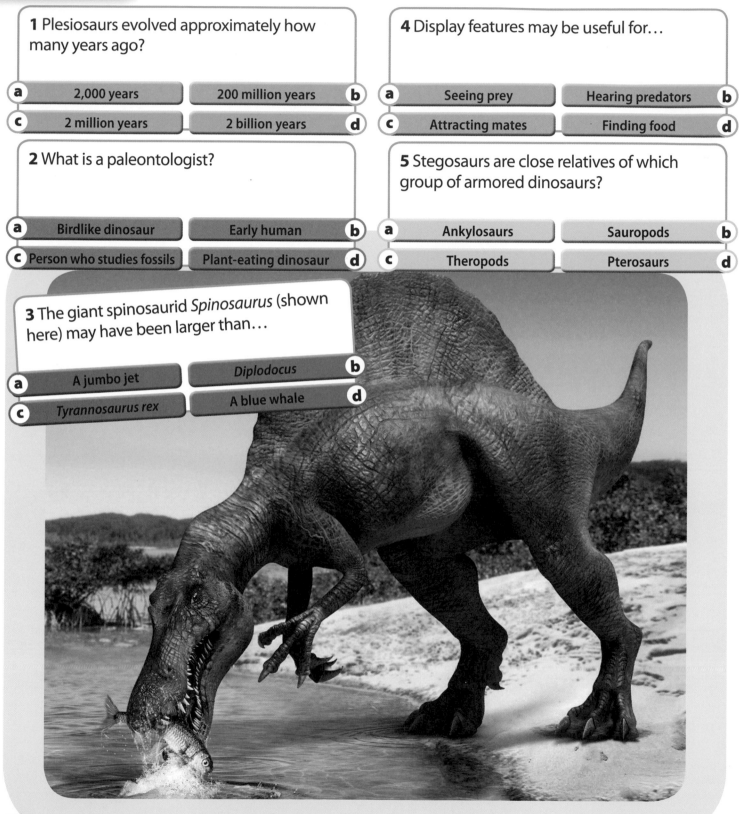

1 Plesiosaurs evolved approximately how many years ago?

- **a** 2,000 years
- **b** 200 million years
- **c** 2 million years
- **d** 2 billion years

2 What is a paleontologist?

- **a** Birdlike dinosaur
- **b** Early human
- **c** Person who studies fossils
- **d** Plant-eating dinosaur

3 The giant spinosaurid *Spinosaurus* (shown here) may have been larger than…

- **a** A jumbo jet
- **b** *Diplodocus*
- **c** *Tyrannosaurus rex*
- **d** A blue whale

4 Display features may be useful for…

- **a** Seeing prey
- **b** Hearing predators
- **c** Attracting mates
- **d** Finding food

5 Stegosaurs are close relatives of which group of armored dinosaurs?

- **a** Ankylosaurs
- **b** Sauropods
- **c** Theropods
- **d** Pterosaurs

birth to their young **tail first**.

6 *Juravenator* was from which period of the Mesozoic?

- **a** Cretaceous
- **b** Silurian
- **c** Hadean
- **d** Jurassic

7 Not all theropod dinosaurs…

- **a** Breathed with lungs
- **b** Were big
- **c** Hatched from eggs
- **d** Had arms

8 Which feature of therizinosaurs was useful in digesting plants?

- **a** Sharp teeth
- **b** Large claws
- **c** Forward-pointing pelvis
- **d** Large guts

9 A species may go extinct if…

- **a** It is hit by lightning
- **b** It cannot adapt
- **c** Its bones are too big
- **d** Its skin burns

10 The species name *antiquus* (in *Thecodontosaurus antiquus*) means what?

- **a** Fresh
- **b** Larger lungs
- **c** Old
- **d** New

11 Which type of fossil helps paleontologists understand how dinosaurs moved?

- **a** Footprints
- **b** Teeth
- **c** Brains
- **d** Skulls

12 What parts of sharks are commonly found as fossils?

- **a** Skin
- **b** Teeth
- **c** Bones
- **d** Braincases

13 Which of the following is not a carnivorous dinosaur?

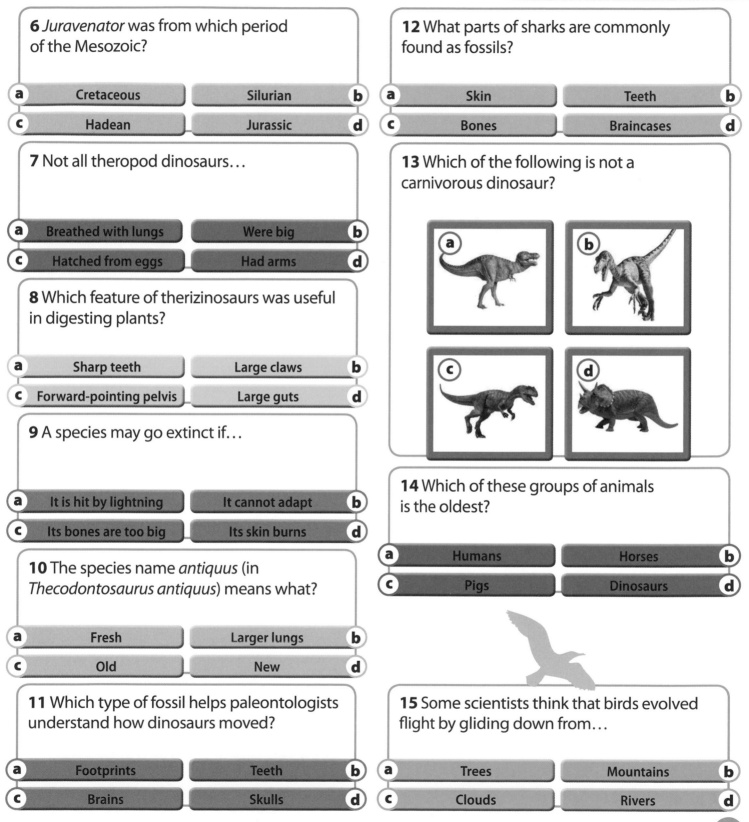

14 Which of these groups of animals is the oldest?

- **a** Humans
- **b** Horses
- **c** Pigs
- **d** Dinosaurs

15 Some scientists think that birds evolved flight by gliding down from…

- **a** Trees
- **b** Mountains
- **c** Clouds
- **d** Rivers

The **tiniest** feathered dinosaurs were

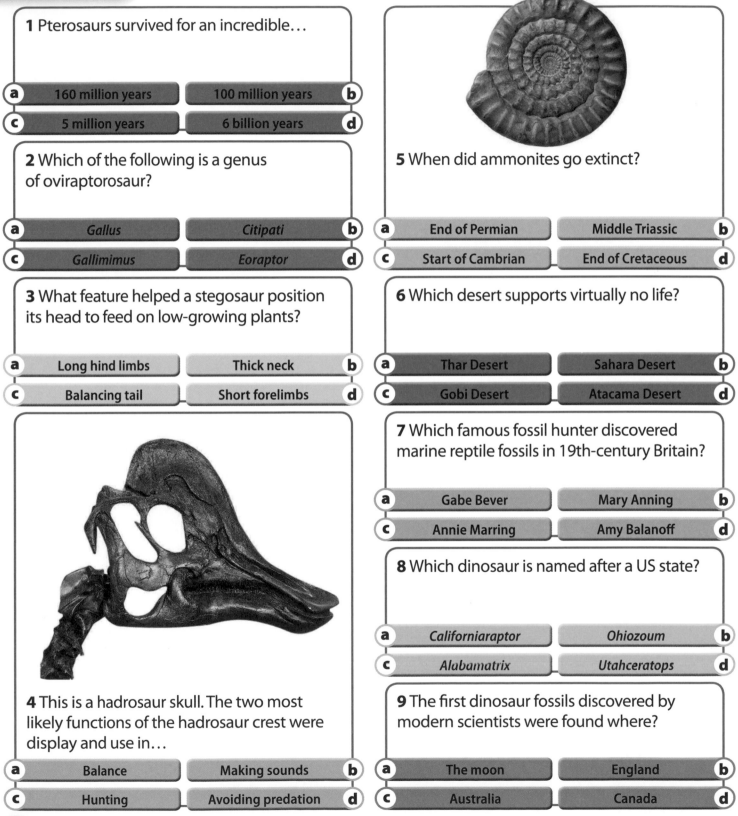

1 Pterosaurs survived for an incredible…

- **a** 160 million years
- **b** 100 million years
- **c** 5 million years
- **d** 6 billion years

2 Which of the following is a genus of oviraptorosaur?

- **a** *Gallus*
- **b** *Citipati*
- **c** *Gallimimus*
- **d** *Eoraptor*

3 What feature helped a stegosaur position its head to feed on low-growing plants?

- **a** Long hind limbs
- **b** Thick neck
- **c** Balancing tail
- **d** Short forelimbs

4 This is a hadrosaur skull. The two most likely functions of the hadrosaur crest were display and use in…

- **a** Balance
- **b** Making sounds
- **c** Hunting
- **d** Avoiding predation

5 When did ammonites go extinct?

- **a** End of Permian
- **b** Middle Triassic
- **c** Start of Cambrian
- **d** End of Cretaceous

6 Which desert supports virtually no life?

- **a** Thar Desert
- **b** Sahara Desert
- **c** Gobi Desert
- **d** Atacama Desert

7 Which famous fossil hunter discovered marine reptile fossils in 19th-century Britain?

- **a** Gabe Bever
- **b** Mary Anning
- **c** Annie Marring
- **d** Amy Balanoff

8 Which dinosaur is named after a US state?

- **a** *Californiaraptor*
- **b** *Ohiozoum*
- **c** *Alabamatrix*
- **d** *Utahceratops*

9 The first dinosaur fossils discovered by modern scientists were found where?

- **a** The moon
- **b** England
- **c** Australia
- **d** Canada

the **scansoriopterygids**.

10 How are abelisaurids distinguished from other theropods?

- **a** Lack of teeth
- **b** Backward-facing pelvis
- **c** Deep skulls
- **d** Small claws

11 Which dinosaur is named after Godzilla?

- **a** *Kileskus*
- **b** *Ojoceratops*
- **c** *Gojirasaurus*
- **d** *Tyrannosaurus*

12 Which type of scientist studies ancient human fossils?

- **a** Paleoanthropologist
- **b** Forensic pathologist
- **c** Paleobotanist
- **d** Geochemist

13 What are correlated changes in the diversity of plants and insects an example of?

- **a** Mass extinction
- **b** Evolutionary radiation
- **c** Coevolution
- **d** Stabilizing selection

14 The Triassic prosauropod *Plateosaurus* has been discovered in vast bone beds in which country?

- **a** Germany
- **b** Australia
- **c** Russia
- **d** El Salvador

15 Mosasaurs are closely related to which living animals?

- **a** Monitor lizards
- **b** Frogs
- **c** Ducks
- **d** Salamanders

16 Hadrosaurs and ceratopsians had more complex feeding habits than sauropods because they could…

- **a** Eat fruit
- **b** Digest food quicker
- **c** Chew food easily
- **d** Eat meat

17 *Euparkeria*, a small Triassic predator, may be closely related to the common ancestor of which major group?

- **a** Plants
- **b** Archosaurs
- **c** Fish
- **d** Trilobites

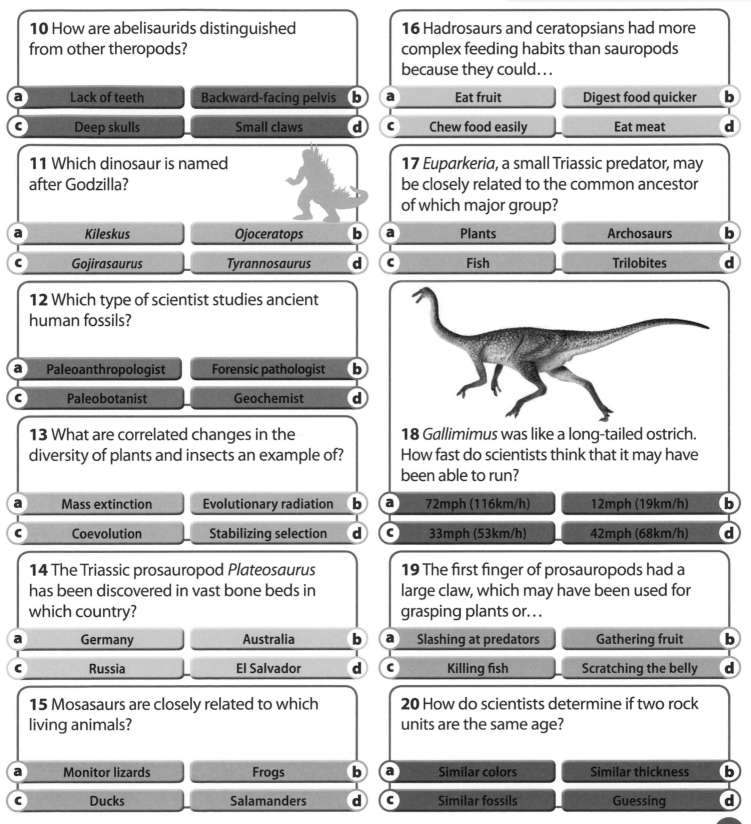

18 *Gallimimus* was like a long-tailed ostrich. How fast do scientists think that it may have been able to run?

- **a** 72mph (116km/h)
- **b** 12mph (19km/h)
- **c** 33mph (53km/h)
- **d** 42mph (68km/h)

19 The first finger of prosauropods had a large claw, which may have been used for grasping plants or…

- **a** Slashing at predators
- **b** Gathering fruit
- **c** Killing fish
- **d** Scratching the belly

20 How do scientists determine if two rock units are the same age?

- **a** Similar colors
- **b** Similar thickness
- **c** Similar fossils
- **d** Guessing

Some *Edmontosaurus* skulls had

1 If the individual bones of a skull are fused together and unable to move independently during feeding, the skull is called…

- **a** Akinetic
- **b** Kinetic
- **c** Static
- **d** Herniated

2 The seeds of which gymnosperm are located at the ends of short stalks?

- **a** Cycad
- **b** Cedar
- **c** Ginkgo
- **d** Pine

3 Which feature helped mosasaurs swallow large prey?

- **a** Hinge in their jaws
- **b** Conical teeth
- **c** Large eyes
- **d** Secondary palate

4 The fossil of the theropod *Scipionyx* was remarkable because…

- **a** It had five skull horns
- **b** Soft tissues were preserved
- **c** It could burrow
- **d** It could swim

5 Which cell replacement process may explain the dramatic changes in pachycephalosaur skulls during growth?

- **a** Metaplasia
- **b** Postdisplacement
- **c** Keratinization
- **d** Transformation

6 Which scientist made the first geological map?

- **a** William Smith
- **b** Lord Kelvin
- **c** O. C. Marsh
- **d** Thomas Carr

7 Which scientist came up with the theory of punctuated equilibrium?

- **a** Shaena Montanari
- **b** Stephen Jay Gould
- **c** George Gaylord Simpson
- **d** Mark Siddall

8 The sauropod name *Brontomerus* means…

- **a** Night-walker
- **b** Obese noodle-neck
- **c** Barrel-chested
- **d** Thunder thighs

9 Why was the carnivorous theropod *Majungasaurus* once thought to be a herbivorous pachycephalosaur?

- **a** Fossils found together
- **b** Both were bipedal
- **c** Both had thick skull domes
- **d** Both lacked teeth

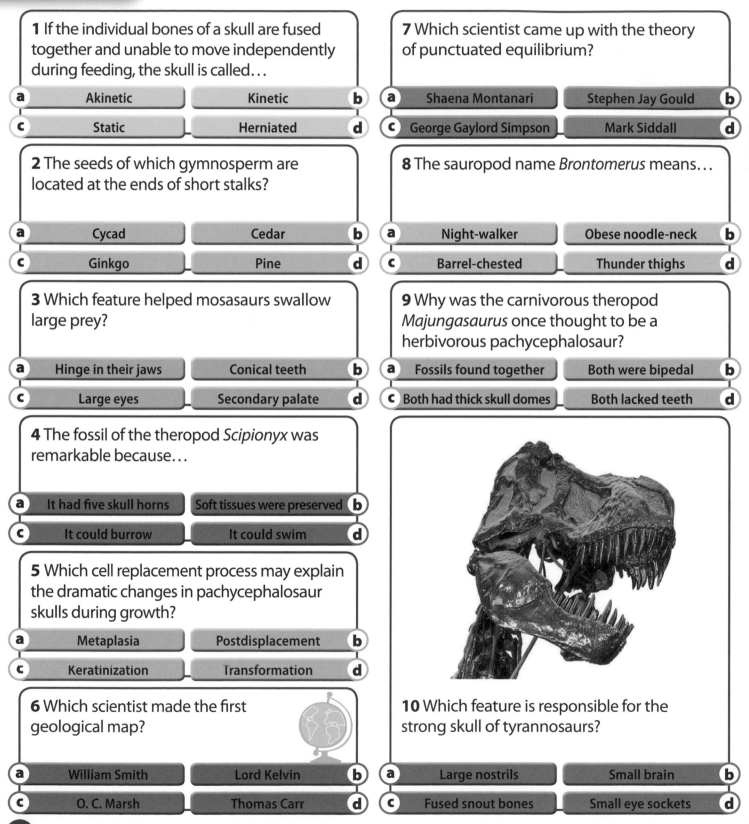

10 Which feature is responsible for the strong skull of tyrannosaurs?

- **a** Large nostrils
- **b** Small brain
- **c** Fused snout bones
- **d** Small eye sockets

more than **1,600 teeth**.

11 The supercontinent that existed before Pangaea is called…

a Protopangaea
b Socratia
c Geologia
d Rodinia

12 Gregor Mendel studied the inheritance of characteristics using which plant species?

a Peas
b Sunflowers
c Oaks
d Mangoes

13 Which of the following is a primitive cousin of ankylosaurs and stegosaurs?

a *Riojasaurus*
b *Shuvosaurus*
c *Camposaurus*
d *Emausaurus*

14 *Stegosaurus* has a series of small osteoderms covering its throat. These formed a structure called a…

a Neck guard
b Gular shield
c Tracheal ring
d Windpipe plate

15 Which of the following is not a sarcopterygian?

a Tetrapod
b Shark
c Lungfish
d Coelacanth

16 One of the closest relatives of pterosaurs is a small archosaur called…

a *Tawa*
b *Syntarsus*
c *Effigia*
d *Scleromochlus*

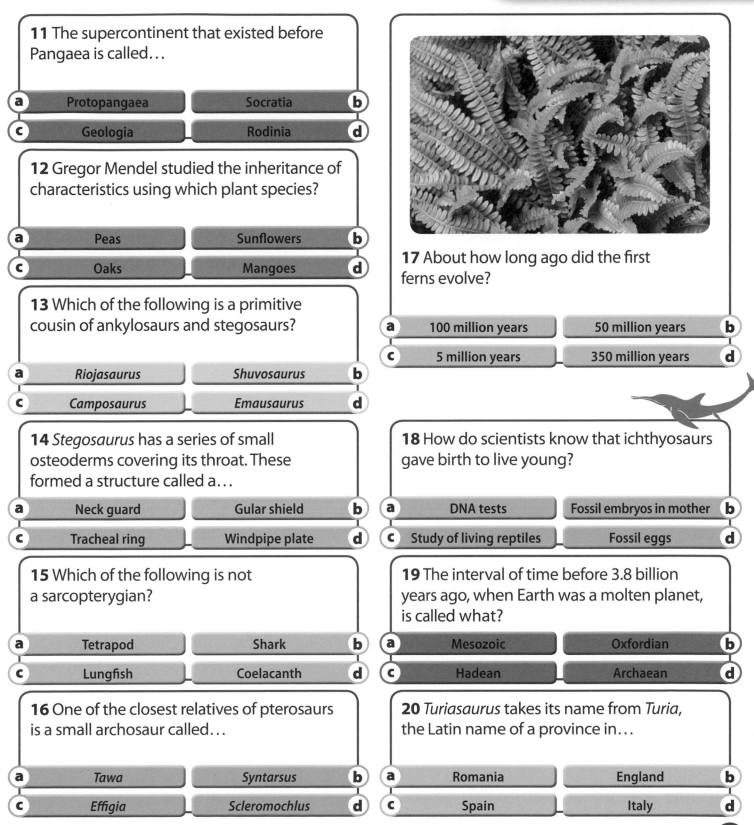

17 About how long ago did the first ferns evolve?

a 100 million years
b 50 million years
c 5 million years
d 350 million years

18 How do scientists know that ichthyosaurs gave birth to live young?

a DNA tests
b Fossil embryos in mother
c Study of living reptiles
d Fossil eggs

19 The interval of time before 3.8 billion years ago, when Earth was a molten planet, is called what?

a Mesozoic
b Oxfordian
c Hadean
d Archaean

20 *Turiasaurus* takes its name from *Turia*, the Latin name of a province in…

a Romania
b England
c Spain
d Italy

Marine **reptile** fossils were found before

1 In addition to fish, what did plesiosaurs often eat?

a Chickens
b Tyrannosaurs
c Squid
d Mice

2 Which of the following is not an ankylosaur?

a *Euoplocephalus*
b *Pteranodon*
c *Ankylosaurus*
d *Pinacosaurus*

3 Tetrapods are defined as vertebrates with…

a Hearts
b Tails
c Limbs and fingers
d Brains

4 *Brachiosaurus*, *Diplodocus*, and *Apatosaurus* belong to which major dinosaur group?

a Sauropoda
b Theropoda
c Synapsida
d Pterosauria

5 The evolution of life on Earth has occurred over…

a 1 year
b Billions of years
c Dozens of years
d Hundreds of years

6 Skeletons of *Compsognathus* have been found in the same rock unit as which fossil bird?

a *Archaeopteryx*
b *Tarbosaurus*
c *Coelophysis*
d *Deinonychus*

7 What feature of ornithischians like *Hypsilophodon* helped make room for their large gut?

a Extra muscles
b Loss of vertebrae
c Backward-facing pubis
d Loss of forearms

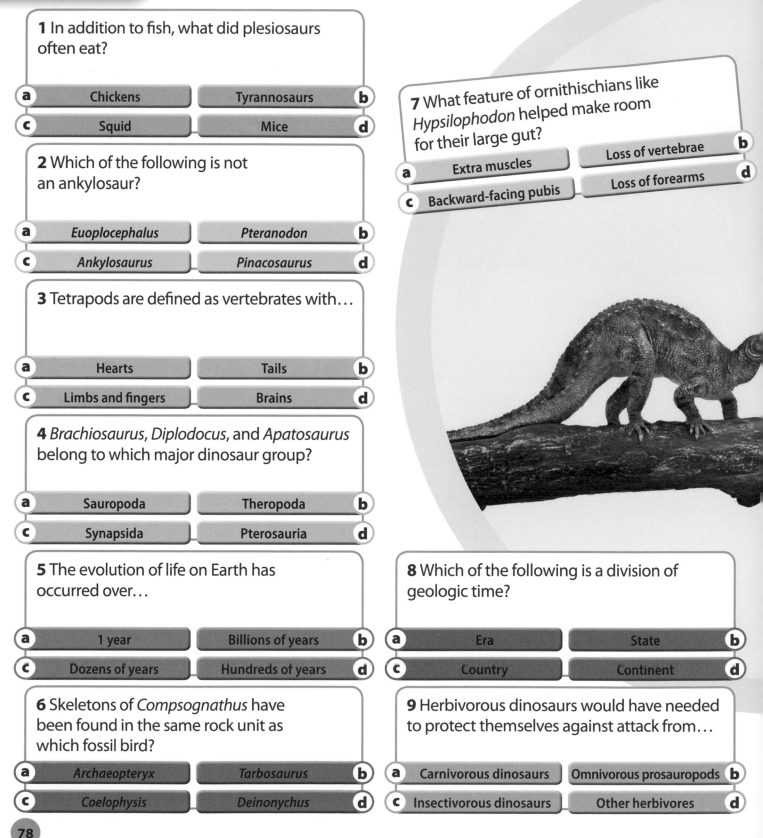

8 Which of the following is a division of geologic time?

a Era
b State
c Country
d Continent

9 Herbivorous dinosaurs would have needed to protect themselves against attack from…

a Carnivorous dinosaurs
b Omnivorous prosauropods
c Insectivorous dinosaurs
d Other herbivores

we knew about **dinosaurs**.

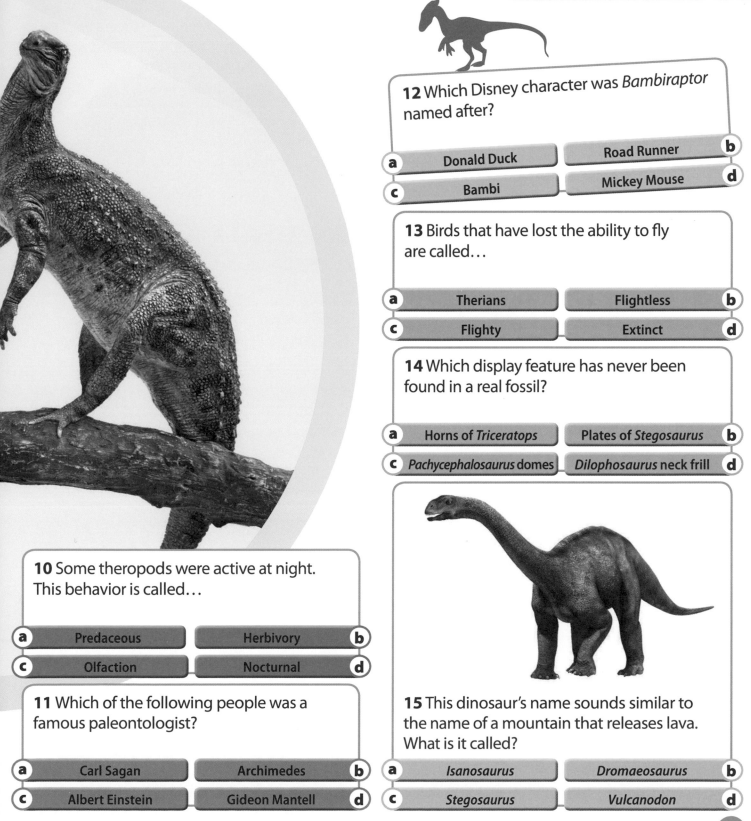

12 Which Disney character was *Bambiraptor* named after?

- **a** Donald Duck
- **b** Road Runner
- **c** Bambi
- **d** Mickey Mouse

13 Birds that have lost the ability to fly are called…

- **a** Therians
- **b** Flightless
- **c** Flighty
- **d** Extinct

14 Which display feature has never been found in a real fossil?

- **a** Horns of *Triceratops*
- **b** Plates of *Stegosaurus*
- **c** *Pachycephalosaurus* domes
- **d** *Dilophosaurus* neck frill

10 Some theropods were active at night. This behavior is called…

- **a** Predaceous
- **b** Herbivory
- **c** Olfaction
- **d** Nocturnal

11 Which of the following people was a famous paleontologist?

- **a** Carl Sagan
- **b** Archimedes
- **c** Albert Einstein
- **d** Gideon Mantell

15 This dinosaur's name sounds similar to the name of a mountain that releases lava. What is it called?

- **a** *Isanosaurus*
- **b** *Dromaeosaurus*
- **c** *Stegosaurus*
- **d** *Vulcanodon*

The **ankylosaur** *Liaoningosaurus*

1 Coprolites are the fossilized remains of what?

a Fingers | Hair b
c Feces | Teeth d

2 In which period did the first turtles appear?

a Triassic | Jurassic b
c Neogene | Devonian d

3 Troodontids are very close relatives of…

a Ornithischians | Birds b
c Tyrannosaurs | *Allosaurus* d

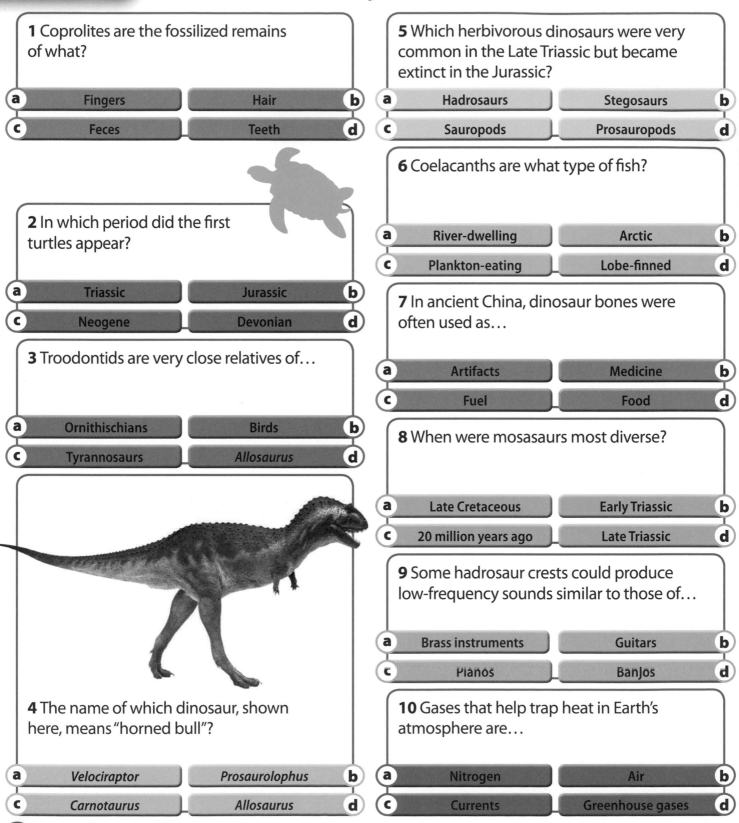

4 The name of which dinosaur, shown here, means "horned bull"?

a *Velociraptor* | *Prosaurolophus* b
c *Carnotaurus* | *Allosaurus* d

5 Which herbivorous dinosaurs were very common in the Late Triassic but became extinct in the Jurassic?

a Hadrosaurs | Stegosaurs b
c Sauropods | Prosauropods d

6 Coelacanths are what type of fish?

a River-dwelling | Arctic b
c Plankton-eating | Lobe-finned d

7 In ancient China, dinosaur bones were often used as…

a Artifacts | Medicine b
c Fuel | Food d

8 When were mosasaurs most diverse?

a Late Cretaceous | Early Triassic b
c 20 million years ago | Late Triassic d

9 Some hadrosaur crests could produce low-frequency sounds similar to those of…

a Brass instruments | Guitars b
c Pianos | Banjos d

10 Gases that help trap heat in Earth's atmosphere are…

a Nitrogen | Air b
c Currents | Greenhouse gases d

had an **armor-plated** belly.

11 Which fossil creature do people associate with the fictional Loch Ness monster?

a *Pentaceratops*
b *Elasmosaurus*
c *Gigantosaurus*
d *Dimorphodon*

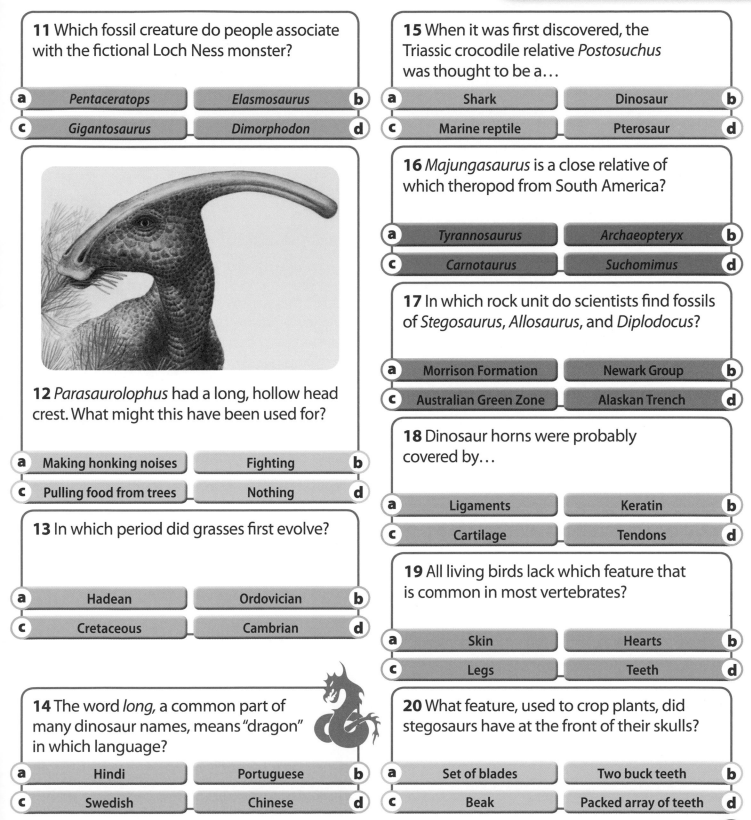

12 *Parasaurolophus* had a long, hollow head crest. What might this have been used for?

a Making honking noises
b Fighting
c Pulling food from trees
d Nothing

13 In which period did grasses first evolve?

a Hadean
b Ordovician
c Cretaceous
d Cambrian

14 The word *long,* a common part of many dinosaur names, means "dragon" in which language?

a Hindi
b Portuguese
c Swedish
d Chinese

15 When it was first discovered, the Triassic crocodile relative *Postosuchus* was thought to be a…

a Shark
b Dinosaur
c Marine reptile
d Pterosaur

16 *Majungasaurus* is a close relative of which theropod from South America?

a *Tyrannosaurus*
b *Archaeopteryx*
c *Carnotaurus*
d *Suchomimus*

17 In which rock unit do scientists find fossils of *Stegosaurus*, *Allosaurus*, and *Diplodocus*?

a Morrison Formation
b Newark Group
c Australian Green Zone
d Alaskan Trench

18 Dinosaur horns were probably covered by…

a Ligaments
b Keratin
c Cartilage
d Tendons

19 All living birds lack which feature that is common in most vertebrates?

a Skin
b Hearts
c Legs
d Teeth

20 What feature, used to crop plants, did stegosaurs have at the front of their skulls?

a Set of blades
b Two buck teeth
c Beak
d Packed array of teeth

Quetzalcoatlus was **named after** the

1 Which type of gymnosperm, which looks like a big pineapple with green fronds, was common during the Mesozoic?

a Cedar | b Fern
c Ginkgo | d Cycad

2 Some sauropods had large claws on their feet, which may have been useful for…

a Digging nests | b Fighting over carcasses
c Attracting mates | d Helping them run

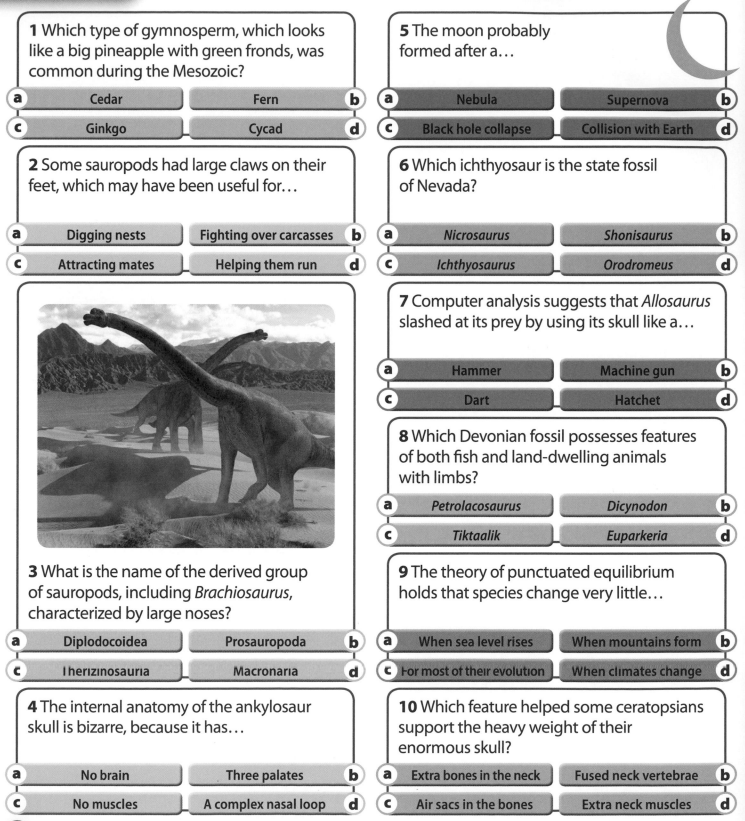

3 What is the name of the derived group of sauropods, including *Brachiosaurus*, characterized by large noses?

a Diplodocoidea | b Prosauropoda
c Therizinosauria | d Macronaria

4 The internal anatomy of the ankylosaur skull is bizarre, because it has…

a No brain | b Three palates
c No muscles | d A complex nasal loop

5 The moon probably formed after a…

a Nebula | b Supernova
c Black hole collapse | d Collision with Earth

6 Which ichthyosaur is the state fossil of Nevada?

a *Nicrosaurus* | b *Shonisaurus*
c *Ichthyosaurus* | d *Orodromeus*

7 Computer analysis suggests that *Allosaurus* slashed at its prey by using its skull like a…

a Hammer | b Machine gun
c Dart | d Hatchet

8 Which Devonian fossil possesses features of both fish and land-dwelling animals with limbs?

a *Petrolacosaurus* | b *Dicynodon*
c *Tiktaalik* | d *Euparkeria*

9 The theory of punctuated equilibrium holds that species change very little…

a When sea level rises | b When mountains form
c For most of their evolution | d When climates change

10 Which feature helped some ceratopsians support the heavy weight of their enormous skull?

a Extra bones in the neck | b Fused neck vertebrae
c Air sacs in the bones | d Extra neck muscles

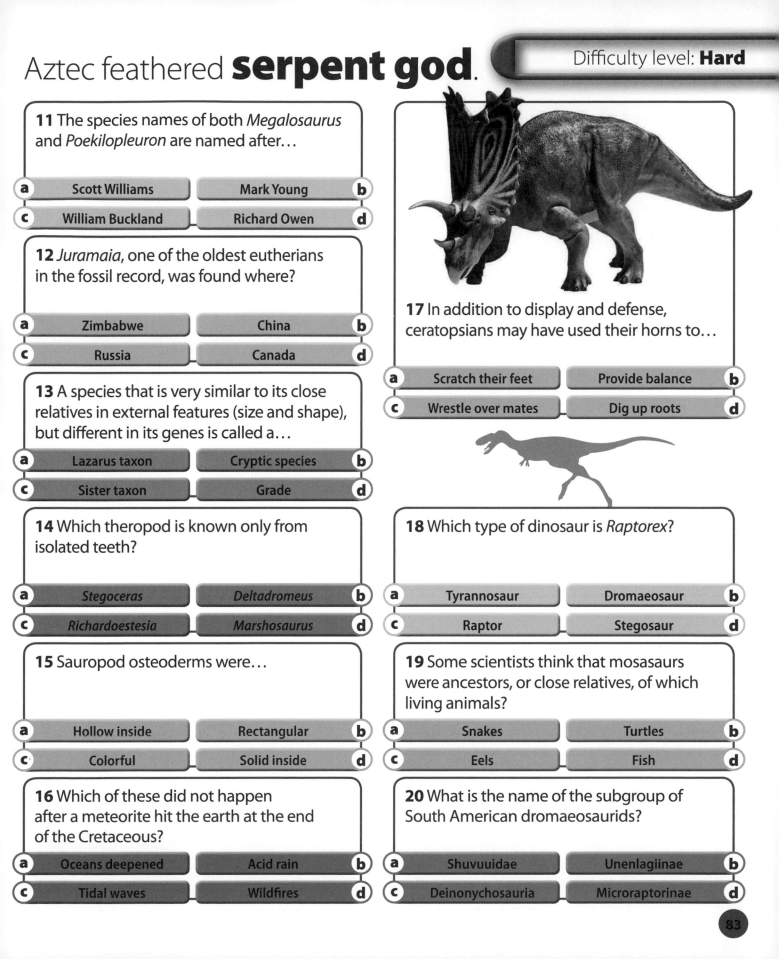

11 The species names of both *Megalosaurus* and *Poekilopleuron* are named after…

a Scott Williams	**b** Mark Young
c William Buckland	**d** Richard Owen

12 *Juramaia*, one of the oldest eutherians in the fossil record, was found where?

a Zimbabwe	**b** China
c Russia	**d** Canada

13 A species that is very similar to its close relatives in external features (size and shape), but different in its genes is called a…

a Lazarus taxon	**b** Cryptic species
c Sister taxon	**d** Grade

14 Which theropod is known only from isolated teeth?

a *Stegoceras*	**b** *Deltadromeus*
c *Richardoestesia*	**d** *Marshosaurus*

15 Sauropod osteoderms were…

a Hollow inside	**b** Rectangular
c Colorful	**d** Solid inside

16 Which of these did not happen after a meteorite hit the earth at the end of the Cretaceous?

a Oceans deepened	**b** Acid rain
c Tidal waves	**d** Wildfires

17 In addition to display and defense, ceratopsians may have used their horns to…

a Scratch their feet	**b** Provide balance
c Wrestle over mates	**d** Dig up roots

18 Which type of dinosaur is *Raptorex*?

a Tyrannosaur	**b** Dromaeosaur
c Raptor	**d** Stegosaur

19 Some scientists think that mosasaurs were ancestors, or close relatives, of which living animals?

a Snakes	**b** Turtles
c Eels	**d** Fish

20 What is the name of the subgroup of South American dromaeosaurids?

a Shuvuuidae	**b** Unenlagiinae
c Deinonychosauria	**d** Microraptorinae

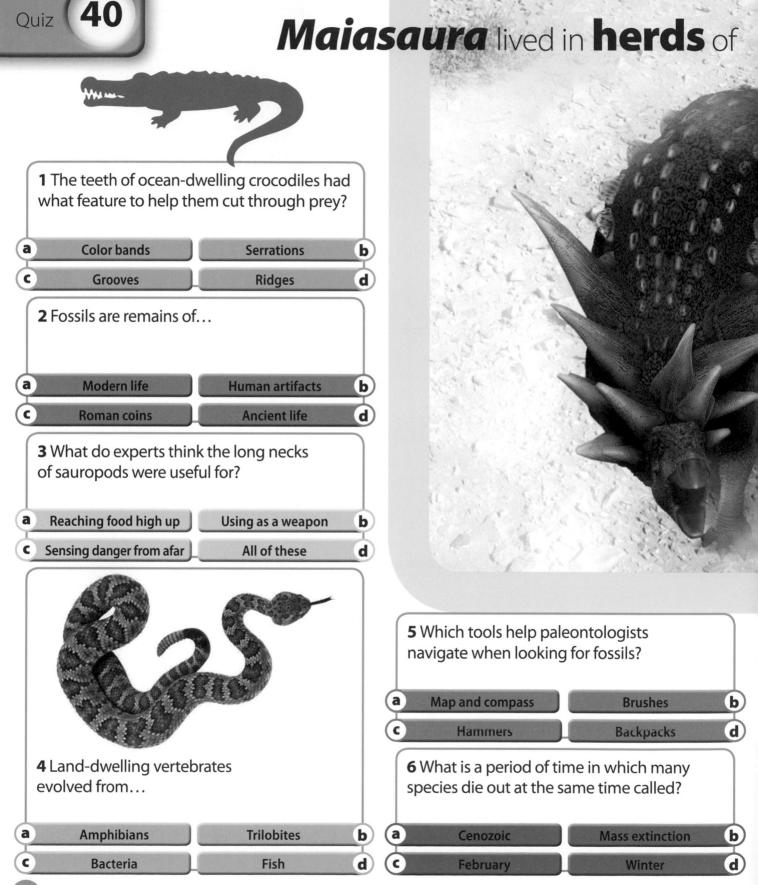

Maiasaura lived in **herds** of

1 The teeth of ocean-dwelling crocodiles had what feature to help them cut through prey?

- **a** Color bands
- **b** Serrations
- **c** Grooves
- **d** Ridges

2 Fossils are remains of…

- **a** Modern life
- **b** Human artifacts
- **c** Roman coins
- **d** Ancient life

3 What do experts think the long necks of sauropods were useful for?

- **a** Reaching food high up
- **b** Using as a weapon
- **c** Sensing danger from afar
- **d** All of these

4 Land-dwelling vertebrates evolved from…

- **a** Amphibians
- **b** Trilobites
- **c** Bacteria
- **d** Fish

5 Which tools help paleontologists navigate when looking for fossils?

- **a** Map and compass
- **b** Brushes
- **c** Hammers
- **d** Backpacks

6 What is a period of time in which many species die out at the same time called?

- **a** Cenozoic
- **b** Mass extinction
- **c** February
- **d** Winter

up to **10,000** individuals.

10 What are the armored ankylosaurs often described as?

a Batlike
b Whalelike
c Tanklike
d Swanlike

11 What is a common word used to describe birds?

a Amphibian
b Suchian
c Avian
d Dinosaurian

12 A mark made by the tooth of one animal on the bone of another animal is a…

a Worthless bit of damage
b Bite mark
c Dental drag
d Tooth spot

7 The armored ankylosaurs resembled which living mammal, which can roll into a ball when threatened?

a Armadillo
b Rat
c Shrew
d Aardvark

13 Which of the following was a plant-eating theropod?

a *Velociraptor*
b *Therizinosaurus*
c *Allosaurus*
d *Deinonychus*

8 Which of the following is not a tyrannosaur?

a *Stegosaurus*
b *Tyrannosaurus rex*
c *Tarbosaurus*
d *Gorgosaurus*

14 The Chinese theropod *Pedopenna's* name means…

a Foot feather
b Ugly dragon
c Green beast
d Fat swimmer

9 *Supersaurus* was given its name because it is…

a Very fast
b Very small
c Very skinny
d Very large

15 Which of the following is not evidence for evolution?

a Laboratory experiments
b Field observations
c Guessing
d Fossils

Ichthyosaurs did not lay eggs—they

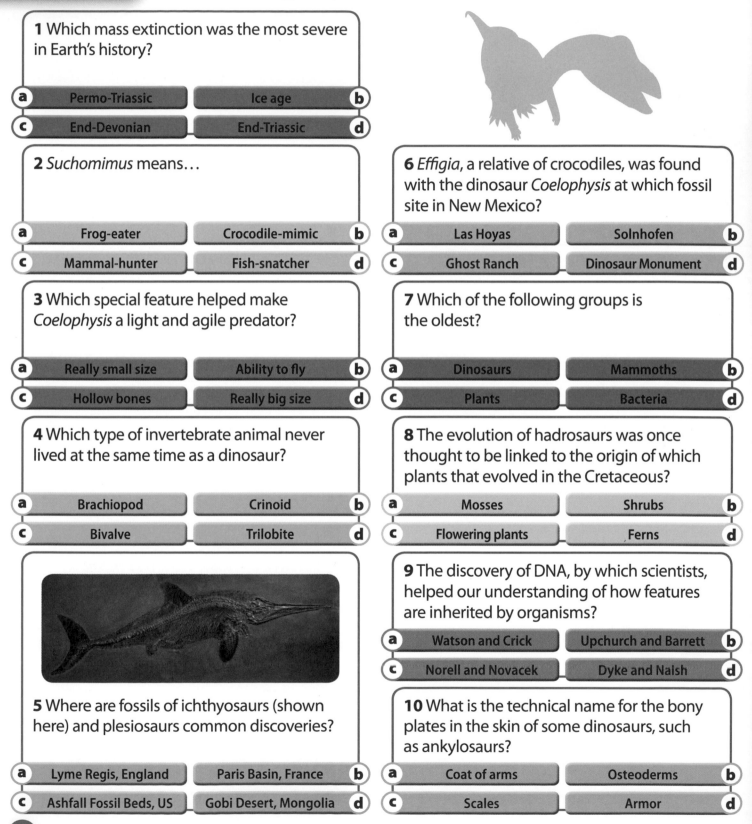

1 Which mass extinction was the most severe in Earth's history?

a Permo-Triassic
b Ice age
c End-Devonian
d End-Triassic

2 *Suchomimus* means…

a Frog-eater
b Crocodile-mimic
c Mammal-hunter
d Fish-snatcher

3 Which special feature helped make *Coelophysis* a light and agile predator?

a Really small size
b Ability to fly
c Hollow bones
d Really big size

4 Which type of invertebrate animal never lived at the same time as a dinosaur?

a Brachiopod
b Crinoid
c Bivalve
d Trilobite

5 Where are fossils of ichthyosaurs (shown here) and plesiosaurs common discoveries?

a Lyme Regis, England
b Paris Basin, France
c Ashfall Fossil Beds, US
d Gobi Desert, Mongolia

6 *Effigia*, a relative of crocodiles, was found with the dinosaur *Coelophysis* at which fossil site in New Mexico?

a Las Hoyas
b Solnhofen
c Ghost Ranch
d Dinosaur Monument

7 Which of the following groups is the oldest?

a Dinosaurs
b Mammoths
c Plants
d Bacteria

8 The evolution of hadrosaurs was once thought to be linked to the origin of which plants that evolved in the Cretaceous?

a Mosses
b Shrubs
c Flowering plants
d Ferns

9 The discovery of DNA, by which scientists, helped our understanding of how features are inherited by organisms?

a Watson and Crick
b Upchurch and Barrett
c Norell and Novacek
d Dyke and Naish

10 What is the technical name for the bony plates in the skin of some dinosaurs, such as ankylosaurs?

a Coat of arms
b Osteoderms
c Scales
d Armor

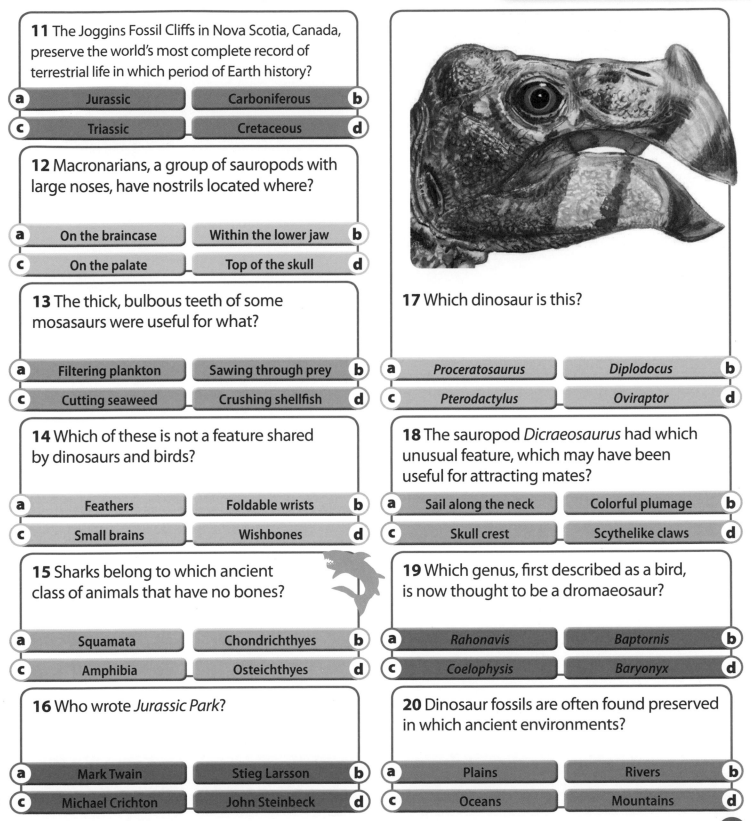

11 The Joggins Fossil Cliffs in Nova Scotia, Canada, preserve the world's most complete record of terrestrial life in which period of Earth history?

a Jurassic | Carboniferous b
c Triassic | Cretaceous d

12 Macronarians, a group of sauropods with large noses, have nostrils located where?

a On the braincase | Within the lower jaw b
c On the palate | Top of the skull d

13 The thick, bulbous teeth of some mosasaurs were useful for what?

a Filtering plankton | Sawing through prey b
c Cutting seaweed | Crushing shellfish d

14 Which of these is not a feature shared by dinosaurs and birds?

a Feathers | Foldable wrists b
c Small brains | Wishbones d

15 Sharks belong to which ancient class of animals that have no bones?

a Squamata | Chondrichthyes b
c Amphibia | Osteichthyes d

16 Who wrote *Jurassic Park*?

a Mark Twain | Stieg Larsson b
c Michael Crichton | John Steinbeck d

17 Which dinosaur is this?

a *Proceratosaurus* | *Diplodocus* b
c *Pterodactylus* | *Oviraptor* d

18 The sauropod *Dicraeosaurus* had which unusual feature, which may have been useful for attracting mates?

a Sail along the neck | Colorful plumage b
c Skull crest | Scythelike claws d

19 Which genus, first described as a bird, is now thought to be a dromaeosaur?

a *Rahonavis* | *Baptornis* b
c *Coelophysis* | *Baryonyx* d

20 Dinosaur fossils are often found preserved in which ancient environments?

a Plains | Rivers b
c Oceans | Mountains d

Seismosaurus was the **longest**

1 Which ceratopsian had two huge horns projecting upward from the back of its frill?

- **a** Styracosaurus
- **b** Chasmosaurus
- **c** Protoceratops
- **d** Diabloceratops

2 Nests, eggs, and embryos associated with which early sauropod cousin were recently discovered in South Africa?

- **a** Plateosaurus
- **b** Thecodontosaurus
- **c** Lessemsaurus
- **d** Massospondylus

3 Pterosaurs had which unique bone in their wrists?

- **a** Carpal
- **b** Sesamoid
- **c** Furcula
- **d** Pteroid

4 A group that includes a common ancestor and all of its descendants is a…

- **a** Clade
- **b** Grade
- **c** Stem group
- **d** Total group

5 The eye socket of many large theropods is what shape?

- **a** Triangle
- **b** Keyhole
- **c** Circle
- **d** Square

6 *Ajkaceratops* is named after Ajka, a town in which country?

- **a** Wales
- **b** Belgium
- **c** Croatia
- **d** Hungary

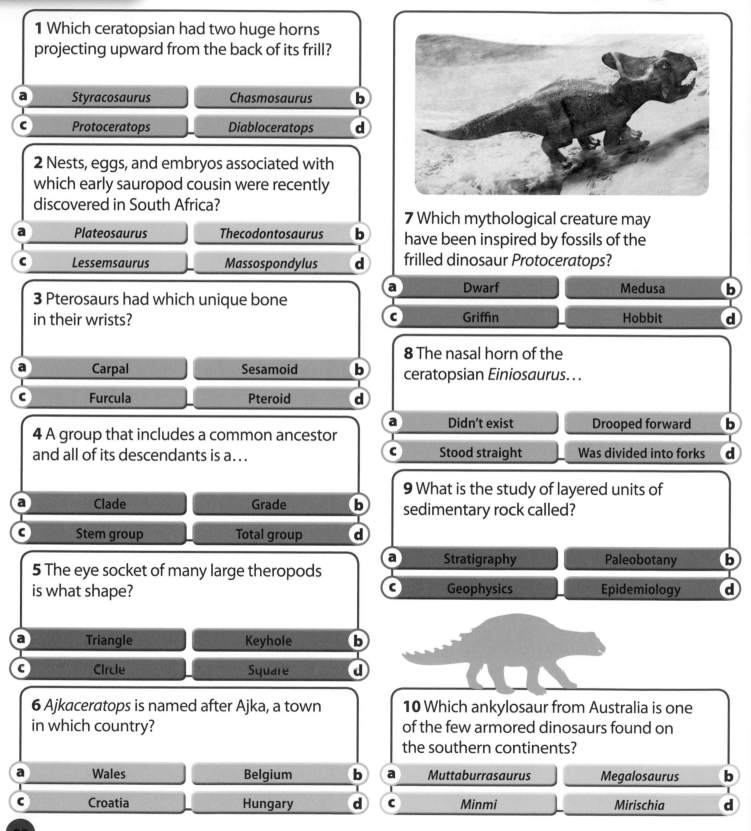

7 Which mythological creature may have been inspired by fossils of the frilled dinosaur *Protoceratops*?

- **a** Dwarf
- **b** Medusa
- **c** Griffin
- **d** Hobbit

8 The nasal horn of the ceratopsian *Einiosaurus*…

- **a** Didn't exist
- **b** Drooped forward
- **c** Stood straight
- **d** Was divided into forks

9 What is the study of layered units of sedimentary rock called?

- **a** Stratigraphy
- **b** Paleobotany
- **c** Geophysics
- **d** Epidemiology

10 Which ankylosaur from Australia is one of the few armored dinosaurs found on the southern continents?

- **a** Muttaburrasaurus
- **b** Megalosaurus
- **c** Minmi
- **d** Mirischia

11 Which of the following is not an ichthyosaur?

a Sordes
b Ichthyosaurus
c Shastasaurus
d Mixosaurus

12 Which tyrannosaur lived in eastern North America?

a Appalachiosaurus
b Tarbosaurus
c Gorgosaurus
d Acrocanthosaurus

13 In the Jurassic period, Pangaea split into Laurasia and which other supercontinent?

a Euramerica
b Eurasia
c Rodinia
d Gondwana

14 *Falcarius* is a primitive member of which unusual group of theropods?

a Aves
b Kentrosauridae
c Therizinosauria
d Deinonychosauria

15 Gymnosperms and angiosperms together make up a larger group of plants called…

a Araucarias
b Gnetophytes
c Spermatophytes
d Grasses

16 What is the name of a famous fossil bird with teeth?

a Troodon
b Corvus
c Ichthyornis
d Gallus

17 *Tyrannotitan* belongs to which theropod subgroup?

a Coelophysidae
b Carcharodontosauridae
c Tyrannosauridae
d Titanosauria

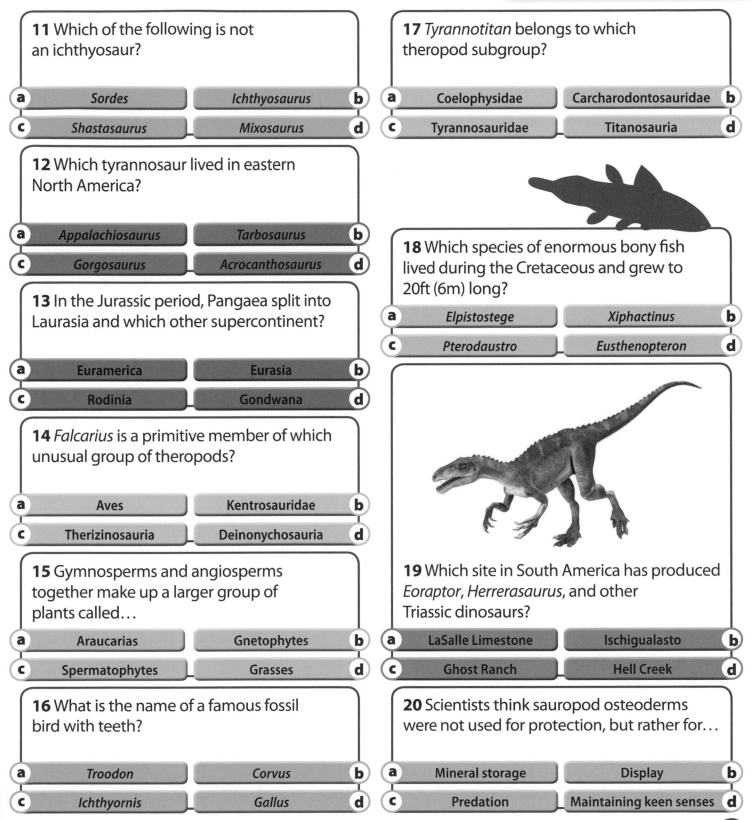

18 Which species of enormous bony fish lived during the Cretaceous and grew to 20ft (6m) long?

a Elpistostege
b Xiphactinus
c Pterodaustro
d Eusthenopteron

19 Which site in South America has produced *Eoraptor*, *Herrerasaurus*, and other Triassic dinosaurs?

a LaSalle Limestone
b Ischigualasto
c Ghost Ranch
d Hell Creek

20 Scientists think sauropod osteoderms were not used for protection, but rather for…

a Mineral storage
b Display
c Predation
d Maintaining keen senses

The **first** complete **ichthyosaur**

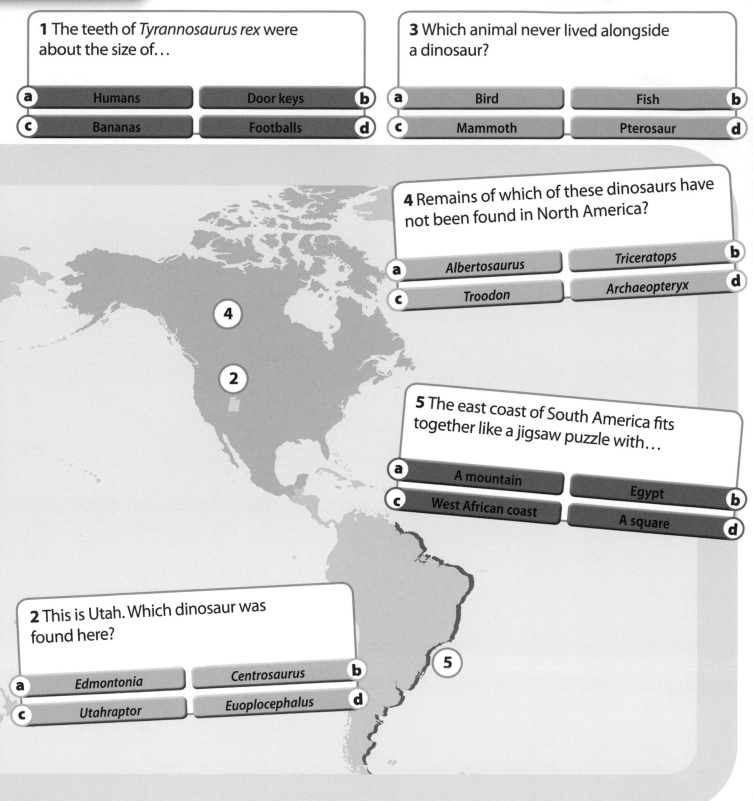

1 The teeth of *Tyrannosaurus rex* were about the size of…

- **a** Humans
- **b** Door keys
- **c** Bananas
- **d** Footballs

3 Which animal never lived alongside a dinosaur?

- **a** Bird
- **b** Fish
- **c** Mammoth
- **d** Pterosaur

4 Remains of which of these dinosaurs have not been found in North America?

- **a** *Albertosaurus*
- **b** *Triceratops*
- **c** *Troodon*
- **d** *Archaeopteryx*

5 The east coast of South America fits together like a jigsaw puzzle with…

- **a** A mountain
- **b** Egypt
- **c** West African coast
- **d** A square

2 This is Utah. Which dinosaur was found here?

- **a** *Edmontonia*
- **b** *Centrosaurus*
- **c** *Utahraptor*
- **d** *Euoplocephalus*

6 *Archaeopteryx*, the first bird, was about the size of a…

a Crow	**b** House	
c School bus	**d** Refrigerator	

7 Only a few dinosaur fossils are known from which continent?

a Antarctica	**b** North America	
c Asia	**d** Australia	

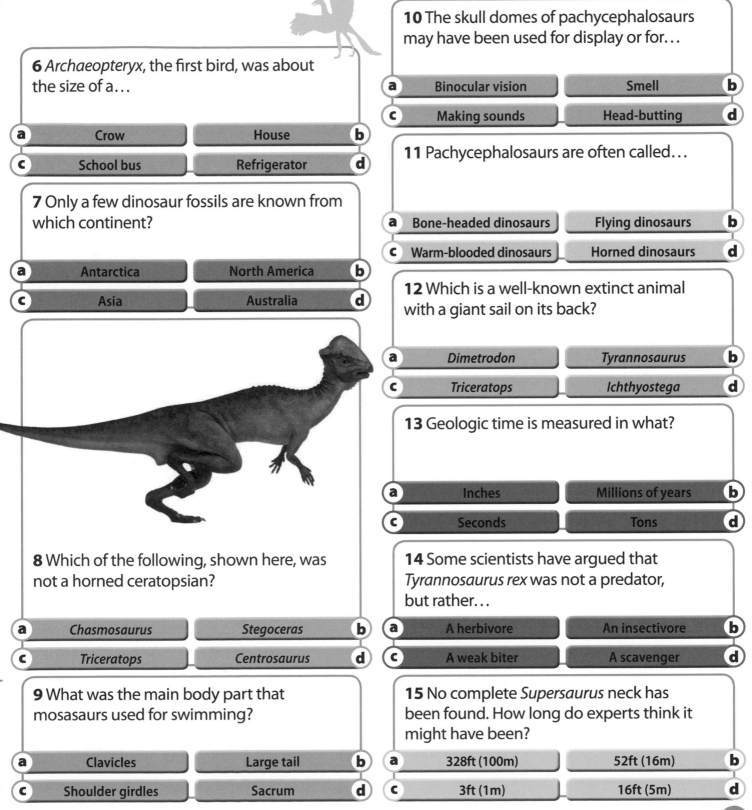

8 Which of the following, shown here, was not a horned ceratopsian?

a Chasmosaurus	**b** Stegoceras	
c Triceratops	**d** Centrosaurus	

9 What was the main body part that mosasaurs used for swimming?

a Clavicles	**b** Large tail	
c Shoulder girdles	**d** Sacrum	

10 The skull domes of pachycephalosaurs may have been used for display or for…

a Binocular vision	**b** Smell	
c Making sounds	**d** Head-butting	

11 Pachycephalosaurs are often called…

a Bone-headed dinosaurs	**b** Flying dinosaurs	
c Warm-blooded dinosaurs	**d** Horned dinosaurs	

12 Which is a well-known extinct animal with a giant sail on its back?

a Dimetrodon	**b** Tyrannosaurus	
c Triceratops	**d** Ichthyostega	

13 Geologic time is measured in what?

a Inches	**b** Millions of years	
c Seconds	**d** Tons	

14 Some scientists have argued that *Tyrannosaurus rex* was not a predator, but rather…

a A herbivore	**b** An insectivore	
c A weak biter	**d** A scavenger	

15 No complete *Supersaurus* neck has been found. How long do experts think it might have been?

a 328ft (100m)	**b** 52ft (16m)	
c 3ft (1m)	**d** 16ft (5m)	

Stomach contents show that some **big**

1 Multiple footprints show that hadrosaurs often…

a Hopped on one leg	**b** Crawled
c Swam	**d** Walked on four legs

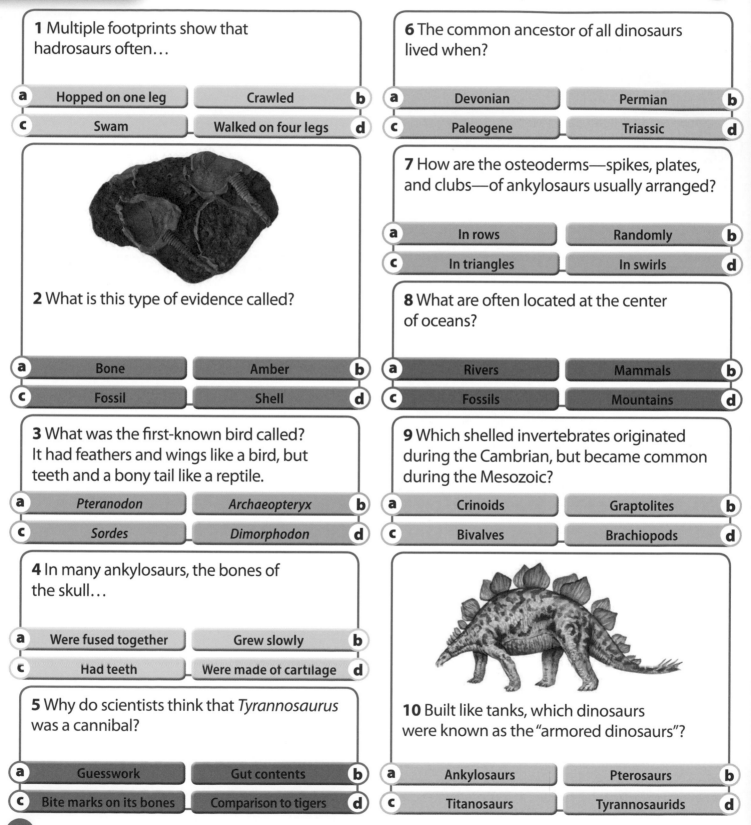

2 What is this type of evidence called?

a Bone	**b** Amber
c Fossil	**d** Shell

3 What was the first-known bird called? It had feathers and wings like a bird, but teeth and a bony tail like a reptile.

a *Pteranodon*	**b** *Archaeopteryx*
c *Sordes*	**d** *Dimorphodon*

4 In many ankylosaurs, the bones of the skull…

a Were fused together	**b** Grew slowly
c Had teeth	**d** Were made of cartilage

5 Why do scientists think that *Tyrannosaurus* was a cannibal?

a Guesswork	**b** Gut contents
c Bite marks on its bones	**d** Comparison to tigers

6 The common ancestor of all dinosaurs lived when?

a Devonian	**b** Permian
c Paleogene	**d** Triassic

7 How are the osteoderms—spikes, plates, and clubs—of ankylosaurs usually arranged?

a In rows	**b** Randomly
c In triangles	**d** In swirls

8 What are often located at the center of oceans?

a Rivers	**b** Mammals
c Fossils	**d** Mountains

9 Which shelled invertebrates originated during the Cambrian, but became common during the Mesozoic?

a Crinoids	**b** Graptolites
c Bivalves	**d** Brachiopods

10 Built like tanks, which dinosaurs were known as the "armored dinosaurs"?

a Ankylosaurs	**b** Pterosaurs
c Titanosaurs	**d** Tyrannosaurids

11 Which of the following is not an explanation for the plates of stegosaurs?

a Temperature control

b Aid in gathering plants

c Defense

d Display

12 Fossils of *Microraptor* have been found with large, vaned feathers on the arms and…

a Tail

b Legs

c Skull

d Back

13 What is the technical name for the wishbone of birds?

a Sternum

b Vertebra

c Femur

d Furcula

14 Stegosaurs and ankylosaurs together form a group called…

a Heterodontosauridae

b Ornithopoda

c Thyreophora

d Titanosauria

15 Which parts of an animal usually degrade during fossilization?

a Shells

b Muscles

c Teeth

d Bones

16 Approximately what percentage of species died in the Permo-Triassic mass extinction?

a 95 percent

b 5 percent

c 15 percent

d 30 percent

17 What is the technical name for plants that have "naked seeds," such as these pine trees?

a Angiosperms

b Ferns

c Reeds

d Gymnosperms

18 Which dinosaur is named after an energy company?

a *Coalraptor*

b *Exxontyrant*

c *Gasosaurus*

d *Oiltitan*

19 Mosasaurs swam in a style similar to…

a Sea snakes

b Dolphins

c Humans

d Starfish

20 Which group of Mesozoic mammals resembled living rodents in their diet and body size?

a Tetrapods

b Multituberculates

c Primates

d Caecilians

The **largest**-known *Tyrannosaurus rex*

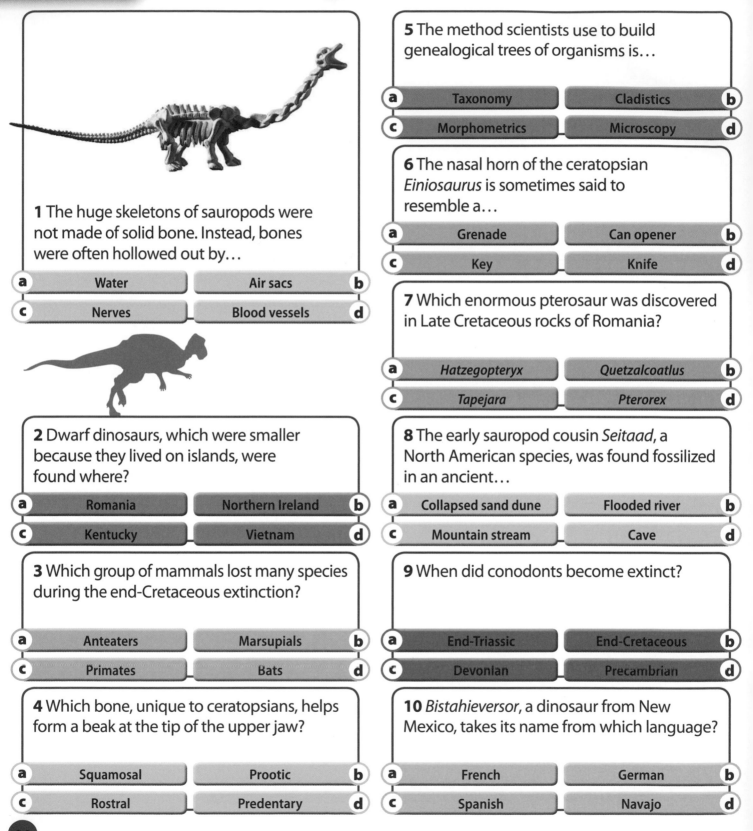

1 The huge skeletons of sauropods were not made of solid bone. Instead, bones were often hollowed out by…

a	Water	Air sacs	b
c	Nerves	Blood vessels	d

2 Dwarf dinosaurs, which were smaller because they lived on islands, were found where?

a	Romania	Northern Ireland	b
c	Kentucky	Vietnam	d

3 Which group of mammals lost many species during the end-Cretaceous extinction?

a	Anteaters	Marsupials	b
c	Primates	Bats	d

4 Which bone, unique to ceratopsians, helps form a beak at the tip of the upper jaw?

a	Squamosal	Prootic	b
c	Rostral	Predentary	d

5 The method scientists use to build genealogical trees of organisms is…

a	Taxonomy	Cladistics	b
c	Morphometrics	Microscopy	d

6 The nasal horn of the ceratopsian *Einiosaurus* is sometimes said to resemble a…

a	Grenade	Can opener	b
c	Key	Knife	d

7 Which enormous pterosaur was discovered in Late Cretaceous rocks of Romania?

a	*Hatzegopteryx*	*Quetzalcoatlus*	b
c	*Tapejara*	*Pterorex*	d

8 The early sauropod cousin *Seitaad*, a North American species, was found fossilized in an ancient…

a	Collapsed sand dune	Flooded river	b
c	Mountain stream	Cave	d

9 When did conodonts become extinct?

a	End-Triassic	End-Cretaceous	b
c	Devonian	Precambrian	d

10 *Bistahieversor*, a dinosaur from New Mexico, takes its name from which language?

a	French	German	b
c	Spanish	Navajo	d

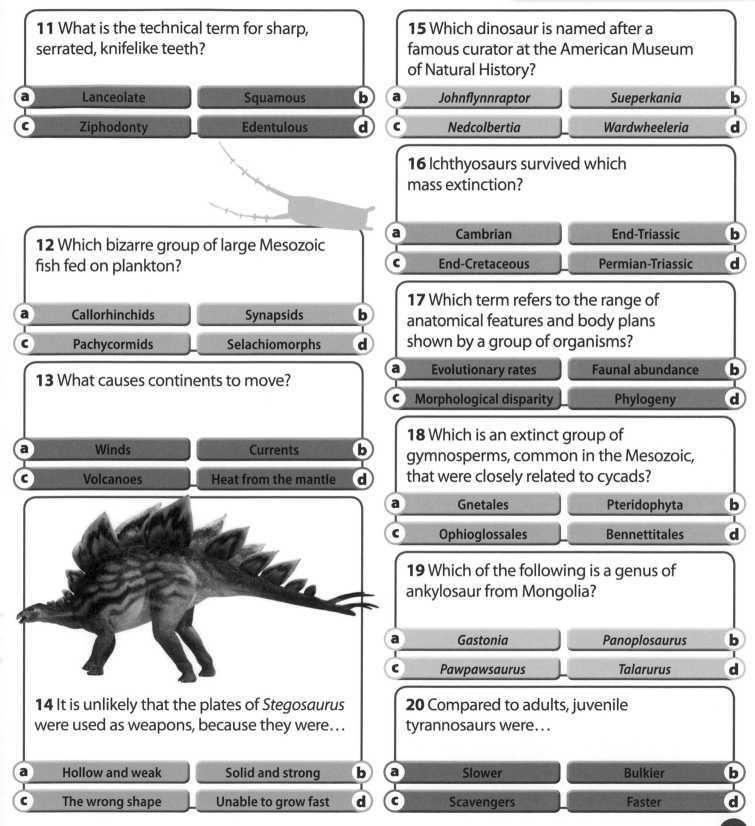

11 What is the technical term for sharp, serrated, knifelike teeth?

a   Lanceolate

b   Squamous

c   Ziphodonty

d   Edentulous

12 Which bizarre group of large Mesozoic fish fed on plankton?

a   Callorhinchids

b   Synapsids

c   Pachycormids

d   Selachiomorphs

13 What causes continents to move?

a   Winds

b   Currents

c   Volcanoes

d   Heat from the mantle

14 It is unlikely that the plates of *Stegosaurus* were used as weapons, because they were…

a   Hollow and weak

b   Solid and strong

c   The wrong shape

d   Unable to grow fast

15 Which dinosaur is named after a famous curator at the American Museum of Natural History?

a   *Johnflynnraptor*

b   *Sueperkania*

c   *Nedcolbertia*

d   *Wardwheeleria*

16 Ichthyosaurs survived which mass extinction?

a   Cambrian

b   End-Triassic

c   End-Cretaceous

d   Permian-Triassic

17 Which term refers to the range of anatomical features and body plans shown by a group of organisms?

a   Evolutionary rates

b   Faunal abundance

c   Morphological disparity

d   Phylogeny

18 Which is an extinct group of gymnosperms, common in the Mesozoic, that were closely related to cycads?

a   Gnetales

b   Pteridophyta

c   Ophioglossales

d   Bennettitales

19 Which of the following is a genus of ankylosaur from Mongolia?

a   *Gastonia*

b   *Panoplosaurus*

c   *Pawpawsaurus*

d   *Talarurus*

20 Compared to adults, juvenile tyrannosaurs were…

a   Slower

b   Bulkier

c   Scavengers

d   Faster

A site in **Spain** contained more than

1 Before scientists accepted the theory of evolution, it was thought that…

a Species never changed

b All species ate meat

c All species lived in forests

d Dragons were real

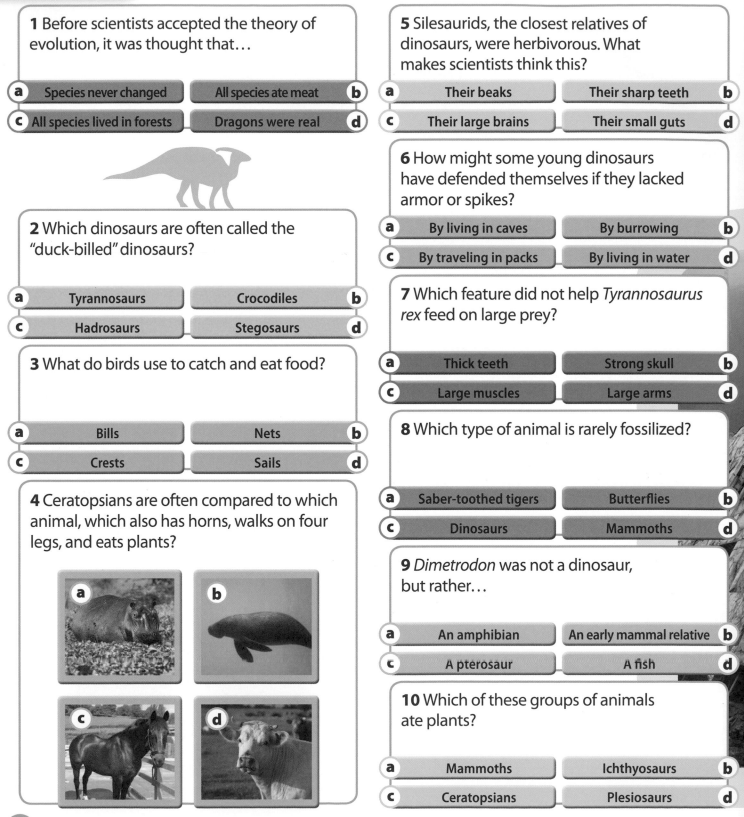

2 Which dinosaurs are often called the "duck-billed" dinosaurs?

a Tyrannosaurs

b Crocodiles

c Hadrosaurs

d Stegosaurs

3 What do birds use to catch and eat food?

a Bills

b Nets

c Crests

d Sails

4 Ceratopsians are often compared to which animal, which also has horns, walks on four legs, and eats plants?

a

b

c

d

5 Silesaurids, the closest relatives of dinosaurs, were herbivorous. What makes scientists think this?

a Their beaks

b Their sharp teeth

c Their large brains

d Their small guts

6 How might some young dinosaurs have defended themselves if they lacked armor or spikes?

a By living in caves

b By burrowing

c By traveling in packs

d By living in water

7 Which feature did not help *Tyrannosaurus rex* feed on large prey?

a Thick teeth

b Strong skull

c Large muscles

d Large arms

8 Which type of animal is rarely fossilized?

a Saber-toothed tigers

b Butterflies

c Dinosaurs

d Mammoths

9 *Dimetrodon* was not a dinosaur, but rather…

a An amphibian

b An early mammal relative

c A pterosaur

d A fish

10 Which of these groups of animals ate plants?

a Mammoths

b Ichthyosaurs

c Ceratopsians

d Plesiosaurs

300,000 fossilized dinosaur **eggs**.

11 Which of the following is not a dinosaur?

a Tyrannosaurus   Brachiosaurus **b**

c Sauropod   Pterosaur **d**

12 What was the body of a mosasaur covered in?

a Dust   Scales **b**

c Feathers   Hair **d**

13 Which of the following is a common type of fossil?

a Arrowhead   Quartz crystal **b**

c Trilobite   Pottery shard **d**

14 Ceratopsians are often called the…

a Swimming dinosaurs   Horned dinosaurs **b**

c Bone-headed dinosaurs   Meat-eating dinosaurs **d**

15 This city has been shaken by an earthquake. An earthquake occurs when…

a It rains   It snows **b**

c It is dark   Rocks move **d**

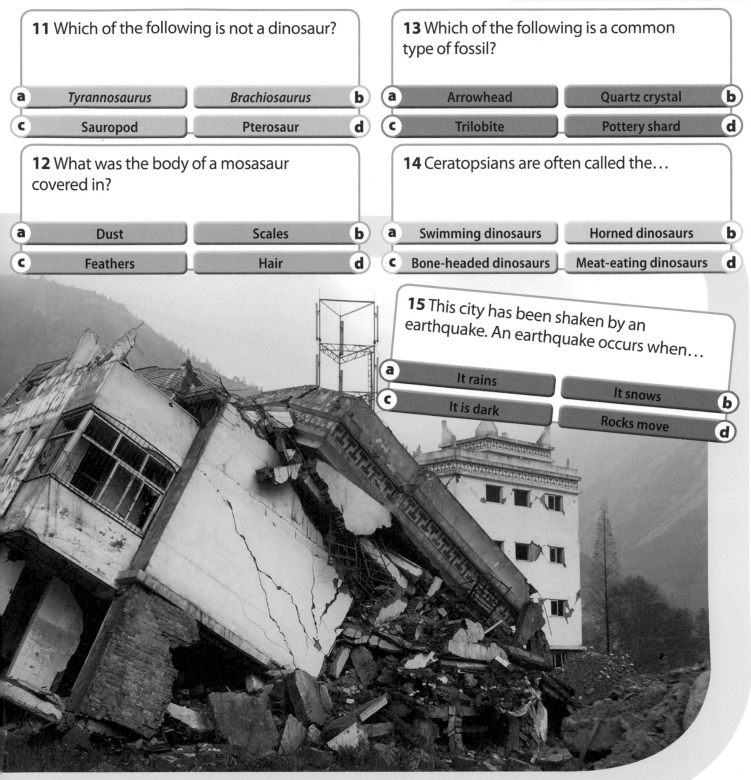

Epidexipteryx used a **long** third **finger** to

1 There are two major subgroups of ankylosaurs, the Ankylosauridae and the…

a Hadrosauridae	Brachiosauridae **b**	
c Nodosauridae	Spinosauridae **d**	

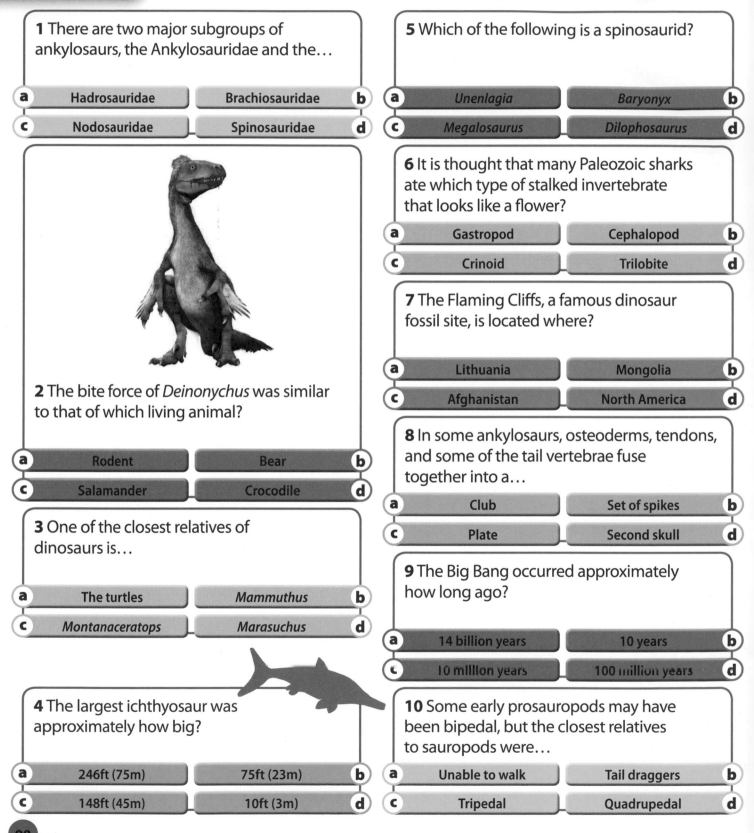

2 The bite force of *Deinonychus* was similar to that of which living animal?

a Rodent	Bear **b**	
c Salamander	Crocodile **d**	

3 One of the closest relatives of dinosaurs is…

a The turtles	*Mammuthus* **b**	
c *Montanaceratops*	*Marasuchus* **d**	

4 The largest ichthyosaur was approximately how big?

a 246ft (75m)	75ft (23m) **b**	
c 148ft (45m)	10ft (3m) **d**	

5 Which of the following is a spinosaurid?

a *Unenlagia*	*Baryonyx* **b**	
c *Megalosaurus*	*Dilophosaurus* **d**	

6 It is thought that many Paleozoic sharks ate which type of stalked invertebrate that looks like a flower?

a Gastropod	Cephalopod **b**	
c Crinoid	Trilobite **d**	

7 The Flaming Cliffs, a famous dinosaur fossil site, is located where?

a Lithuania	Mongolia **b**	
c Afghanistan	North America **d**	

8 In some ankylosaurs, osteoderms, tendons, and some of the tail vertebrae fuse together into a…

a Club	Set of spikes **b**	
c Plate	Second skull **d**	

9 The Big Bang occurred approximately how long ago?

a 14 billion years	10 years **b**	
c 10 million years	100 million years **d**	

10 Some early prosauropods may have been bipedal, but the closest relatives to sauropods were…

a Unable to walk	Tail draggers **b**	
c Tripedal	Quadrupedal **d**	

extract **bugs** from tree crevices.

11 Which dinosaur was discovered after a forest fire, as reflected in its name?

a Megaraptor
b Orkoraptor
c Pyroraptor
d Unenlagia

12 Which of the following is a major fault in Earth's crust?

a New York
b Russian
c Cenozoic
d San Andreas

13 Which of these is a genus of mosasaur?

a Tylosaurus
b Deinosuchus
c Carcharodontosaurus
d Quetzalcoatlus

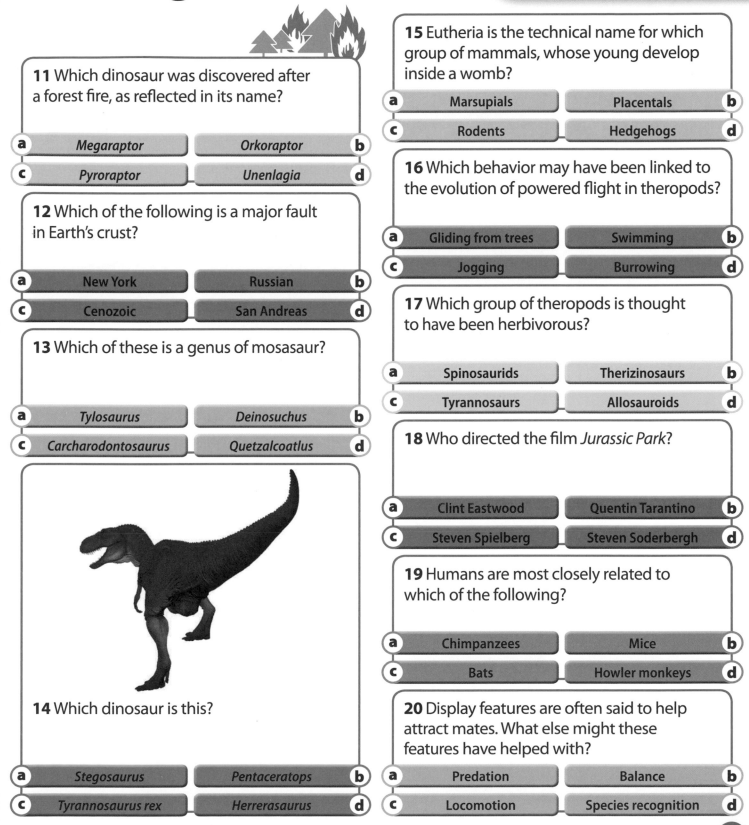

14 Which dinosaur is this?

a Stegosaurus
b Pentaceratops
c Tyrannosaurus rex
d Herrerasaurus

15 Eutheria is the technical name for which group of mammals, whose young develop inside a womb?

a Marsupials
b Placentals
c Rodents
d Hedgehogs

16 Which behavior may have been linked to the evolution of powered flight in theropods?

a Gliding from trees
b Swimming
c Jogging
d Burrowing

17 Which group of theropods is thought to have been herbivorous?

a Spinosaurids
b Therizinosaurs
c Tyrannosaurs
d Allosauroids

18 Who directed the film *Jurassic Park*?

a Clint Eastwood
b Quentin Tarantino
c Steven Spielberg
d Steven Soderbergh

19 Humans are most closely related to which of the following?

a Chimpanzees
b Mice
c Bats
d Howler monkeys

20 Display features are often said to help attract mates. What else might these features have helped with?

a Predation
b Balance
c Locomotion
d Species recognition

The **oldest dinosaur** types are about

1 Which of these is a specific habitat or lifestyle that an organism is well adapted to?

- **a** Preference
- **b** Ecology
- **c** Niche
- **d** Home base

2 The "heyday" of the ichthyosaurs, when they were most common and diverse, was…

- **a** Middle Devonian
- **b** Early Jurassic
- **c** Late Cretaceous
- **d** Middle Triassic

3 *Duriavenator* and *Duriatitan* are named after an ancient name of which British county?

- **a** Somerset
- **b** Flanders
- **c** Yorkshire
- **d** Dorset

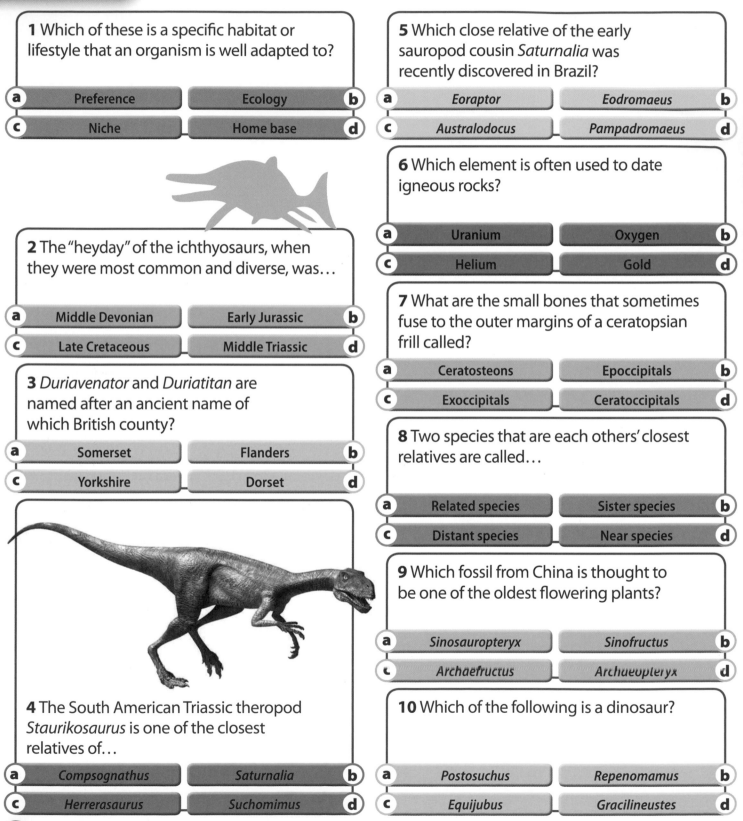

4 The South American Triassic theropod *Staurikosaurus* is one of the closest relatives of…

- **a** Compsognathus
- **b** Saturnalia
- **c** Herrerasaurus
- **d** Suchomimus

5 Which close relative of the early sauropod cousin *Saturnalia* was recently discovered in Brazil?

- **a** *Eoraptor*
- **b** *Eodromaeus*
- **c** *Australodocus*
- **d** *Pampadromaeus*

6 Which element is often used to date igneous rocks?

- **a** Uranium
- **b** Oxygen
- **c** Helium
- **d** Gold

7 What are the small bones that sometimes fuse to the outer margins of a ceratopsian frill called?

- **a** Ceratosteons
- **b** Epoccipitals
- **c** Exoccipitals
- **d** Ceratoccipitals

8 Two species that are each others' closest relatives are called…

- **a** Related species
- **b** Sister species
- **c** Distant species
- **d** Near species

9 Which fossil from China is thought to be one of the oldest flowering plants?

- **a** *Sinosauropteryx*
- **b** *Sinofructus*
- **c** *Archaefructus*
- **d** *Archaeopteryx*

10 Which of the following is a dinosaur?

- **a** *Postosuchus*
- **b** *Repenomamus*
- **c** *Equijubus*
- **d** *Gracilineustes*

230 million years old.

11 Which feature may have helped some theropods feed on large prey?

a Fusion of jaw symphysis | Jaws that could open wide b
c Extra teeth on the palate | Ability to suction feed d

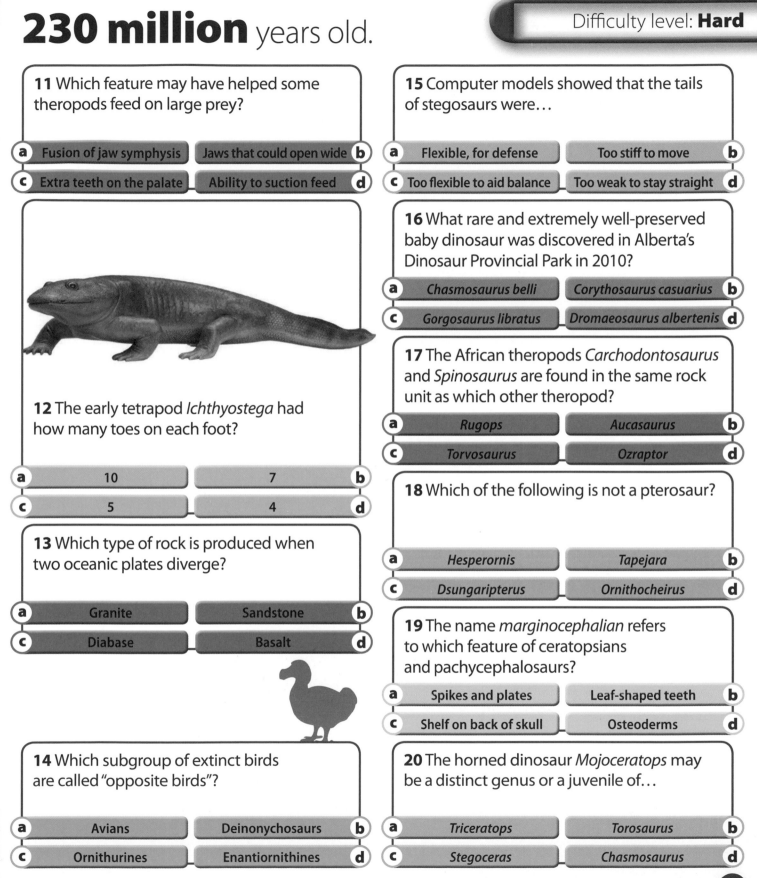

12 The early tetrapod *Ichthyostega* had how many toes on each foot?

a 10 | 7 b
c 5 | 4 d

13 Which type of rock is produced when two oceanic plates diverge?

a Granite | Sandstone b
c Diabase | Basalt d

14 Which subgroup of extinct birds are called "opposite birds"?

a Avians | Deinonychosaurs b
c Ornithurines | Enantiornithines d

15 Computer models showed that the tails of stegosaurs were…

a Flexible, for defense | Too stiff to move b
c Too flexible to aid balance | Too weak to stay straight d

16 What rare and extremely well-preserved baby dinosaur was discovered in Alberta's Dinosaur Provincial Park in 2010?

a *Chasmosaurus belli* | *Corythosaurus casuarius* b
c *Gorgosaurus libratus* | *Dromaeosaurus albertenis* d

17 The African theropods *Carchodontosaurus* and *Spinosaurus* are found in the same rock unit as which other theropod?

a *Rugops* | *Aucasaurus* b
c *Torvosaurus* | *Ozraptor* d

18 Which of the following is not a pterosaur?

a *Hesperornis* | *Tapejara* b
c *Dsungaripterus* | *Ornithocheirus* d

19 The name *marginocephalian* refers to which feature of ceratopsians and pachycephalosaurs?

a Spikes and plates | Leaf-shaped teeth b
c Shelf on back of skull | Osteoderms d

20 The horned dinosaur *Mojoceratops* may be a distinct genus or a juvenile of…

a *Triceratops* | *Torosaurus* b
c *Stegoceras* | *Chasmosaurus* d

It took **30 years** for a **sauropod**

1 What feature do birds often use for attracting mates?

a Colorful feathers	Sharp teeth **b**
c Tail spikes	Back plates **d**

2 Stegosaurs were…

a Herbivores	Carnivores **b**
c Omnivores	Scavengers **d**

4 Which type of fossil is often found alongside the bones of plant-eating dinosaurs?

a Seashells	Starfish **b**
c Teeth of meat-eaters	Trilobites **d**

5 Which of the following is one of Earth's layers?

a Core	Skin **b**
c Muscle	Volcano **d**

3 This is the head of a *Giganotosaurus*. How long do experts think its skull was?

a 6ft (1.8m)	10ft (3m) **b**
c 16ft (5m)	33ft (10m) **d**

6 Which of the following was not a mosasaur?

a	*Clidastes*	*Stegosaurus*	**b**
c	*Mosasaurus*	*Platecarpus*	**d**

7 Amphibians lay their eggs...

a	In trees	On mountains	**b**
c	In water	On land	**d**

8 Which dinosaurs are often called the "horned and frilled" dinosaurs?

a	Theropods	Birds	**b**
c	Ceratopsians	Stegosaurs	**d**

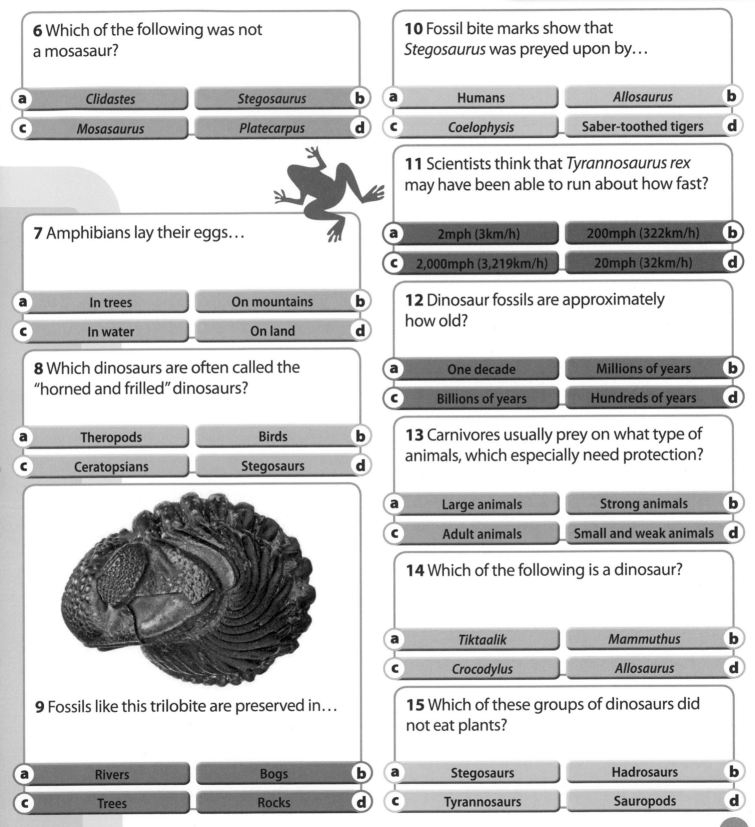

9 Fossils like this trilobite are preserved in...

a	Rivers	Bogs	**b**
c	Trees	Rocks	**d**

10 Fossil bite marks show that *Stegosaurus* was preyed upon by...

a	Humans	*Allosaurus*	**b**
c	*Coelophysis*	Saber-toothed tigers	**d**

11 Scientists think that *Tyrannosaurus rex* may have been able to run about how fast?

a	2mph (3km/h)	200mph (322km/h)	**b**
c	2,000mph (3,219km/h)	20mph (32km/h)	**d**

12 Dinosaur fossils are approximately how old?

a	One decade	Millions of years	**b**
c	Billions of years	Hundreds of years	**d**

13 Carnivores usually prey on what type of animals, which especially need protection?

a	Large animals	Strong animals	**b**
c	Adult animals	Small and weak animals	**d**

14 Which of the following is a dinosaur?

a	*Tiktaalik*	*Mammuthus*	**b**
c	*Crocodylus*	*Allosaurus*	**d**

15 Which of these groups of dinosaurs did not eat plants?

a	Stegosaurs	Hadrosaurs	**b**
c	Tyrannosaurs	Sauropods	**d**

Scientists have now **named** more

1 Which scientist proposed that an asteroid caused the dinosaur extinction?

- **a** Luis Alvarez
- **b** Charles Darwin
- **c** Stephen Hawking
- **d** Isaac Newton

2 What is the name given to someone who studies dinosaurs?

- **a** Entomologist
- **b** Meteorologist
- **c** Paleontologist
- **d** Zoologist

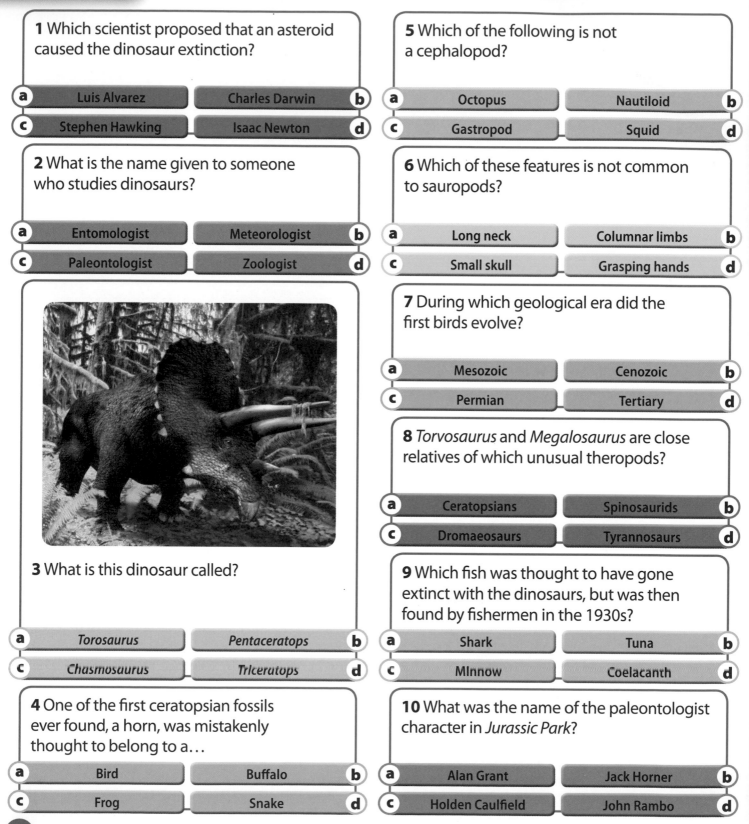

3 What is this dinosaur called?

- **a** *Torosaurus*
- **b** *Pentaceratops*
- **c** *Chasmosaurus*
- **d** *Triceratops*

4 One of the first ceratopsian fossils ever found, a horn, was mistakenly thought to belong to a…

- **a** Bird
- **b** Buffalo
- **c** Frog
- **d** Snake

5 Which of the following is not a cephalopod?

- **a** Octopus
- **b** Nautiloid
- **c** Gastropod
- **d** Squid

6 Which of these features is not common to sauropods?

- **a** Long neck
- **b** Columnar limbs
- **c** Small skull
- **d** Grasping hands

7 During which geological era did the first birds evolve?

- **a** Mesozoic
- **b** Cenozoic
- **c** Permian
- **d** Tertiary

8 *Torvosaurus* and *Megalosaurus* are close relatives of which unusual theropods?

- **a** Ceratopsians
- **b** Spinosaurids
- **c** Dromaeosaurs
- **d** Tyrannosaurs

9 Which fish was thought to have gone extinct with the dinosaurs, but was then found by fishermen in the 1930s?

- **a** Shark
- **b** Tuna
- **c** Minnow
- **d** Coelacanth

10 What was the name of the paleontologist character in *Jurassic Park*?

- **a** Alan Grant
- **b** Jack Horner
- **c** Holden Caulfield
- **d** John Rambo

11 The stubby forelimbs of alvarezsaurs may have been used to rip open logs to feed on which animals?

a Insects   **b** Frogs

c Bats   **d** Gastropods

12 Which primitive cousin of ankylosaurs had a series of small, oval-shaped osteoderms along its flanks?

a *Scelidosaurus*   **b** *Heterodontosaurus*

c *Hypsilophodon*   **d** *Orodromeus*

13 The oldest known dinosaur fossils are from…

a Hungary   **b** Argentina

c China   **d** United States

14 Which famous French scientist determined that mosasaurs were reptiles and not fish?

a Sébastien Steyer   **b** Ronan Allain

c Romain Amiot   **d** Georges Cuvier

15 The oldest known rocks on Earth are how old?

a 1 billion years   **b** 100 million years

c 1 million years   **d** 4 billion years

16 *Albertonykus* and *Albertosaurus* are both named after…

a Alberton, North Dakota   **b** Allemagne

c Alberta, Canada   **d** Albert Prieto-Marquez

17 Fossils of *Archaeopteryx* are well preserved because they formed in a…

a Delta   **b** Mountain stream

c Lagoon   **d** Desert

18 Which small dinosaur was named after a furry mammal?

a *Pugtyrant*   **b** *Mussaurus*

c *Ratoraptor*   **d** *Catlong*

19 Just like their mammalian descendants, extinct species of cynodonts are thought to have possessed…

a Uniform teeth   **b** Hair

c Night vision   **d** The ability to fly

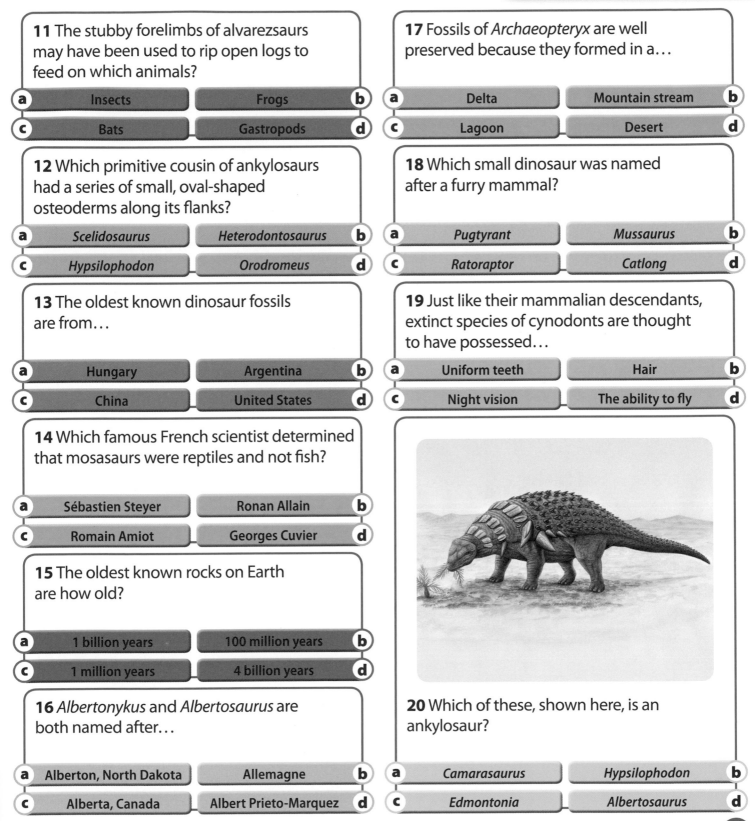

20 Which of these, shown here, is an ankylosaur?

a *Camarasaurus*   **b** *Hypsilophodon*

c *Edmontonia*   **d** *Albertosaurus*

Stegosaurus had a **brain**

1 Which South African genus is one of the oldest true sauropods ever found?

- **a** *Antetonitrus*
- **b** *Apatosaurus*
- **c** *Paludititan*
- **d** *Rapetosaurus*

2 The name Plesiosauria comes from which Greek term?

- **a** Near to lizard
- **b** Swimming lizard
- **c** Lightweight lizard
- **d** Obese lizard

3 In which ceratopsian was the nasal horn replaced by a thick, gnarly pad?

- **a** *Pentaceratops*
- **b** *Pachyrhinosaurus*
- **c** *Triceratops*
- **d** *Chasmosaurus*

4 Which scientist developed the now-rejected idea of inheritance of acquired characters?

- **a** Michael LaBarbera
- **b** Jean-Baptiste Lamarck
- **c** Charles Darwin
- **d** O. C. Marsh

5 How many layers make up Earth's atmosphere?

- **a** 2
- **b** 10
- **c** 4
- **d** 1

6 The duck-billed dinosaur *Gilshades ericksoni* is named after which paleontologist?

- **a** Erick Gregory
- **b** Gil Gualda
- **c** Shadi Gilman
- **d** Gregory Erickson

7 Which famous Devonian fossil assemblage has preserved specimens of early plants?

- **a** Solnhofen Limestone
- **b** Stonesfield Slate
- **c** Francis Creek Shale
- **d** Rhynie Chert

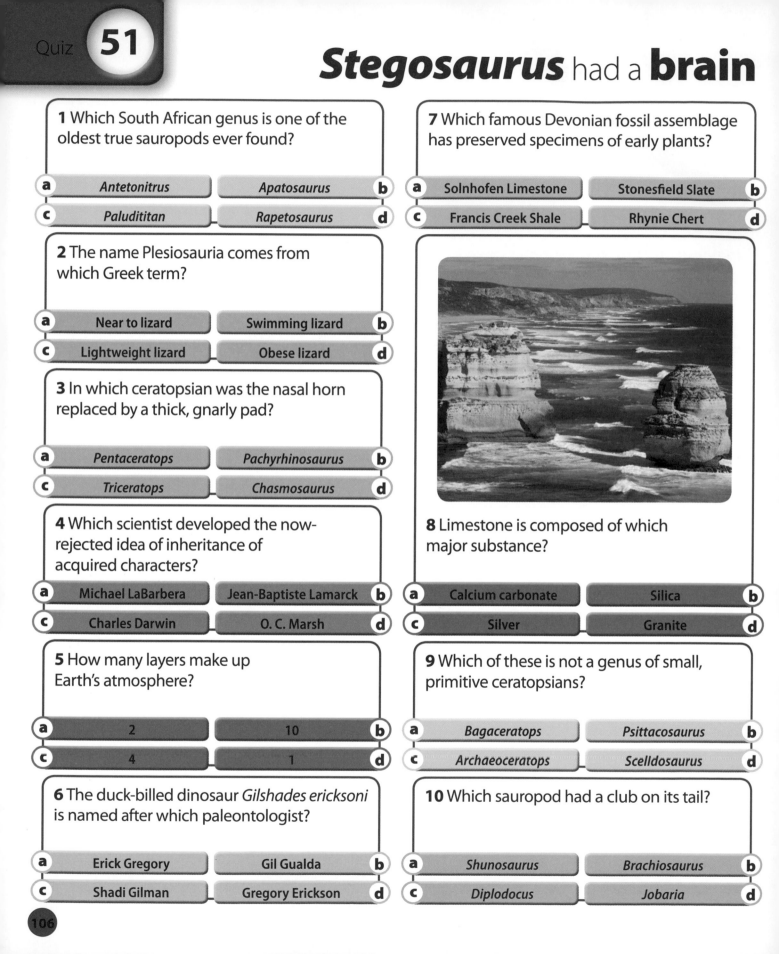

8 Limestone is composed of which major substance?

- **a** Calcium carbonate
- **b** Silica
- **c** Silver
- **d** Granite

9 Which of these is not a genus of small, primitive ceratopsians?

- **a** *Bagaceratops*
- **b** *Psittacosaurus*
- **c** *Archaeoceratops*
- **d** *Scelldosaurus*

10 Which sauropod had a club on its tail?

- **a** *Shunosaurus*
- **b** *Brachiosaurus*
- **c** *Diplodocus*
- **d** *Jobaria*

the **size** of a **walnut**.

11 Which of the following is not a dinosaur?

a *Caudipteryx*	*Barsboldia* **b**
c *Tyrannoneustes*	*Saturnalia* **d**

12 The Jurassic genus *Chunerpeton* from China is a fossil member of which group?

a Lizards	Turtles **b**
c Salamanders	Frogs **d**

13 Which scientist created the modern method for building genealogical trees?

a Willi Hennig	Carl Linnaeus **b**
c Steve Jobs	Steve Wang **d**

14 What effect did elongate prezygapophyses in the lower part of the spine have on some theropods?

a Armor plates	Large neural canal **b**
c Stiffened tails	Fused skin **d**

15 Which mammal-like creatures, some of the closest relatives of living mammals, lived during the Mesozoic?

a Condylarths	Tritylodonts **b**
c Gorgonopsians	Taeniodonts **d**

16 What is a gap of missing time in a unit of rocks called?

a Conformity	Extinction **b**
c Elimination	Unconformity **d**

17 Scientists think that most ornithischians had…

a Five-chambered hearts	Large biceps **b**
c Cheeks	Night vision **d**

18 Which tyrannosaur is unique in having a long snout?

a *Dryptosaurus*	*Alioramus* **b**
c *Tarbosaurus*	*Albertosaurus* **d**

19 Which dinosaur is named after a famous Roman general?

a *Berlusconirex*	*Scipionyx* **b**
c *Caesarsaurus*	*Markantonyus* **d**

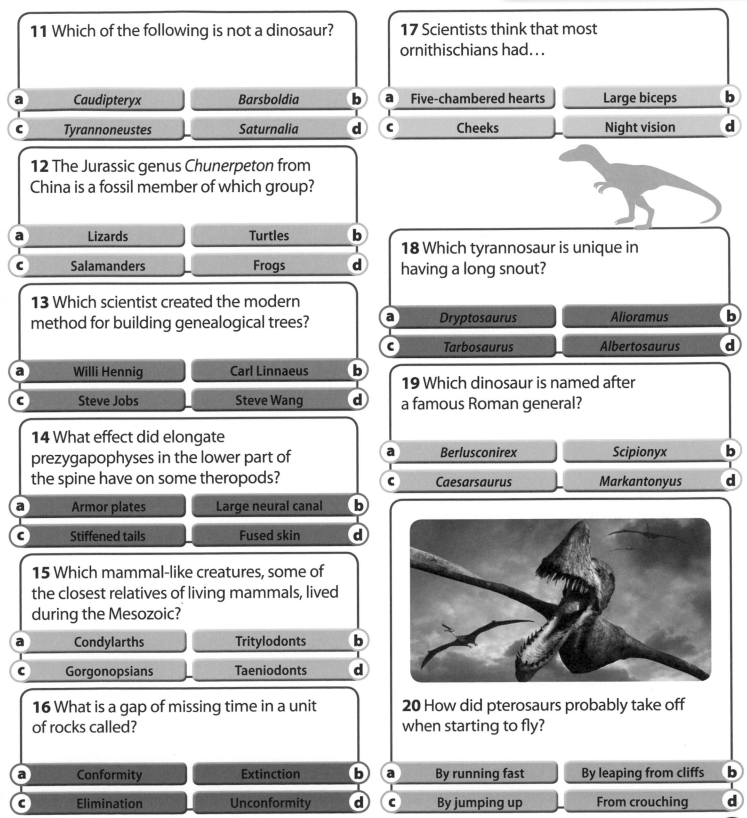

20 How did pterosaurs probably take off when starting to fly?

a By running fast	By leaping from cliffs **b**
c By jumping up	From crouching **d**

The **earliest fossils** are of bacteria-like

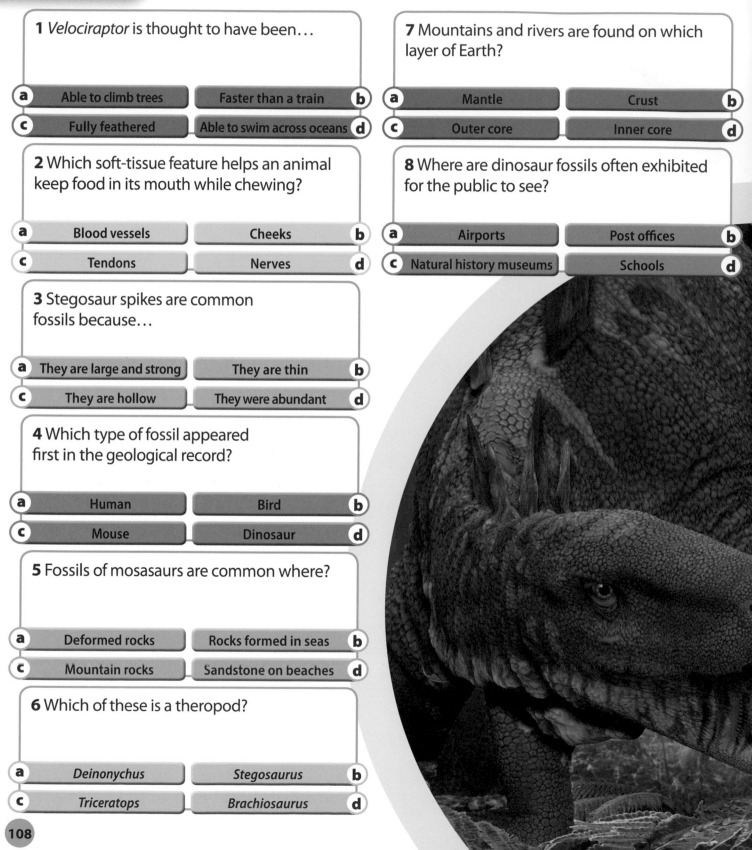

1 *Velociraptor* is thought to have been…

a Able to climb trees
b Faster than a train
c Fully feathered
d Able to swim across oceans

2 Which soft-tissue feature helps an animal keep food in its mouth while chewing?

a Blood vessels
b Cheeks
c Tendons
d Nerves

3 Stegosaur spikes are common fossils because…

a They are large and strong
b They are thin
c They are hollow
d They were abundant

4 Which type of fossil appeared first in the geological record?

a Human
b Bird
c Mouse
d Dinosaur

5 Fossils of mosasaurs are common where?

a Deformed rocks
b Rocks formed in seas
c Mountain rocks
d Sandstone on beaches

6 Which of these is a theropod?

a *Deinonychus*
b *Stegosaurus*
c *Triceratops*
d *Brachiosaurus*

7 Mountains and rivers are found on which layer of Earth?

a Mantle
b Crust
c Outer core
d Inner core

8 Where are dinosaur fossils often exhibited for the public to see?

a Airports
b Post offices
c Natural history museums
d Schools

cells, **3.5 billion** years old.

9 Phytosaurs were long-snouted Triassic predators that lived near water. Which living animals did they resemble?

a Birds

b Marsupials

c Salamanders

d Crocodiles

10 Ankylosaurs probably moved…

a As fast as a sprinter

b By flying

c Very slowly

d By leaping

11 What is the name of this dinosaur, which is famous for the plates along its back?

a Diplodocus

b Stegosaurus

c Tyrannosaurus rex

d Allosaurus

12 In a scene from the film *Jurassic Park,* what does the *Tyrannosaurus rex* do that is unrealistic?

a Chase a fast-moving jeep

b Eat meat

c Walk on two legs

d Breathe through its nostrils

13 Which of the following types of fossils can usually only be seen under a microscope?

a Bacteria

b Dinosaur bone

c Feather

d Teeth

14 *Archaeopteryx's* claim to fame is that it…

a Had the longest neck

b Was the fastest animal

c Was the biggest dinosaur

d Is the oldest known bird

15 What feature of the skeleton did hadrosaurs use to eat plants?

a Head crest

b Large nostrils

c Shearing teeth

d Ducklike beak

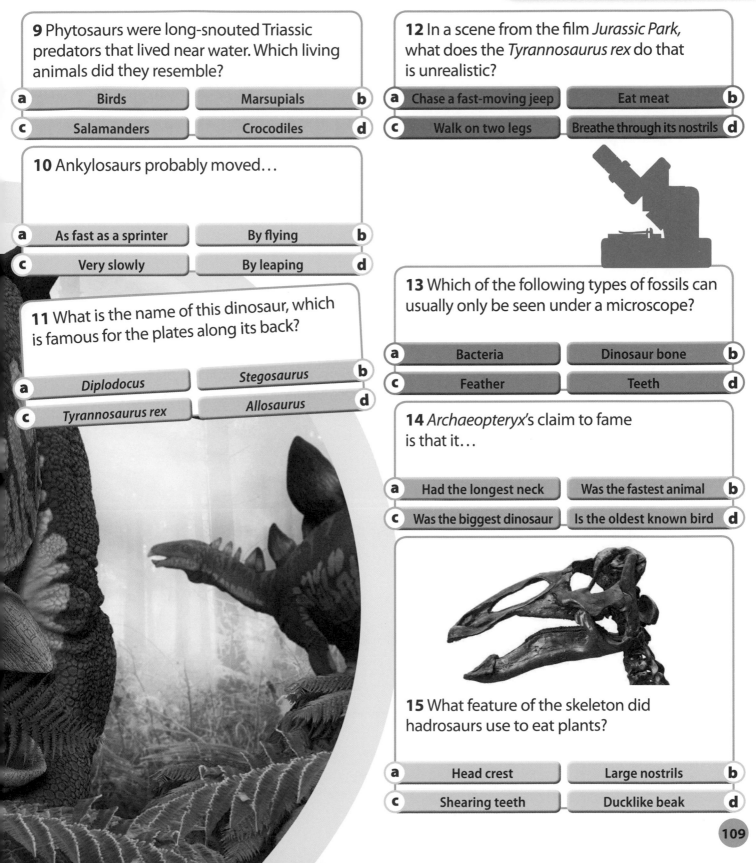

More than **7,000** dinosaur **bones**

1 Which direct type of fossil evidence tells scientists that the ankylosaur *Minmi* was a herbivore?

- **a** Bone structure
- **b** Skull anatomy
- **c** Fossil gut contents
- **d** Fossil bite marks

2 Which mountains formed when India collided with Asia?

- **a** Rocky Mountains
- **b** Alps
- **c** Atlas Mountains
- **d** Himalayas

3 The common ancestor of all mammals was probably about the size of…

- **a** *Tyrannosaurus*
- **b** A mouse
- **c** A dog
- **d** A rhinoceros

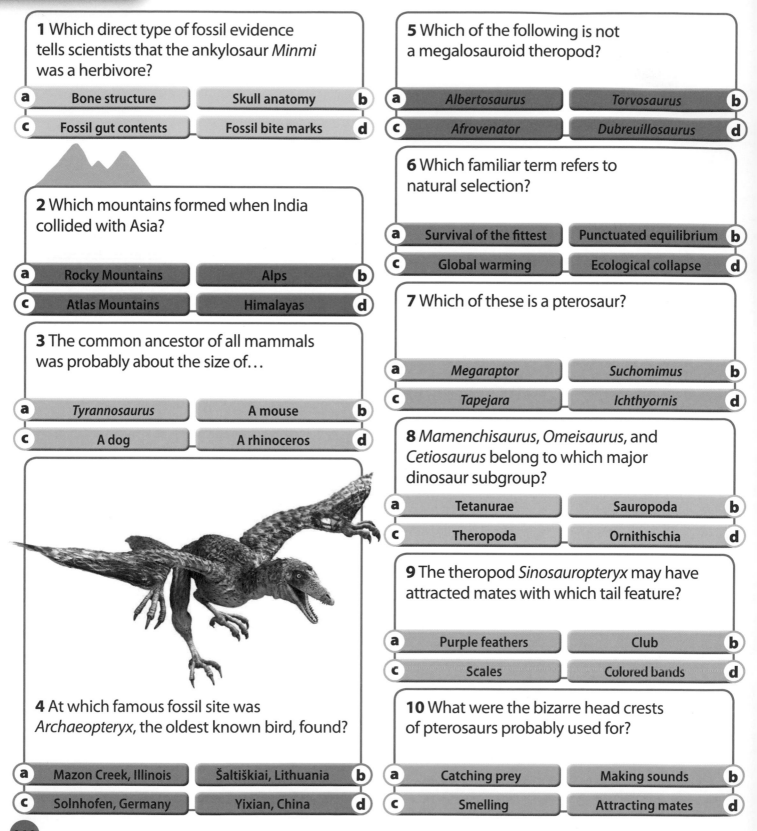

4 At which famous fossil site was *Archaeopteryx*, the oldest known bird, found?

- **a** Mazon Creek, Illinois
- **b** Šaltiškiai, Lithuania
- **c** Solnhofen, Germany
- **d** Yixian, China

5 Which of the following is not a megalosauroid theropod?

- **a** *Albertosaurus*
- **b** *Torvosaurus*
- **c** *Afrovenator*
- **d** *Dubreuillosaurus*

6 Which familiar term refers to natural selection?

- **a** Survival of the fittest
- **b** Punctuated equilibrium
- **c** Global warming
- **d** Ecological collapse

7 Which of these is a pterosaur?

- **a** *Megaraptor*
- **b** *Suchomimus*
- **c** *Tapejara*
- **d** *Ichthyornis*

8 *Mamenchisaurus*, *Omeisaurus*, and *Cetiosaurus* belong to which major dinosaur subgroup?

- **a** Tetanurae
- **b** Sauropoda
- **c** Theropoda
- **d** Ornithischia

9 The theropod *Sinosauropteryx* may have attracted mates with which tail feature?

- **a** Purple feathers
- **b** Club
- **c** Scales
- **d** Colored bands

10 What were the bizarre head crests of pterosaurs probably used for?

- **a** Catching prey
- **b** Making sounds
- **c** Smelling
- **d** Attracting mates

11 Which stegosaur had a series of spikes along its back, instead of broad plates like *Stegosaurus*?

a *Kentrosaurus*

b *Monkonosaurus*

c *Edmontonia*

d *Eotyrannus*

12 Which group of dinosaurs were the largest creatures ever to walk the earth?

a Hadrosaurids

b Ceratopsians

c Mosasaurs

d Sauropods

13 Which of these is not generally required for life to exist?

a Water

b Company

c Light

d Heat

14 Compared to other dinosaurs, sauropods had large…

a Heads

b Brains

c Jaws

d Guts

15 What refers to the use of minerals to date rocks?

a Radiometric dating

b Speed dating

c Ecology

d Geology

16 *Australovenator* was discovered in…

a Austral, Canada

b Sierra Leone

c Australia

d Austin, Texas

17 What led scientists to hypothesize that some ornithomimosaurian theropods were herbivores?

a Peglike teeth

b Stomach stones

c Bite marks

d Soft tissues

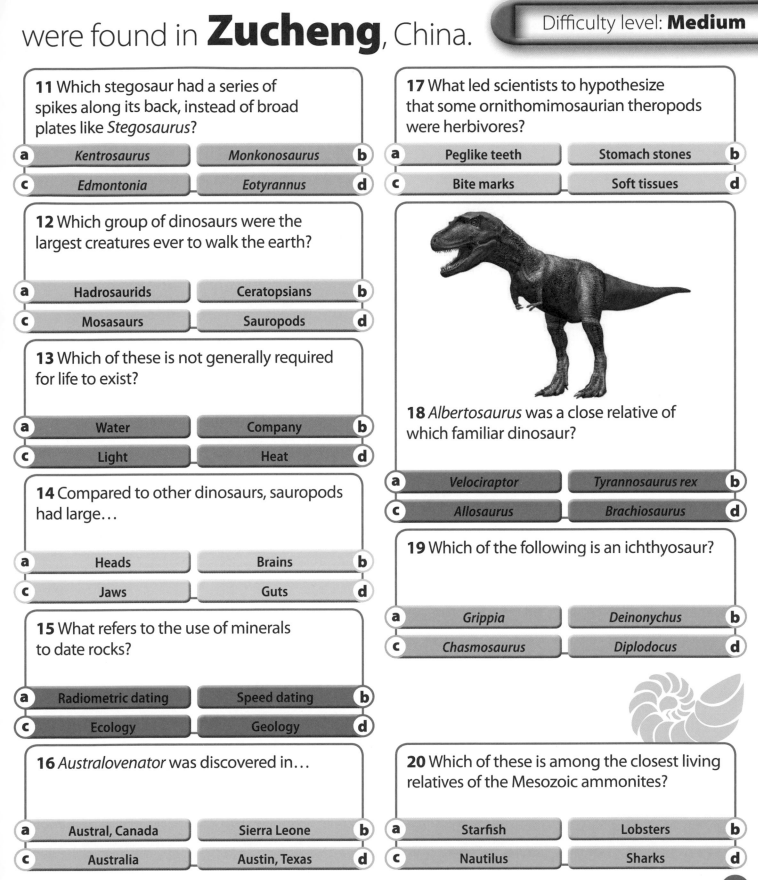

18 *Albertosaurus* was a close relative of which familiar dinosaur?

a *Velociraptor*

b *Tyrannosaurus rex*

c *Allosaurus*

d *Brachiosaurus*

19 Which of the following is an ichthyosaur?

a *Grippia*

b *Deinonychus*

c *Chasmosaurus*

d *Diplodocus*

20 Which of these is among the closest living relatives of the Mesozoic ammonites?

a Starfish

b Lobsters

c Nautilus

d Sharks

Azhdarchids, the biggest pterosaurs,

1 Isotopic studies have suggested that the frill of ceratopsians was useful for…

a Detecting predators	Releasing excess heat **b**
c Swimming	Echolocation **d**

2 Which finger of the hand was elongated to help support the wing membrane of pterosaurs?

a Fourth	First **b**
c Sixth	Eighth **d**

3 Several specimens of duck-billed dinosaurs have been found with preserved…

a Brains	Hearts **b**
c Skin	Nerves **d**

4 Earth's core is made up of how many layers?

a 2	1 **b**
c 5	13 **d**

5 The extinction of many plant species at the Permian-Triassic boundary resulted in what?

a Evolution of grasses	Evolution of dinosaurs **b**
c Coal gap in fossil record	Total extinction of ferns **d**

6 *Iguanacolossus* is a close relative of…

a Iguanas	*Colossaurus* **b**
c *Iguanasaurus*	*Iguanodon* **d**

7 A large set of stomach stones, which are used together to digest plants, is called a…

a Gastrolith bunch	Gizzard **b**
c Crop	Gastric mill **d**

8 Many ceratosaurs share which feature?

a Enlarged nostrils	Stubby forelimbs **b**
c Fusion of pelvic bones	Scythelike claws **d**

9 The flippers of most plesiosaurs are…

a Made of long fingernails	Large and paddlelike **b**
c Small and circular	Lacking bones **d**

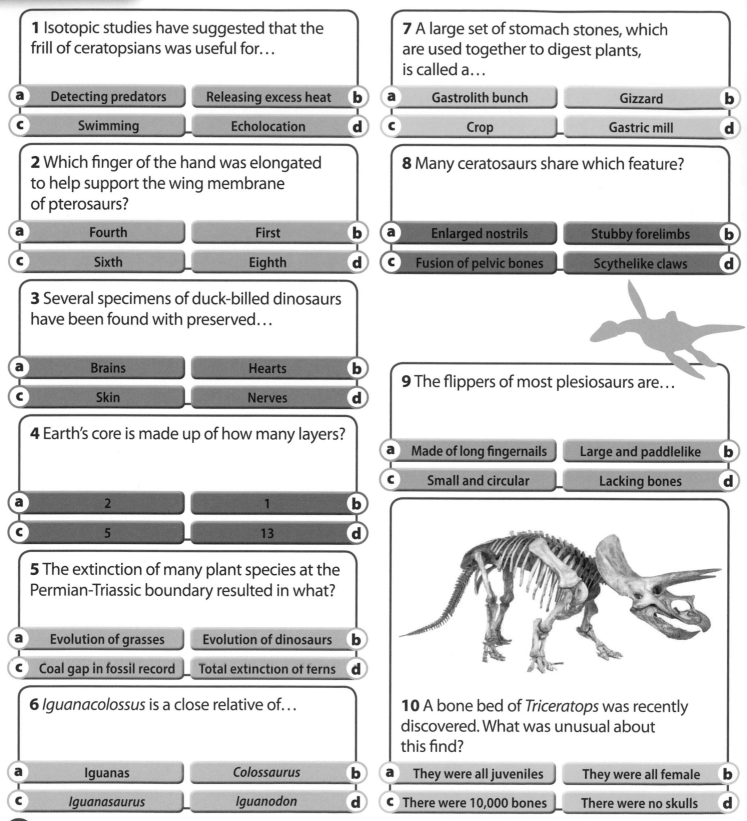

10 A bone bed of *Triceratops* was recently discovered. What was unusual about this find?

a They were all juveniles	They were all female **b**
c There were 10,000 bones	There were no skulls **d**

liked to **walk** as well as **fly**.

11 The closest relatives of the carnivorous dinosaurs are…

a Pterosaurs
b Sauropods
c Triceratops
d Stegosaurs

12 Which type of rock do glaciers leave behind when they melt?

a Mudstone
b Chert
c Blocks
d Erratics

13 A close relative of *Tyrannosaurus* is…

a Camposaurus
b Telmatosaurus
c Alioramus
d Chindesaurus

14 What is the term for chemical residues that are left by an ancient organism and can be studied by scientists?

a Biomarkers
b Liquid fossils
c Water fossils
d Chemicofossils

15 The Early Cretaceous European theropod *Neovenator* lived alongside…

a Archaeopteryx
b Eotyrannus
c Balaur
d Hesperornis

16 Which species of dromaeosaur was originally identified as a bird when it was found?

a Deinonychus
b Sinovenator
c Syntarsus
d Rahonavis

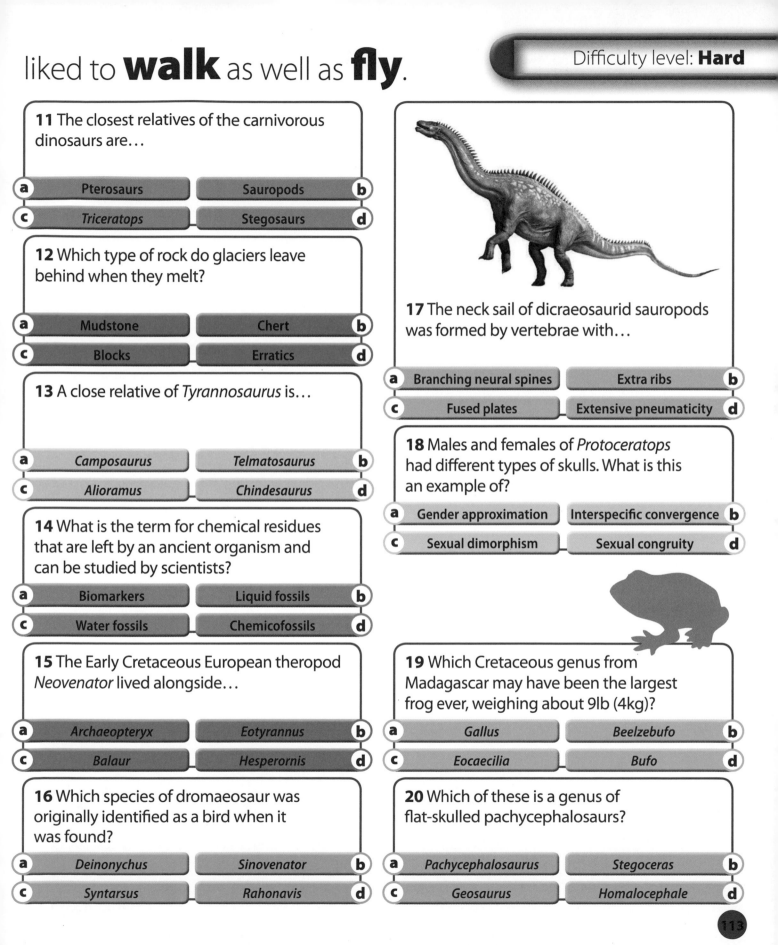

17 The neck sail of dicraeosaurid sauropods was formed by vertebrae with…

a Branching neural spines
b Extra ribs
c Fused plates
d Extensive pneumaticity

18 Males and females of *Protoceratops* had different types of skulls. What is this an example of?

a Gender approximation
b Interspecific convergence
c Sexual dimorphism
d Sexual congruity

19 Which Cretaceous genus from Madagascar may have been the largest frog ever, weighing about 9lb (4kg)?

a Gallus
b Beelzebufo
c Eocaecilia
d Bufo

20 Which of these is a genus of flat-skulled pachycephalosaurs?

a Pachycephalosaurus
b Stegoceras
c Geosaurus
d Homalocephale

In the **Mesozoic**, there was **less**

1 Scientists think some dinosaurs used feathers for display. Which bird uses its colorful feathers in this way?

a Sparrow | Peacock b
c Ostrich | Penguin d

2 All theropods walked on how many limbs?

a 6 | 2 b
c 3 | 4 d

3 Which feature of ceratopsians, like this *Einiosaurus*, was not used for feeding on plants?

a Beak | Teeth b
c Gut | Skull horns d

4 *Velociraptor* was no bigger than…

a A horse | An elephant b
c A wolf | A camel d

5 Mosasaurs were the dominant predators in the ocean during which period?

a Silurian | Cretaceous b
c Permian | Devonian d

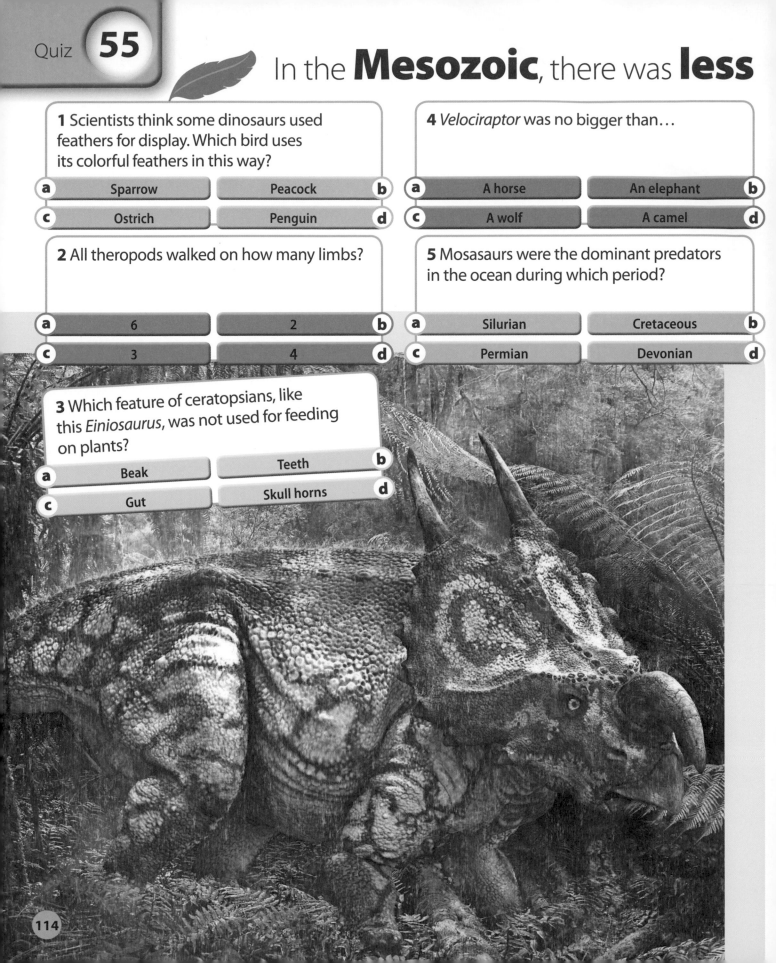

oxygen and **more** carbon dioxide.

6 Which of these is an ornithischian?

a | *Diplodocus*
b | *Homo sapiens*
c | *Stegosaurus*
d | *Tyrannosaurus*

7 Pterosaurs were not dinosaurs. How were they different?

a | They flew
b | They didn't lay eggs
c | They were tiny
d | They lived underwater

8 Which tool do paleontologists use to dig out dinosaur fossils?

a | Computer
b | Rock hammer
c | Microscope
d | Thermometer

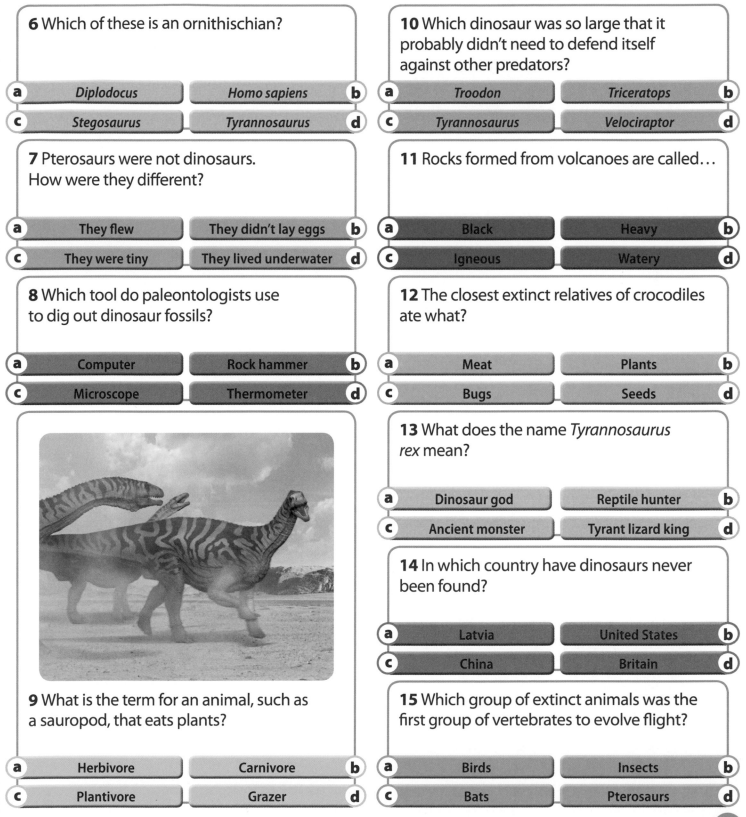

9 What is the term for an animal, such as a sauropod, that eats plants?

a | Herbivore
b | Carnivore
c | Plantivore
d | Grazer

10 Which dinosaur was so large that it probably didn't need to defend itself against other predators?

a | *Troodon*
b | *Triceratops*
c | *Tyrannosaurus*
d | *Velociraptor*

11 Rocks formed from volcanoes are called…

a | Black
b | Heavy
c | Igneous
d | Watery

12 The closest extinct relatives of crocodiles ate what?

a | Meat
b | Plants
c | Bugs
d | Seeds

13 What does the name *Tyrannosaurus rex* mean?

a | Dinosaur god
b | Reptile hunter
c | Ancient monster
d | Tyrant lizard king

14 In which country have dinosaurs never been found?

a | Latvia
b | United States
c | China
d | Britain

15 Which group of extinct animals was the first group of vertebrates to evolve flight?

a | Birds
b | Insects
c | Bats
d | Pterosaurs

A giant **sauropod** could **weigh** as

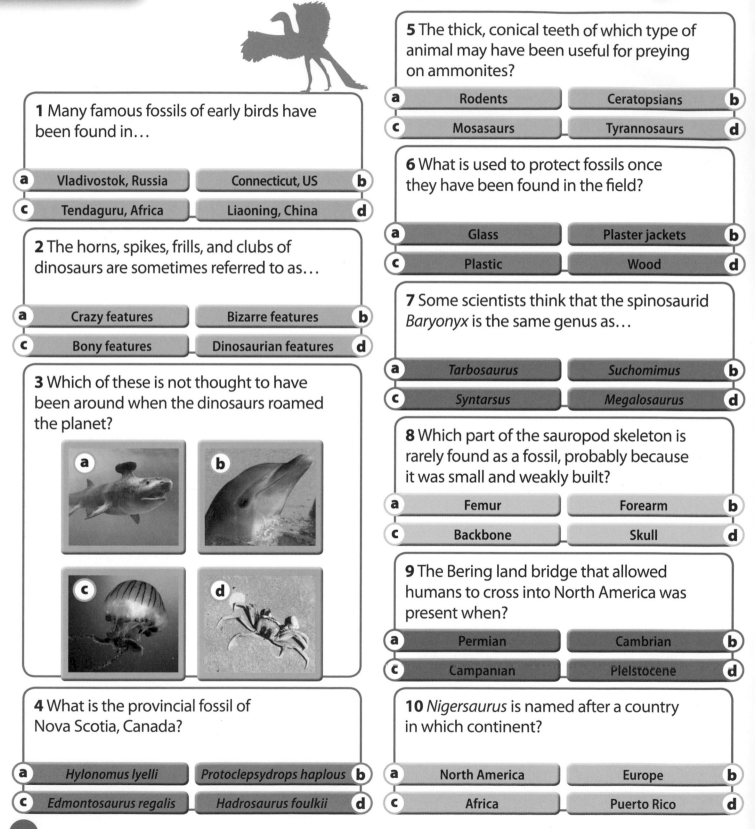

1 Many famous fossils of early birds have been found in…

- **a** Vladivostok, Russia
- **b** Connecticut, US
- **c** Tendaguru, Africa
- **d** Liaoning, China

2 The horns, spikes, frills, and clubs of dinosaurs are sometimes referred to as…

- **a** Crazy features
- **b** Bizarre features
- **c** Bony features
- **d** Dinosaurian features

3 Which of these is not thought to have been around when the dinosaurs roamed the planet?

- **a**
- **b**
- **c**
- **d**

4 What is the provincial fossil of Nova Scotia, Canada?

- **a** *Hylonomus lyelli*
- **b** *Protoclepsydrops haplous*
- **c** *Edmontosaurus regalis*
- **d** *Hadrosaurus foulkii*

5 The thick, conical teeth of which type of animal may have been useful for preying on ammonites?

- **a** Rodents
- **b** Ceratopsians
- **c** Mosasaurs
- **d** Tyrannosaurs

6 What is used to protect fossils once they have been found in the field?

- **a** Glass
- **b** Plaster jackets
- **c** Plastic
- **d** Wood

7 Some scientists think that the spinosaurid *Baryonyx* is the same genus as…

- **a** *Tarbosaurus*
- **b** *Suchomimus*
- **c** *Syntarsus*
- **d** *Megalosaurus*

8 Which part of the sauropod skeleton is rarely found as a fossil, probably because it was small and weakly built?

- **a** Femur
- **b** Forearm
- **c** Backbone
- **d** Skull

9 The Bering land bridge that allowed humans to cross into North America was present when?

- **a** Permian
- **b** Cambrian
- **c** Campanian
- **d** Pleistocene

10 *Nigersaurus* is named after a country in which continent?

- **a** North America
- **b** Europe
- **c** Africa
- **d** Puerto Rico

much as **13 elephants**.

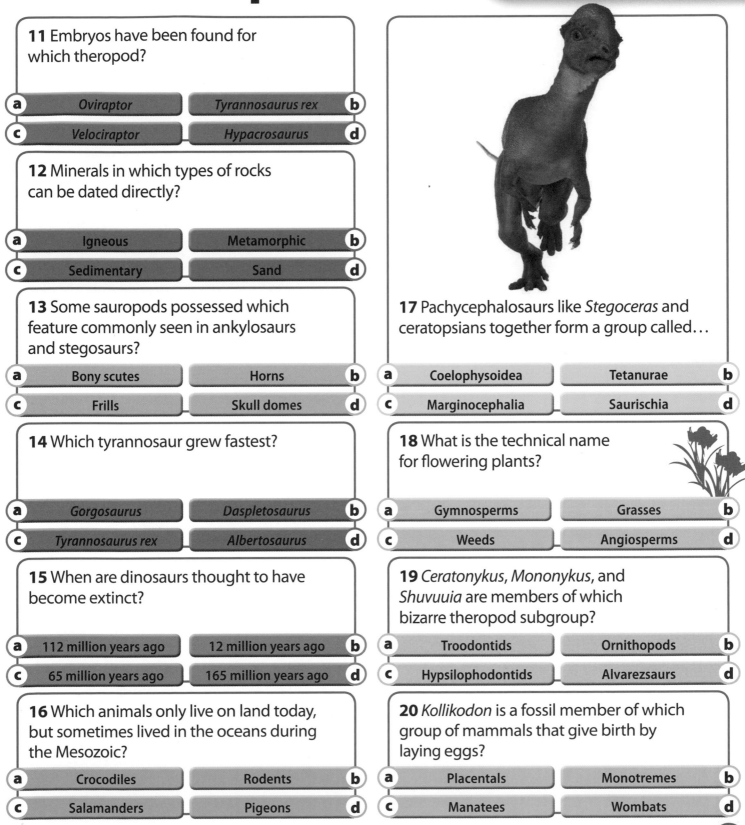

11 Embryos have been found for which theropod?

a *Oviraptor*

b *Tyrannosaurus rex*

c *Velociraptor*

d *Hypacrosaurus*

12 Minerals in which types of rocks can be dated directly?

a Igneous

b Metamorphic

c Sedimentary

d Sand

13 Some sauropods possessed which feature commonly seen in ankylosaurs and stegosaurs?

a Bony scutes

b Horns

c Frills

d Skull domes

14 Which tyrannosaur grew fastest?

a *Gorgosaurus*

b *Daspletosaurus*

c *Tyrannosaurus rex*

d *Albertosaurus*

15 When are dinosaurs thought to have become extinct?

a 112 million years ago

b 12 million years ago

c 65 million years ago

d 165 million years ago

16 Which animals only live on land today, but sometimes lived in the oceans during the Mesozoic?

a Crocodiles

b Rodents

c Salamanders

d Pigeons

17 Pachycephalosaurs like *Stegoceras* and ceratopsians together form a group called…

a Coelophysoidea

b Tetanurae

c Marginocephalia

d Saurischia

18 What is the technical name for flowering plants?

a Gymnosperms

b Grasses

c Weeds

d Angiosperms

19 *Ceratonykus, Mononykus*, and *Shuvuuia* are members of which bizarre theropod subgroup?

a Troodontids

b Ornithopods

c Hypsilophodontids

d Alvarezsaurs

20 *Kollikodon* is a fossil member of which group of mammals that give birth by laying eggs?

a Placentals

b Monotremes

c Manatees

d Wombats

Small **plesiosaurs** probably crawled to

1 *Amargasaurus*, a small sauropod with tall spines on its neck and back, is a member of which subgroup?

- **a** Dicraeosauridae
- **b** Shunosauridae
- **c** Titanosauria
- **d** Brachiosauridae

2 The common Mesozoic plant genus *Araucaria* is better known as…

- **a** Oak
- **b** Poison ivy
- **c** Fig
- **d** Monkey puzzle tree

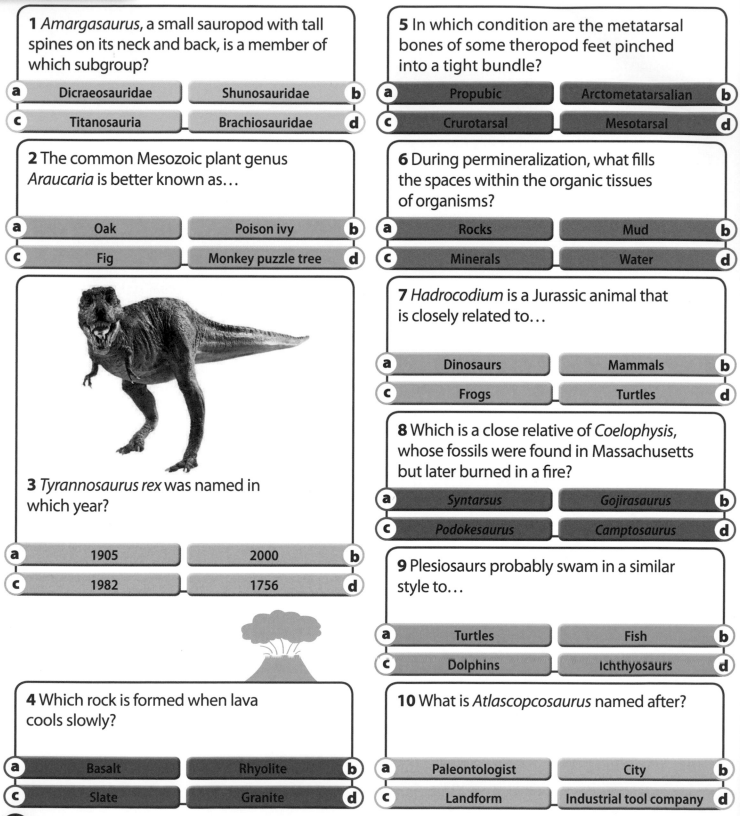

3 *Tyrannosaurus rex* was named in which year?

- **a** 1905
- **b** 2000
- **c** 1982
- **d** 1756

4 Which rock is formed when lava cools slowly?

- **a** Basalt
- **b** Rhyolite
- **c** Slate
- **d** Granite

5 In which condition are the metatarsal bones of some theropod feet pinched into a tight bundle?

- **a** Propubic
- **b** Arctometatarsalian
- **c** Crurotarsal
- **d** Mesotarsal

6 During permineralization, what fills the spaces within the organic tissues of organisms?

- **a** Rocks
- **b** Mud
- **c** Minerals
- **d** Water

7 *Hadrocodium* is a Jurassic animal that is closely related to…

- **a** Dinosaurs
- **b** Mammals
- **c** Frogs
- **d** Turtles

8 Which is a close relative of *Coelophysis*, whose fossils were found in Massachusetts but later burned in a fire?

- **a** *Syntarsus*
- **b** *Gojirasaurus*
- **c** *Podokesaurus*
- **d** *Camptosaurus*

9 Plesiosaurs probably swam in a similar style to…

- **a** Turtles
- **b** Fish
- **c** Dolphins
- **d** Ichthyosaurs

10 What is *Atlascopcosaurus* named after?

- **a** Paleontologist
- **b** City
- **c** Landform
- **d** Industrial tool company

11 Computer modeling shows that the broad and vaulted shape of the ceratopsian frill made it…

a Weaker
b Stronger
c More aerodynamic
d Stay in place

12 Which ceratopsian is now thought not to be a distinct genus, but rather adults of *Triceratops*?

a *Torvosaurus*
b *Centrosaurus*
c *Protoceratops*
d *Torosaurus*

13 The therizinosaurid dinosaur *Neimongosaurus* is named after what?

a A river in Thailand
b Inner Mongolia
c Neiman Province, Taiwan
d Artist Neiman Mongo

14 Which of the following is not a type of contact where two tectonic plates meet?

a Upthrust
b Convergent
c Divergent
d Strike-slip

15 The gaudy ceratopsian *Kosmoceratops* had how many small horns surrounding its frill?

a 10
b 3
c 20
d 7

16 Which group of bizarre, tree-dwelling reptiles are only known from rare Triassic fossils?

a Suchians
b Phytosaurs
c Drepanosaurids
d Trematosaurids

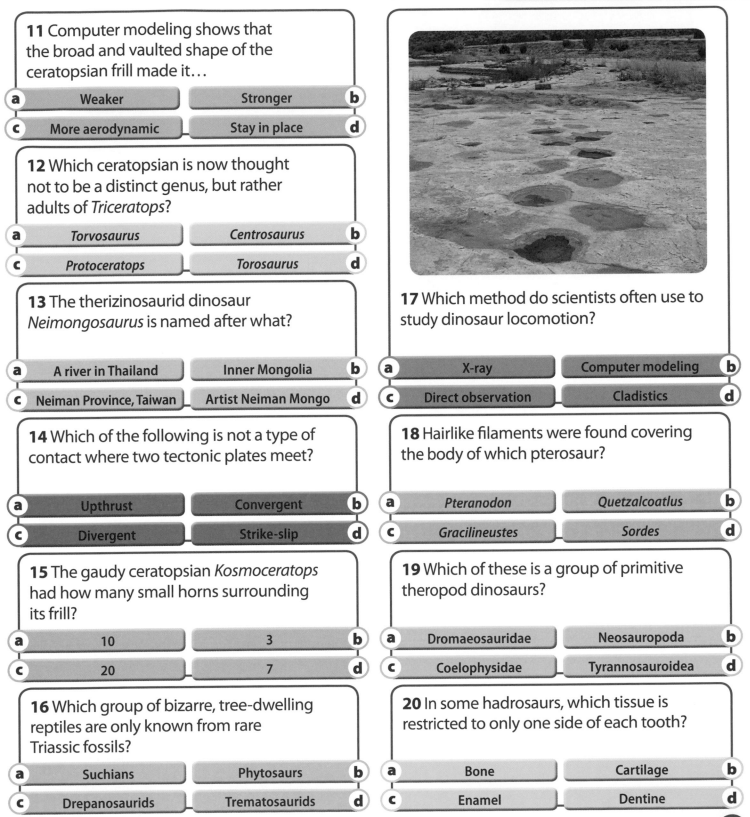

17 Which method do scientists often use to study dinosaur locomotion?

a X-ray
b Computer modeling
c Direct observation
d Cladistics

18 Hairlike filaments were found covering the body of which pterosaur?

a *Pteranodon*
b *Quetzalcoatlus*
c *Gracilineustes*
d *Sordes*

19 Which of these is a group of primitive theropod dinosaurs?

a Dromaeosauridae
b Neosauropoda
c Coelophysidae
d Tyrannosauroidea

20 In some hadrosaurs, which tissue is restricted to only one side of each tooth?

a Bone
b Cartilage
c Enamel
d Dentine

More than **100** different **sauropods**

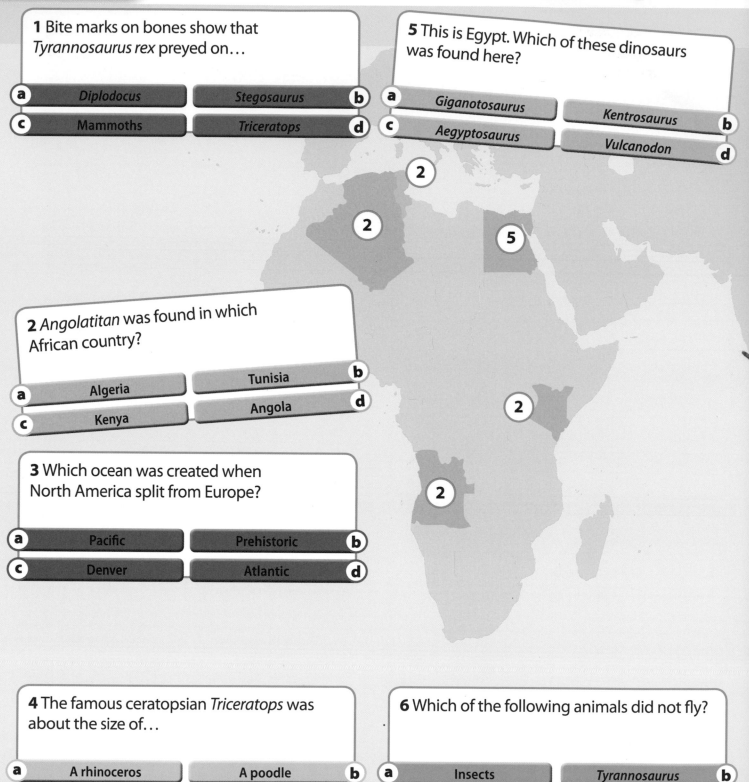

1 Bite marks on bones show that
Tyrannosaurus rex preyed on…

- **a** Diplodocus
- **b** Stegosaurus
- **c** Mammoths
- **d** Triceratops

5 This is Egypt. Which of these dinosaurs was found here?

- **a** Giganotosaurus
- **b** Kentrosaurus
- **c** Aegyptosaurus
- **d** Vulcanodon

2 *Angolatitan* was found in which African country?

- **a** Algeria
- **b** Tunisia
- **c** Kenya
- **d** Angola

3 Which ocean was created when North America split from Europe?

- **a** Pacific
- **b** Prehistoric
- **c** Denver
- **d** Atlantic

4 The famous ceratopsian *Triceratops* was about the size of…

- **a** A rhinoceros
- **b** A poodle
- **c** Tyrannosaurus
- **d** A baleen whale

6 Which of the following animals did not fly?

- **a** Insects
- **b** Tyrannosaurus
- **c** Pterosaurs
- **d** Birds

have been **named.**

7 What is it called when a group of paleontologists travel in search of new dinosaur fossils?

a Graduation | Expedition **b**
c Vacation | Trial **d**

8 Which element is necessary for animals to breathe?

a Plutonium | Mercury **b**
c Oxygen | Gold **d**

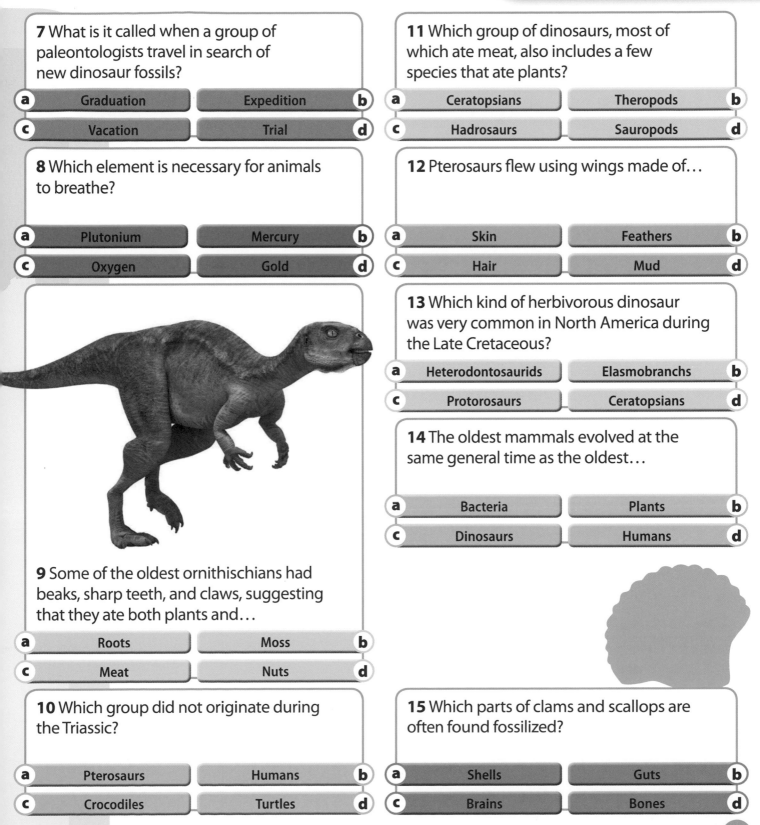

9 Some of the oldest ornithischians had beaks, sharp teeth, and claws, suggesting that they ate both plants and…

a Roots | Moss **b**
c Meat | Nuts **d**

10 Which group did not originate during the Triassic?

a Pterosaurs | Humans **b**
c Crocodiles | Turtles **d**

11 Which group of dinosaurs, most of which ate meat, also includes a few species that ate plants?

a Ceratopsians | Theropods **b**
c Hadrosaurs | Sauropods **d**

12 Pterosaurs flew using wings made of…

a Skin | Feathers **b**
c Hair | Mud **d**

13 Which kind of herbivorous dinosaur was very common in North America during the Late Cretaceous?

a Heterodontosaurids | Elasmobranchs **b**
c Protorosaurs | Ceratopsians **d**

14 The oldest mammals evolved at the same general time as the oldest…

a Bacteria | Plants **b**
c Dinosaurs | Humans **d**

15 Which parts of clams and scallops are often found fossilized?

a Shells | Guts **b**
c Brains | Bones **d**

In **1823**, Mary Anning found the first

1 Which feature helped stiffen the tail of many ornithischian dinosaurs?

a Extra vertebrae   Interlocking scales b
c Bony tendons   Hard muscles d

2 In which of these locations have no tyrannosaur fossils yet been found?

a Europe   Antarctica b
c North America   Asia d

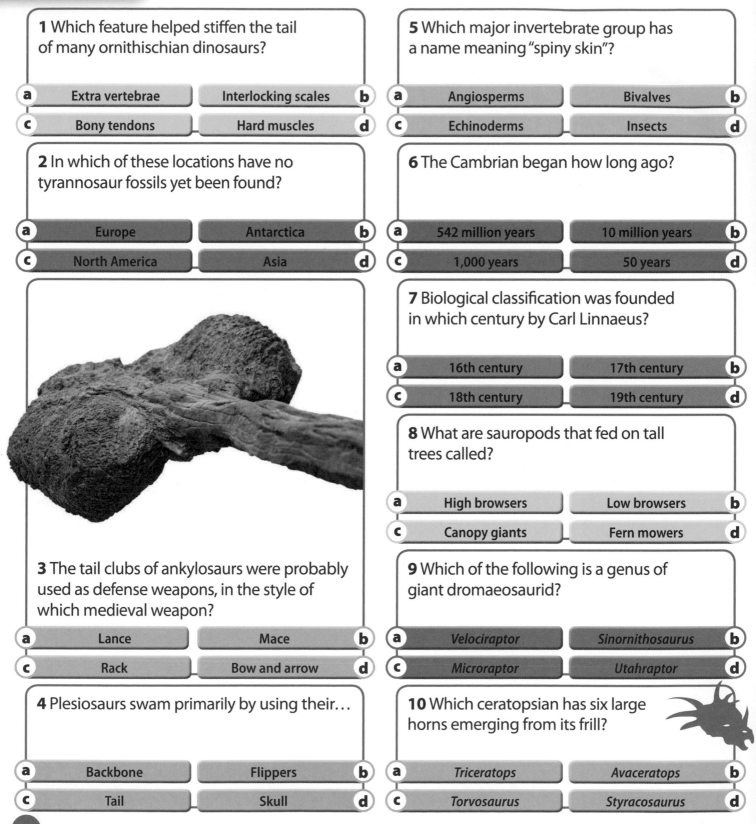

3 The tail clubs of ankylosaurs were probably used as defense weapons, in the style of which medieval weapon?

a Lance   Mace b
c Rack   Bow and arrow d

4 Plesiosaurs swam primarily by using their…

a Backbone   Flippers b
c Tail   Skull d

5 Which major invertebrate group has a name meaning "spiny skin"?

a Angiosperms   Bivalves b
c Echinoderms   Insects d

6 The Cambrian began how long ago?

a 542 million years   10 million years b
c 1,000 years   50 years d

7 Biological classification was founded in which century by Carl Linnaeus?

a 16th century   17th century b
c 18th century   19th century d

8 What are sauropods that fed on tall trees called?

a High browsers   Low browsers b
c Canopy giants   Fern mowers d

9 Which of the following is a genus of giant dromaeosaurid?

a *Velociraptor*   *Sinornithosaurus* b
c *Microraptor*   *Utahraptor* d

10 Which ceratopsian has six large horns emerging from its frill?

a *Triceratops*   *Avaceratops* b
c *Torvosaurus*   *Styracosaurus* d

known **plesiosaur** skeleton.

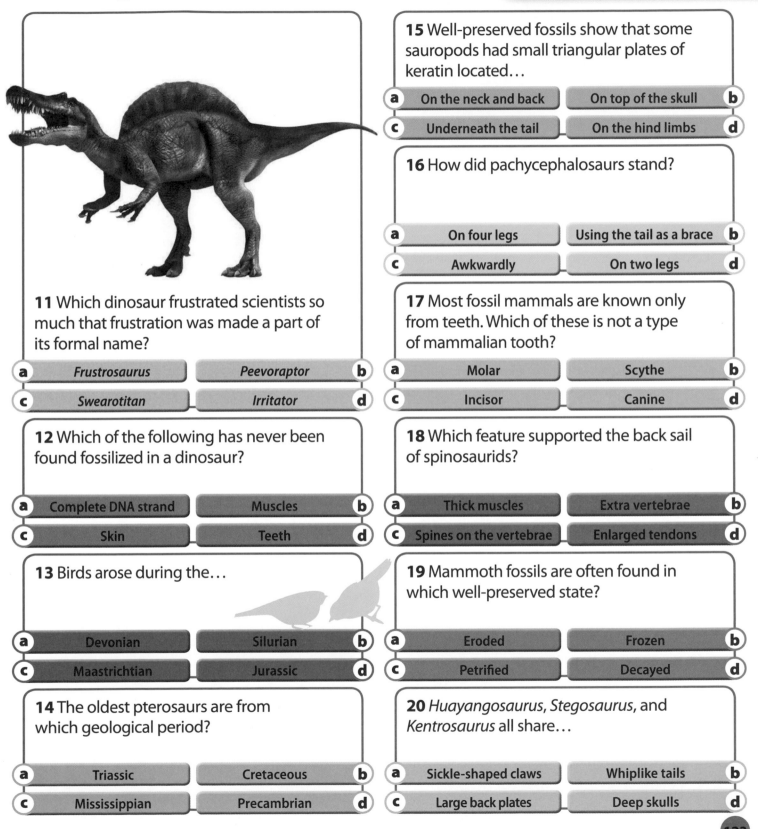

11 Which dinosaur frustrated scientists so much that frustration was made a part of its formal name?

a *Frustrosaurus*
b *Peevoraptor*
c *Swearotitan*
d *Irritator*

12 Which of the following has never been found fossilized in a dinosaur?

a Complete DNA strand
b Muscles
c Skin
d Teeth

13 Birds arose during the…

a Devonian
b Silurian
c Maastrichtian
d Jurassic

14 The oldest pterosaurs are from which geological period?

a Triassic
b Cretaceous
c Mississippian
d Precambrian

15 Well-preserved fossils show that some sauropods had small triangular plates of keratin located…

a On the neck and back
b On top of the skull
c Underneath the tail
d On the hind limbs

16 How did pachycephalosaurs stand?

a On four legs
b Using the tail as a brace
c Awkwardly
d On two legs

17 Most fossil mammals are known only from teeth. Which of these is not a type of mammalian tooth?

a Molar
b Scythe
c Incisor
d Canine

18 Which feature supported the back sail of spinosaurids?

a Thick muscles
b Extra vertebrae
c Spines on the vertebrae
d Enlarged tendons

19 Mammoth fossils are often found in which well-preserved state?

a Eroded
b Frozen
c Petrified
d Decayed

20 *Huayangosaurus*, *Stegosaurus*, and *Kentrosaurus* all share…

a Sickle-shaped claws
b Whiplike tails
c Large back plates
d Deep skulls

Fossils of more than **1,000** dinosaur

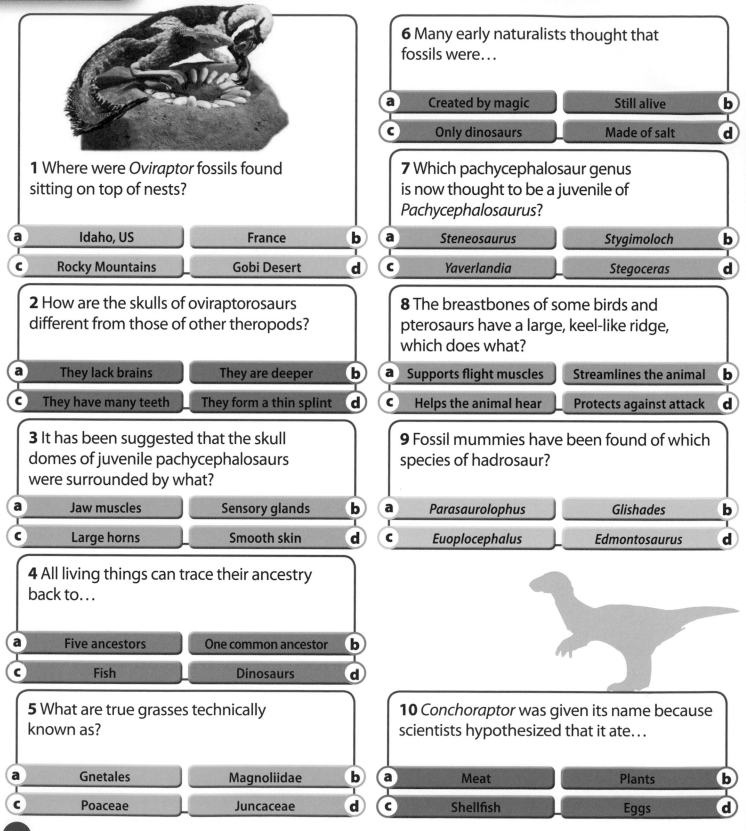

1 Where were *Oviraptor* fossils found sitting on top of nests?

- **a** Idaho, US
- **b** France
- **c** Rocky Mountains
- **d** Gobi Desert

2 How are the skulls of oviraptorosaurs different from those of other theropods?

- **a** They lack brains
- **b** They are deeper
- **c** They have many teeth
- **d** They form a thin splint

3 It has been suggested that the skull domes of juvenile pachycephalosaurs were surrounded by what?

- **a** Jaw muscles
- **b** Sensory glands
- **c** Large horns
- **d** Smooth skin

4 All living things can trace their ancestry back to…

- **a** Five ancestors
- **b** One common ancestor
- **c** Fish
- **d** Dinosaurs

5 What are true grasses technically known as?

- **a** Gnetales
- **b** Magnoliidae
- **c** Poaceae
- **d** Juncaceae

6 Many early naturalists thought that fossils were…

- **a** Created by magic
- **b** Still alive
- **c** Only dinosaurs
- **d** Made of salt

7 Which pachycephalosaur genus is now thought to be a juvenile of *Pachycephalosaurus*?

- **a** *Steneosaurus*
- **b** *Stygimoloch*
- **c** *Yaverlandia*
- **d** *Stegoceras*

8 The breastbones of some birds and pterosaurs have a large, keel-like ridge, which does what?

- **a** Supports flight muscles
- **b** Streamlines the animal
- **c** Helps the animal hear
- **d** Protects against attack

9 Fossil mummies have been found of which species of hadrosaur?

- **a** *Parasaurolophus*
- **b** *Glishades*
- **c** *Euoplocephalus*
- **d** *Edmontosaurus*

10 *Conchoraptor* was given its name because scientists hypothesized that it ate…

- **a** Meat
- **b** Plants
- **c** Shellfish
- **d** Eggs

species have been **found**.

11 Which country is located above the place where two ocean plates meet?

a Britain | b Cuba
c Australia | d Iceland

12 Which of these is a member of Titanosauria, a derived group of sauropods common on the southern continents?

a Rapetosaurus | b Camarasaurus
c Omeisaurus | d Nigersaurus

13 Which ceratosaur has been found in the famous Tendaguru fossil beds of Africa?

a Coelophysis | b Allosaurus
c Segisaurus | d Elaphrosaurus

14 Which small dinosaur may be a pachycephalosaur, but no skull has ever been found to prove this?

a Stenopelix | b Yaverlandia
c Texacephale | d Dimetrodon

15 One of the largest plesiosaurs was…

a Nothosaurus | b Mauisaurus
c Pliosaurus | d Plioplatecarpus

16 What is the gradual pace of extinctions in normal times called?

a Background extinction | b Mass extinction
c Steady extinction | d Evolution

17 Which of these is not a member of Poposauroidea, a group of bipedal, fast-moving crocodile relatives?

a Poposaurus | b Ornithosuchus
c Shuvosaurus | d Effigia

18 Which scientist first understood that species go extinct?

a W. D. Matthew | b Grzegorz Niedzwiedzki
c Georges Cuvier | d Karl Marx

19 Which dinosaur is named after an Ancient Roman festival?

a Tawa | b Kelmayisaurus
c Saturnalia | d Prenocephale

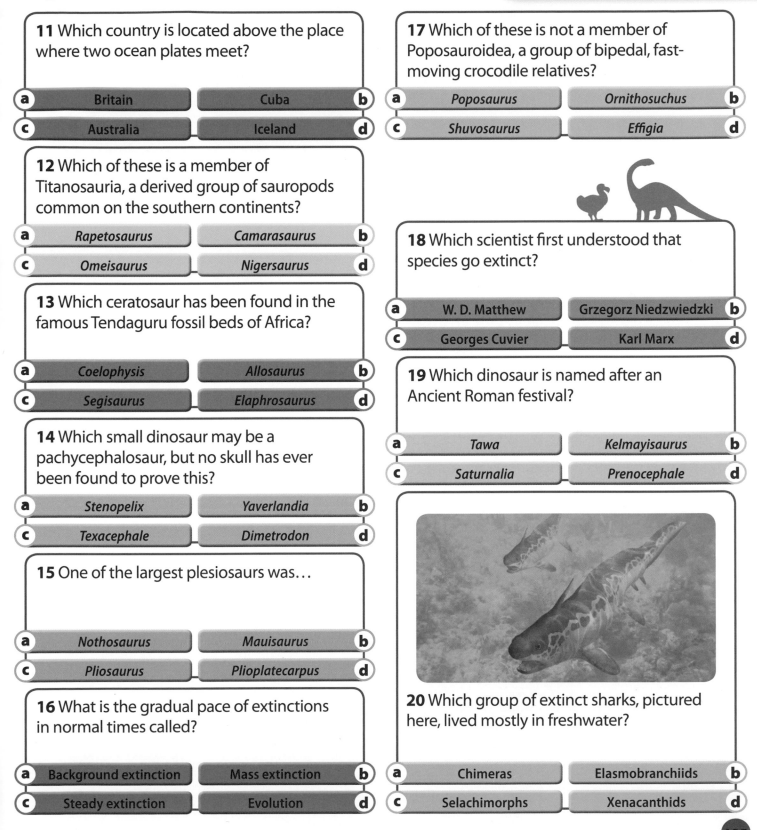

20 Which group of extinct sharks, pictured here, lived mostly in freshwater?

a Chimeras | b Elasmobranchiids
c Selachimorphs | d Xenacanthids

Dinosaur timeline

The biggest, most spectacular land animals that ever walked the earth evolved during the Mesozoic era. This vast span of time began 251 million years ago and ended in global catastrophe 186 million years later. It is divided into three periods—the Triassic, Jurassic, and Cretaceous. The earliest dinosaurs emerged in the Triassic period, but they did not dominate life on land until the Jurassic, when the first of the real ground-shaking giants appeared.

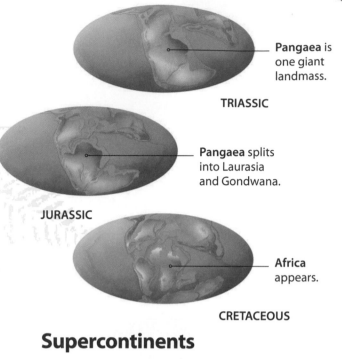

Pangaea is one giant landmass.

TRIASSIC

Pangaea splits into Laurasia and Gondwana.

JURASSIC

Africa appears.

CRETACEOUS

Supercontinents

As the plates of Earth's crust shift around, they take the continents with them. In the Triassic, they formed a single supercontinent, which split in two during the Jurassic. The modern continents emerged in the Cretaceous.

Changing climates

During the Triassic, the arid heart of Pangaea was a vast desert. But by the Late Cretaceous, the supercontinent had split up into smaller continents with wetter climates and lush vegetation.

ERA	MESOZOIC ERA		
PERIOD	Triassic	Jurassic	
MILLIONS OF YEARS AGO	251	199	145

The first dinosaurs

The earliest dinosaurs evolved about 230 million years ago, in the mid-Triassic. Part of a reptile group called the archosaurs, they were small, long-necked animals with broad diets. Many walked on their hind legs.

Thecodontosaurus was mainly a plant-eater.

Success story

Dinosaurs dominated life on land for 165 million years—an immense tract of time that enabled them to evolve into an amazing variety of species. In addition, since dinosaurs also gave rise to birds, they are still with us.

Mass extinction

Just over 65 million years ago, the Mesozoic era came to an end with a mass extinction of life—probably caused by an enormous asteroid crashing into what is now Mexico. All the big dinosaurs died out and only the small, feathered ones survived.

Timeline

The Mesozoic era lasted almost three times as long as the Cenozoic era—the 65 million years that separate the Mesozoic from our own time. The first animals to resemble humans appeared less than 5 million years ago.

	CENOZOIC ERA		
Cretaceous	Paleogene	Neogene	
65	23		0

Fossil evidence

We know that giant dinosaurs existed, because their remains have survived in the form of stony fossils. But the chances of animal remains becoming fossilized are incredibly slim, so every fossil is precious evidence, like a clue at a crime scene. Even the smallest fragment may hold the key to a mystery, or reveal the existence of a creature previously unknown to science.

Stroke of luck

Fossils are the remains of dead organisms that escape being eaten and survive the normal processes of decay—usually by being buried in soft, airless mud. This rarely happens, especially on land, so every fossil is a fluke of nature.

Feathers show on recent fossil finds.

Shells, teeth, and bones

Most fossils preserve the hard parts of animals—their shells, teeth, and bones. These persist for much longer than the soft parts, giving the organic material time to be replaced by minerals, and thus be fossilized.

Dinosaur skeleton is preserved in rock.

Amazing discoveries

Usually, all the soft parts of an animal are lost, but some fossils preserve traces of skin, scales, and even feathers—as on this fossil of a Jurassic bird. New techniques also allow scientists to analyze fossils in much greater detail than before.

Color leaves microscopic traces.

Vital clues

Sometimes whole skeletons are preserved, but most fossils are just odd bones, teeth, or even claws like this one. But a skilled scientist can usually identify them— or, more excitingly, confirm that they are the fragmentary remains of an animal that has not been found before.

In the lab

Fossils have to be carefully recovered, cleaned, and conserved, which can be painstaking work. Then, they can be studied and identified—a process that may involve using advanced tools such as electron microscopes and medical scanners.

Back to life

All the clues are put together to create a reconstruction of the living animal. However, we can never be certain that it is accurate, and new discoveries may prove it wrong. We now know, for example, that many small dinosaurs were covered with feathers, which earlier reconstructions do not show.

What is a dinosaur?

Dinosaurs were reptiles, but they were not like typical reptiles. Even though the word dinosaur means "terrible lizard," they did not stand or move like lizards, and some even had feathers. This probably means that their bodies worked more like those of birds or mammals.

Tyrannosaurus walked tall.

Reptiles with attitude

Imagine a reptile and you might think of a crocodile, lizard, or snake. But the dinosaurs were not like these sprawling, slithering creatures. They were clearly dynamic, agile animals, and some were fast movers too.

Walking tall

One thing that we have always known about dinosaurs is that they walked with their legs beneath their bodies, like birds or mammals—and not like lizards. We know this from the details of their hip and leg bones.

Long tail improved balance at high speeds.

Feathers retained body heat.

Warm blood

The dynamic stance of dinosaurs suggests that they were warm-blooded, like modern mammals or birds. This would explain why many small dinosaurs like this *Gallimimus* had insulating feathers. It also fits in with the fast growth rate of the bigger dinosaurs. However, scientists still disagree about this.

Strong legs were built for running.

Eggs and nests

As far as we know, all dinosaurs laid eggs with hard, brittle shells, similar to birds' eggs. Many of the smaller dinosaurs almost certainly incubated their eggs in nests like birds, and some nested in big breeding colonies. There is even evidence that some brought food to the nest to feed their hungry nestlings.

Thyreophorans

Ornithischians had backward-pointing pubis bones.

Ornithopods

Marginocephalians

Dinosaurs

Theropods

Saurischians usually had forward-pointing pubis bones.

Sauropodomorphs

Family tree

There were two main types of dinosaurs: saurischians and ornithischians. The saurischians included the big, leaf-eating sauropodomorphs and the predatory theropods. The plant-eating ornithischians were divided into the thyreophorans, ornithopods, and marginocephalians.

Pterosaurs and sea monsters

Dinosaurs lived alongside many other types of animals. The most spectacular were the winged pterosaurs and marine reptiles. Some of these were giants, rivaling the big predatory dinosaurs in ferocity. The most powerful pterosaurs may even have preyed on small dinosaurs.

Wing-finger

The first fossil pterosaur to be found was called *Pterodactylus*, which means "wing-finger." This is because the outer part of a pterosaur's batlike wing was supported by the bones of a single, hugely elongated finger.

Long tails

Pterosaurs appeared in the Triassic period. They were crow-sized, with long, bony tails, short necks, and long snouts with sharp teeth. They had furry bodies, so they were probably warm-blooded, like birds.

Extended fourth finger supported wing.

Quetzalcoatlus had a distinctive crest on its head.

Body was very light for its size.

Soaring giants

Later pterosaurs had very short tails, long necks, beaklike snouts, and long legs. Many had spectacular crests. Some, such as *Quetzalcoatlus*, were the size of a light aircraft. They could fly well but also hunted on the ground, walking on all fours with their outer wings folded up.

Marine reptiles

Although some marine reptiles looked a lot like dinosaurs, the two groups were only distantly related. Marine reptiles were more likely to have been cold-blooded, with scaly skin. Early Triassic types such as *Nothosaurus* probably lived partly onshore, like modern sea lions.

Sleek swimmers

By the Late Triassic, some marine reptiles were living entirely at sea. The most highly adapted for marine life were the ichthyosaurs—streamlined, fast-swimming hunters that were the Mesozoic equivalent of dolphins. Their fossils (above) were among the first to be recognized by scientists.

Sea dragons

When their fossils were first found, the long-necked plesiosaurs were known as sea dragons. They probably used their extended flippers to "fly" through the water, reaching down with their long necks to search the seabed for shellfish.

Nightmare hunters

Pliosaurs such as *Kronosaurus* had huge jaws up to 10ft (3m) long, bristling with fearsome teeth. They were the most powerful hunters in the oceans, able to kill and devour anything they ran into.

Hunters and scavengers

The most famous dinosaurs are gigantic hunters such as the mighty *Tyrannosaurus rex*—heavily armed monsters that preyed on plant-eating giants. But predatory dinosaurs came in all shapes and sizes, and would have taken on a wide range of prey, both living and dead.

Tyrannosaurus had forward-facing eyes.

Compsognathus was the size of a chicken.

Fast and ferocious

Nearly all the carnivorous dinosaurs were theropods— saurischians that stood on their hind legs and had grasping hands. They were mostly fast, agile creatures, just like their modern descendants, the birds.

Steak-knife teeth

Typical theropod teeth were serrated blades for slicing through skin and flesh. Hunters like *Allosaurus* used them to target the soft, vulnerable parts of their victims, avoiding any thick armor.

Killer claws

Most predatory theropods also had sharp claws. Dromaeosaurs such as *Deinonychus* were armed with a wickedly long "killer claw" sticking up from each foot, which they probably used as their main attack weapon.

Long legs provided lethal speed.

Bone-crushers

The tyrannosaurs of the Late Cretaceous had massive skulls and jaws, armed with very strong teeth adapted for biting through bone as well as flesh. This made them the most powerful land predators that have ever lived.

Fishing giant

The biggest hunter found so far is *Spinosaurus*, a monster with a strange "sail" on its back. It had long jaws like those of a crocodile, which it used to catch fish in shallow water—although it devoured other dinosaurs if it got the chance.

Beaked and bizarre

Many weird kinds of theropods started appearing in the late Mesozoic. Some had beaks instead of teeth, while others looked and probably behaved like ostriches. Many had feathers, with long plumes on their arms.

Citipati may have been an egg-eater.

Taking off

Relatives of animals like *Citipati* and *Deinonychus* were the ancestors of modern birds. The earliest ones, such as *Archaeopteryx*, were clumsy gliders—but by the end of the Mesozoic the skies were full of them.

Giant plant-eaters

Most dinosaurs were plant-eaters. These included the very biggest dinosaurs—the colossal sauropods—and nearly all of the most flamboyantly horned and crested types. The earlier plant-eaters had only simple teeth, but over time several groups of dinosaurs evolved special adaptations for reducing their tough food to a digestible pulp.

Big gut allowed long digestion.

High-fiber diet

Dinosaurs ate the leaves of plants like this ginkgo. They are difficult to digest because their juicy cells are walled with tough cellulose fiber. Chewing the cells releases their nutritious juices, but ideally a plant-eater has a big digestive system that turns the cellulose to sugar.

Long-necked giants

The biggest herbivores were the long-necked, leaf-eating sauropods. Their simple, peglike teeth were good for stripping leaves from twigs but not for chewing. They would have swallowed the leaves whole and relied on their enormous digestive systems to break them down and release their nutrients.

Sharp teeth could kill small prey.

Picking and choosing

Some plant-eating dinosaurs such as this *Heterodontosaurus* avoided the toughest, most fibrous foods by picking only tender young foliage and juicy roots. They probably also ate insects and worms, and sometimes scavenged meat from dead animals. They were omnivores, much like modern pigs.

Long neck for feeding in treetops.

Heavyweight browsers

The thyreophorans included armored ankylosaurs like this *Scelidosaurus*, as well as stegosaurs—famous for the rows of plates on their backs. They had beaks to select tender plant food, but relied on their digestive systems to process it.

Leaf-grinders

Early ornithopods had simple teeth, but the "duck-billed" hadrosaurs that lived later in the Cretaceous period were equipped with batteries of massive cheek teeth for pulping leafy food. Their teeth were continually replaced, so they never wore out. The pulped leaves were easier to digest, so hadrosaurs did not need to eat them in huge quantities.

Shearing blades

Ceratopsians such as *Triceratops* had sharp beaks and special cheek teeth that were adapted for chopping leaves into very small pieces. Like normal chewing, this made the leaves more digestible.

137

Defense and display

Plant-eating dinosaurs had some formidable enemies—heavily armed, agile predators that were a lot smarter than we usually imagine. Evolution equipped their prey with a variety of defenses, ranging from sheer speed to weapons of their own. But many features that look like armor or weapons were probably mainly for show.

Quick getaway

Many small dinosaurs were very quick on their feet, and they would have relied on this to escape being eaten. Others may have depended on camouflage to conceal them. Some dug burrows, bolting into them like rabbits at any hint of danger.

Armor plate

Some animals depended on thick body armor for defense against the slender, bladelike teeth of typical hunters. The most heavily armored were ankylosaurs such as the Late-Cretaceous *Ankylosaurus*, which had to contend with bone-crunching tyrannosaurs.

Spikes and clubs

A few of the bigger plant-eaters were able to fight off their enemies. Stegosaurs had wicked spikes on the tips of their tails that they could use to impale or cripple an attacker, and the ankylosaurs had heavy, bony, leg-breaking tail clubs.

Horns and crowns

Some dinosaurs like *Styracosaurus* had features that looked like weapons or armor, but were either too elaborate for the job or just not strong enough. They must have been at least partly for show, to impress rivals rather than deter predators.

Tupandactylus had a huge crest.

Spectacular crests

Several dinosaurs and pterosaurs had dramatic crests on their heads. These must have been for display, like the antlers of male deer. It's possible that the animals with the biggest crests were males, but we just don't know.

Fine feathers

Recent fossil discoveries prove that many small dinosaurs had feathers. The fossil remains of some, such as the chicken-sized hunter *Anchiornis*, contain microscopic evidence of color—showing that they had bright plumage just like many modern birds.

Other Mesozoic life

The dinosaurs, pterosaurs, and marine reptiles were the biggest, most dramatic animals of the Mesozoic era, but they could not have survived without a rich variety of other life. The giant, plant-eating dinosaurs had big appetites, and many of the smaller hunters probably preyed mainly on small animals such as insects.

Plant life

In the Mesozoic era, the dominant plants were primitive nonflowering forms such as horsetails, mosses, club-mosses, ferns, cycads, and conifer trees. Flowering plants did not evolve until the Early Cretaceous. For most of the Mesozoic, there was no such thing as grass, but grasses may have appeared by the end of the era.

Insects and spiders

Insects flourished throughout the Mesozoic, but there were no nectar-feeders such as bees until they evolved in parallel with flowering plants in the Cretaceous period. By the end of the era, most of the modern insect groups had appeared—and just like today they were falling prey to a variety of spiders.

Spider trapped in ancient amber.

Marine life

Fish of all kinds were common, including sharks that were very similar to the ones alive today. The oceans also swarmed with invertebrate life such as ammonites—spiral-shelled relatives of cuttlefish that became extinct at the end of the era but left abundant fossils like this one in the rocks.

Prosalirus lived in the Early Jurassic.

Amphibians

During the Devonian period—long before the Mesozoic—amphibians had evolved from fish to become the first vertebrates (animals with backbones) capable of living on land. By the beginning of the Mesozoic era, salamanders were common, but frogs did not appear until the Jurassic period.

Protosuchus was a small Jurassic crocodile.

Scaly reptiles

When dinosaurs appeared, they were just one group of reptiles among many. Others included turtles and tortoises, lizards, and a group called the crurotarsans, which included crocodiles. Most of the bigger crurotarsans died out at the end of the Triassic, but others lived on.

Furry mammals

Mammals evolved from reptilian-looking ancestors that mostly died out at the end of the Triassic. By the Cretaceous, their descendants had diversified into a variety of small, furry animals such as this 4in (10cm) long *Nemegtbaatar*. Even the biggest were only the size of a badger.

141

Answers

1 1c, 2a, 3a, 4c, 5d, 6a, 7b, 8c, 9d, 10a, 11b, 12d, 13b, 14d, 15c

2 1b, 2c, 3d, 4a, 5c, 6b, 7a, 8c, 9d, 10b, 11d, 12a, 13c, 14a, 15d, 16c, 17a, 18b, 19b, 20d

3 1a, 2a, 3c, 4b, 5a, 6c, 7a, 8d, 9c, 10b, 11c, 12b, 13d, 14d, 15b, 16d, 17c, 18b, 19a, 20d

4 1d, 2a, 3c, 4b, 5b, 6d, 7d, 8c, 9b, 10a, 11d, 12a, 13a, 14c, 15b

5 1c, 2c, 3a, 4d, 5b, 6a, 7a, 8d, 9d, 10b, 11c, 12d, 13b, 14c, 15d, 16a, 17b, 18b, 19c, 20a

6 1a, 2c, 3b, 4d, 5a, 6a, 7b, 8d, 9c, 10c, 11a, 12b, 13d, 14c, 15a, 16d, 17b, 18d, 19b, 20c

7 1a, 2d, 3d, 4a, 5b, 6a, 7b, 8a, 9c, 10b, 11d, 12b, 13c, 14c, 15c

8 1c, 2d, 3d, 4b, 5a, 6a, 7c, 8c, 9c, 10c, 11d, 12b, 13a, 14a, 15b, 16b, 17d, 18d, 19a, 20b

9 1a, 2b, 3a, 4d, 5d, 6c, 7b, 8a, 9b, 10a, 11d, 12b, 13c, 14c, 15d, 16d, 17a, 18c, 19b, 20c

10 1d, 2b, 3a, 4b, 5a, 6d, 7a, 8c, 9b, 10b, 11c, 12d, 13c, 14c, 15d

11 1d, 2d, 3d, 4b, 5b, 6a, 7c, 8c, 9a, 10b, 11d, 12a, 13c, 14b, 15a, 16d, 17c, 18c, 19a, 20b

12 1c, 2c, 3a, 4d, 5a, 6a, 7b, 8a, 9d, 10b, 11a, 12c, 13c, 14d, 15b, 16b, 17c, 18b, 19d, 20d

13 1b, 2d, 3d, 4c, 5c, 6a, 7b, 8a, 9b, 10a, 11d, 12a, 13c, 14c, 15d

14 1a, 2c, 3b, 4a, 5b, 6b, 7c, 8d, 9a, 10b, 11d, 12d, 13d, 14c, 15c, 16a, 17b, 18d, 19c, 20a

15 1a, 2c, 3d, 4b, 5d, 6c, 7c, 8a, 9b, 10c, 11a, 12d, 13d, 14a, 15d, 16b, 17c, 18a, 19b, 20b

16 1d, 2a, 3d, 4d, 5b, 6a, 7a, 8b, 9a, 10c, 11c, 12b, 13d, 14c, 15b

17 1a, 2b, 3a, 4b, 5d, 6b, 7b, 8d, 9c, 10a, 11d, 12d, 13c, 14b, 15a, 16c, 17d, 18c, 19a, 20c

18 1b, 2a, 3a, 4a, 5c, 6b, 7c, 8c, 9a, 10a, 11d, 12b, 13d, 14d, 15c, 16d, 17d, 18c, 19b, 20b

19 1a, 2d, 3c, 4c, 5d, 6a, 7c, 8b, 9a, 10d, 11b, 12a, 13c, 14b, 15b

20 1a, 2b, 3a, 4a, 5d, 6b, 7b, 8a, 9c, 10c, 11b, 12c, 13c, 14b, 15d, 16d, 17d, 18d, 19a, 20c

21 1a, 2a, 3c, 4d, 5c, 6b, 7b, 8c, 9d, 10a, 11b, 12c, 13a, 14b, 15b, 16d, 17a, 18c, 19d, 20d

22 1a, 2d, 3b, 4d, 5c, 6a, 7d, 8c, 9b, 10b, 11c, 12c, 13b, 14a, 15d

23 1a, 2d, 3c, 4c, 5a, 6a, 7a, 8c, 9c, 10b, 11d, 12c, 13b, 14b, 15a, 16b, 17d, 18d, 19b, 20d

24 1b, 2a, 3b, 4c, 5d, 6a, 7a, 8c, 9b, 10a, 11d, 12d, 13b, 14a, 15d, 16d, 17c, 18b, 19c, 20c

25 1d, 2c, 3d, 4d, 5a, 6d, 7c, 8b, 9a, 10a, 11b, 12d, 13a, 14c, 15c

26 1b, 2d, 3b, 4b, 5a, 6b, 7a, 8c, 9a, 10c, 11c, 12d, 13d, 14c, 15c, 16a, 17a, 18d, 19b, 20d

27 1d, 2c, 3a, 4a, 5c, 6b, 7a, 8d, 9b, 10c, 11c, 12d, 13b, 14b, 15d, 16b, 17c, 18d, 19a, 20a

28 1b, 2c, 3c, 4d, 5b, 6c, 7a, 8d, 9b, 10b, 11d, 12a, 13a, 14b, 15a

29 1d, 2b, 3d, 4a, 5a, 6b, 7a, 8d, 9d, 10c, 11b, 12c, 13a, 14a, 15b, 16d, 17c, 18c, 19b, 20c

30 1d, 2a, 3c, 4a, 5a, 6d, 7b, 8b, 9b, 10c, 11c, 12c, 13d, 14a, 15b, 16d, 17d, 18c, 19b, 20a

31 1b, 2b, 3b, 4d, 5d, 6c, 7d, 8c, 9c, 10a, 11a, 12b, 13a, 14c, 15a

32 1a, 2a, 3c, 4c, 5c, 6b, 7d, 8c, 9d, 10b, 11b, 12c, 13a, 14a, 15d, 16b, 17b, 18d, 19a, 20d

33 1c, 2d, 3d, 4d, 5d, 6c, 7a, 8a, 9a, 10c, 11b, 12b, 13b, 14b, 15d, 16a, 17b, 18c, 19c, 20a

34 1b, 2c, 3c, 4c, 5a, 6d, 7b, 8d, 9b, 10c, 11a, 12b, 13d, 14d, 15a

35 1a, 2b, 3d, 4b, 5d, 6d, 7b, 8d, 9b, 10c, 11c, 12a, 13c, 14a, 15a, 16c, 17b, 18d, 19a, 20c

36 1a, 2c, 3a, 4b, 5a, 6a, 7b, 8d, 9c, 10c, 11d, 12a, 13d, 14b, 15b, 16d, 17d, 18b, 19c, 20c

37 1c, 2b, 3c, 4a, 5b, 6a, 7c, 8a, 9a, 10d, 11d, 12c, 13b, 14d, 15d

38 1c, 2a, 3b, 4c, 5d, 6d, 7b, 8a, 9a, 10d, 11b, 12a, 13c, 14d, 15b, 16c, 17a, 18b, 19d, 20c

39 1d, 2a, 3d, 4d, 5d, 6b, 7d, 8c, 9c, 10b, 11c, 12b, 13b, 14c, 15a, 16a, 17c, 18a, 19a, 20b

40 1b, 2d, 3d, 4d, 5a, 6b, 7a, 8a, 9d, 10c, 11c, 12b, 13b, 14a, 15c

41 1a, 2b, 3c, 4d, 5a, 6c, 7d, 8c, 9a, 10b, 11b, 12d, 13d, 14c, 15b, 16c, 17d, 18a, 19a, 20b

42 1d, 2d, 3d, 4a, 5b, 6d, 7c, 8b, 9a, 10c, 11a, 12a, 13d, 14c, 15c, 16c, 17b, 18b, 19b, 20a

43 1c, 2c, 3c, 4d, 5c, 6a, 7a, 8b, 9b, 10d, 11a, 12a, 13b, 14d, 15b

44 1d, 2c, 3b, 4a, 5c, 6d, 7a, 8d, 9c, 10a, 11b, 12b, 13d, 14c, 15b, 16a, 17d, 18c, 19a, 20b

45 1b, 2a, 3b, 4c, 5b, 6b, 7a, 8a, 9a, 10d, 11c, 12c, 13d, 14a, 15c, 16b, 17c, 18d, 19d, 20d

46 1a, 2c, 3a, 4d, 5a, 6c, 7d, 8b, 9b, 10c, 11d, 12b, 13c, 14b, 15d

47 1c, 2d, 3d, 4b, 5b, 6c, 7b, 8a, 9a, 10d, 11c, 12d, 13a, 14c, 15b, 16a, 17b, 18c, 19a, 20d

48 1c, 2b, 3d, 4c, 5d, 6a, 7b, 8b, 9a, 10c, 11b, 12b, 13d, 14d, 15a, 16a, 17a, 18a, 19c, 20d

49 1a, 2a, 3a, 4c, 5a, 6b, 7c, 8c, 9d, 10b, 11d, 12b, 13d, 14d, 15c

50 1a, 2c, 3d, 4b, 5c, 6d, 7a, 8b, 9d, 10a, 11a, 12a, 13b, 14d, 15d, 16c, 17c, 18b, 19b, 20c

51 1a, 2a, 3b, 4b, 5c, 6d, 7d, 8a, 9d, 10a, 11c, 12c, 13a, 14c, 15b, 16d, 17c, 18b, 19b, 20d

52 1c, 2b, 3a, 4d, 5b, 6a, 7b, 8c, 9d, 10c, 11b, 12a, 13a, 14d, 15d

53 1c, 2d, 3b, 4c, 5a, 6a, 7c, 8b, 9d, 10d, 11a, 12d, 13b, 14d, 15a, 16c, 17b, 18b, 19a, 20c

54 1b, 2a, 3c, 4a, 5c, 6d, 7d, 8c, 9b, 10a, 11b, 12d, 13c, 14a, 15b, 16d, 17a, 18c, 19b, 20d

55 1b, 2b, 3d, 4c, 5b, 6c, 7a, 8b, 9a, 10c, 11c, 12a, 13d, 14a, 15d

56 1d, 2b, 3b, 4a, 5c, 6b, 7b, 8d, 9d, 10c, 11a, 12a, 13a, 14c, 15c, 16a, 17c, 18d, 19d, 20b

57 1a, 2d, 3a, 4d, 5b, 6c, 7b, 8c, 9a, 10d, 11b, 12d, 13b, 14a, 15a, 16c, 17b, 18d, 19c, 20c

58 1d, 2d, 3d, 4a, 5c, 6b, 7b, 8c, 9c, 10b, 11b, 12a, 13d, 14c, 15a

59 1c, 2b, 3b, 4b, 5c, 6a, 7c, 8a, 9d, 10d, 11d, 12a, 13d, 14a, 15a, 16d, 17b, 18c, 19b, 20c

60 1d, 2b, 3c, 4b, 5c, 6a, 7b, 8a, 9d, 10c, 11d, 12a, 13d, 14a, 15b, 16a, 17b, 18c, 19c, 20d

Acknowledgments

DK would like to thank: Jenny Sich for proofreading; Roma Malik, James Mitchem, and Archana Ramachandran for additional editorial work; and Sanjay Chauhan, Arup Giri, and Isha Nagar for additional design work.

The publisher would like to thank the following for their kind permission to reproduce their photographs:
(Key: a–above; b–below/bottom; c–center; f–far; l–left; r–right; t–top)

6 Dorling Kindersley: Jon Hughes (tl). **6–7 Dorling Kindersley:** Jon Hughes. **11 Dorling Kindersley:** Robert L. Braun – modelmaker (tr). **12 Dorling Kindersley:** Jon Hughes. **12–13 Corbis:** Dave Reede / AgStock Images. **13 Dorling Kindersley:** Natural History Museum, London (br). **14 Dorling Kindersley:** Jerry Young (cr). **16 Dreamstime.com:** Robert Byron (tl). **25 Dorling Kindersley:** Thomas Marent (cb). **26 Dorling Kindersley:** Centaur Studios – modelmakers (bl). **28 Dorling Kindersley:** Royal Tyrrell Museum of Palaeontology, Alberta, Canada (cra). **29 Dorling Kindersley:** Barrie Watts (tr); Franklin Park Zoo, Boston (tc); Thomas Marent (cra). **32 Dorling Kindersley:** Jerry Young (cla). **33 Dorling Kindersley:** Royal Tyrrell Museum of Palaeontology, Alberta, Canada (br). **34 Dorling Kindersley:** Staatliches Museum fur Naturkunde Stuttgart (br). **36–37 Dorling Kindersley:** Jon Hughes. **37 Dreamstime.com:** Yekaixp. **40 Dorling Kindersley:** State Museum of Nature, Stuttgart (bl). **41 Dorling Kindersley:** Natural History Museum, London (tr). **46 Dorling Kindersley:** Peter Minister, Digital Sculptor (tl). **47 Dorling Kindersley:** Peter Minister, Digital Sculptor (bl). **48 Dorling Kindersley:** Jon Hughes (tr). **55 Dorling Kindersley:** The Academy of Natural Sciences (br). **56 Dorling Kindersley:** David Donkin – modelmaker (cr). **57 Dorling Kindersley:** Trustees of the National Museums Of Scotland (br). **59 Dorling Kindersley:** Natural History Museum, London (tr). **60 Dorling Kindersley:** John Holmes – modelmaker (tr). **63 Dorling Kindersley:** Jon Hughes / Bedrock Studios (tl). **65 Dorling Kindersley:** Royal Tyrrell Museum of Palaeontology, Alberta, Canada (cr). **66–67 Dorling Kindersley:** Natural History Museum, London. **69 Dorling Kindersley:** John Holmes – modelmaker (cr); Jon Hughes (bl). **70 Dorling Kindersley:** The American Museum of Natural History (br). **72 Dorling Kindersley:** Jon Hughes. **73 Dorling Kindersley:** Graham High at Centaur Studios – modelmaker (ca); Graham High and Jeremy Hunt Centaur Studios – modelmaker (cr); Jon Hughes (cb). **76 Dorling Kindersley:** The American Museum of Natural History (br). **78–79 Dorling Kindersley:** Natural History Museum, London. **79 Getty Images:** De Agostini (br). **80 Dorling Kindersley:** Robert L. Braun – modelmaker (bl). **82 Dorling Kindersley:** Jon Hughes (cl). **88 Dorling Kindersley:** John hughes (tr). **95 Dorling Kindersley:** Robert L. Braun – modelmaker (bl). **101 Dorling Kindersley:** Trustees of the National Museums Of Scotland (tl). **102 Dorling Kindersley:** Jonathan Hateley – modelmaker. **104 Dorling Kindersley:** Jon Hughes (cl). **106 Dorling Kindersley:** Graham High at Centaur Studios – modelmaker (cl). **108–109 Dorling Kindersley:** Peter Minister, Digital Sculptor. **112 Dorling Kindersley:** Royal Tyrrell Museum of Palaeontology, Alberta, Canada (br). **115 Dorling Kindersley:** Peter Minister, Digital Sculptor (bl). **117 Dorling Kindersley:** Royal Tyrrell Museum of Palaeontology, Alberta, Canada (tr). **122–123 Dorling Kindersley:** Peter Minister, Digital Sculptor. **126 Corbis:** Richard Eastwood (bl). **127 Dorling Kindersley:** Peter Minister, Digital Sculptor (cr). **Dreamstime.com:** Satori13 (cl). **128 Dorling Kindersley:** Royal Tyrrell Museum of Palaeontology, Alberta, Canada (crb). **128–129 Dorling Kindersley:** Jonathan Hateley – modelmaker. **129 Dorling Kindersley:** Natural History Museum, London (c). **130 Dorling Kindersley:** American Museum of Natural History (tr). **131 Dorling Kindersley:** Graham High at Centaur Studios – modelmaker (crb); John Holmes – modelmaker (tr); Robert L. Braun – modelmaker (cra); Jon Hughes (br). **132 Dorling Kindersley:** Jon Hughes (cl); Senckenberg Nature Museum, Frankfurt (tr); Peter Minister, Digital Sculptor (b). **133 Dorling Kindersley:** Peter Minister, Digital Sculptor (t, bl). **134 Dorling Kindersley:** Peter Minister, Digital Sculptor (bl); Staatliches Museum fur Naturkunde Stuttgart (crb). **134–135 Dorling Kindersley:** Peter Minister, Digital Sculptor. **135 Dorling Kindersley:** Jon Hughes (tr); Peter Minister, Digital Sculptor (br). **136 Dorling Kindersley:** Peter Minister, Digital Sculptor (br). **137 Dorling Kindersley:** Jon Hughes (b); Peter Minister, Digital Sculptor (cr). **138 Corbis:** Lake County Museum (br). **Dorling Kindersley:** John Holmes – modelmaker (tr); Jon Hughes (cl). **139 Dorling Kindersley:** Peter Minister, Digital Sculptor (c); The American Museum of Natural (tl). **Science Photo Library:** Julius T Csotonyi (bl). **141 Dorling Kindersley:** The Oxford University Museum of Natural History (tl)

All other images © Dorling Kindersley

For further information see:
www.dkimages.com